MW01275106

John A. Crane

Directions for Social Welfare
in Canada:
The Public's View

With Contributions by Chris McNiven and Beverley Scott

A Publication of the Directions for Social Welfare Project
School of Social Work, University of British Columbia

ISBN 0-88865-523-1 (hardcover)
ISBN 0-88865-524-X (paperback)

Cataloguing in Publication Data
Crane, John A.
    Directions for social welfare in Canada
    Includes bibliographical references.
    ISBN 0-88865-0523-1 (bound). – ISBN 0-88865-0524-X (pbk.)
    1. Public welfare – Canada – Public opinion. 2. Public opinion – Canada.
I. University of British Columbia. School of Social Work. II. Title.

HV105.C72 1994   361.971   C94-910401-9

The Direction for Social Welfare Project is funded by National Welfare grants,
Health and Welfare Canada, Ottawa.

Set in Stone by Val Speidel
Printed and bound by D.W. Friesen & Sons Ltd.

Distributed by UBC Press
University of British Columbia
6344 Memorial Road
Vancouver, BC V6T 1Z2
(604) 822-3259
Fax: (604) 822-6083

Contents

Preface and Acknowledgments

A useful justification for this study was furnished by two academics who were impatiently trying to explain to me that it has no justification.

"Why? Why do this study?" demanded one, a social planner whose apparent mission is to protect the academic purity of policy research. When I suggested that the public might have a valuable contribution to make on directions for social welfare in Canada, he smiled at me tolerantly. Perhaps, he conceded, a poll could be conducted and the results used by a political party, say the NDP, to manipulate public opinion. But then why not just turn the project over to a polling agency?

His companion, a self-described "hired gun" of social research (a self-contradictory concept) added that the public's opinions are determined mainly by what it saw the previous evening on television. If this happened to be a touching case of physical disability the public is all for supporting the disabled. If it happened to be a grisly murder case, what a pollster will get the next day is a demand for tough crime control. But what about reliability? And after all, what good is such data?

It was clear that my critics were identifying the general public with the stock character "John Q. Public," who is impulsive, easily swayed by images on television, and hardly capable of serious analysis of public policy issues. It follows from this image of the public that we must rely on another stock character, the "wise and informed professional," to protect us from the impulsive fluctuations of public opinion. Public opinion is to be manipulated and controlled, not looked to for guidance.

At this point I realized that my critics might have identified a useful pair of stock characters, but with their roles reversed. One can make a case that we more often need "John Q. Public" to protect us from the "wise and informed professionals" than the reverse. We always need to consult the public on policy issues because public opinion data, with its greater mass and variability, and its unconcern for pecking orders amongst academic fields, can help us avoid some of the more arrogant departures of academic wisdom. I'm grateful to my critics for providing such an effective demonstration of the need to consult the public.

I return to the topic of public opinion versus expert opinion below and particularly in Chapter 11, "Social Policy Implications." I use the remainder of this preface mainly to outline the plan of this Report.

First, I must note that this Report is one of three main publications forthcoming from the Directions for Social Welfare Project. It aims to be a straightforward account of the plan, findings, and implications (for policy and for research) of this project.

About to be released as well is a Workbook entitled *Critical Choices, Turbulent Times: A Community Workbook on Social Programs,* by Nancy Pollak. This Workbook places the research findings in the context of some of the major issues with which the social services are confronted today. Drawing on our focus group data, it is able to include a First Nations, not just a "mainstream," perspective on these issues.

In preparation is a theoretical monograph, *Social Interests and Social Welfare,* which elaborates the theoretical model set forth in the final chapter of this Report.

The plan of this Report is as follows: Part I begins with a brief account of some of the trials and tribulations of social programs in Canada in the last couple of decades and states as the central problem for study *the degree to which the Canadian public still expects government to aim for traditional welfare state goals.* A mixed, not altogether orthodox, methodological strategy for researching this topic is presented, to which I will return later in this preface.

Though we prepared a formal review of the literature at the outset of the project, I opted against including this as a chapter of this Report.[1] Though at one time such a review was considered a *sine qua non* of research reporting, Rachel Marks pointed out, as far back as 1975, that "this convention has been changing" in favour of more focussed use of the literature as it applies "immediately to those matters considered" in different parts of the Report.[2] In keeping with this I have found it most helpful to draw upon the literature whenever it could usefully be related to the immediate task in hand.

There are several bodies of literature that are important to this study. First there is an extensive literature on the powerful attack on social programs from the right over the last two decades, and the responses by defenders of social programs. This is explored in Chapters 6 and 7. Then there is a vast body of writing on social programs and issues in the Press to which the public has been exposed in recent years. It is important to take this into account. Chris McNiven looks at some 1,700 items of this kind in Chapter 5.

In Chapter 10, I have compared our results against national and international survey and poll results that are in the public domain. Much of the data important for our purposes is, unfortunately, private property: such is the sorry state of social policy research in Canada today. Finally, though much less extensively, in Chapter 12 I look at the literature of social welfare ideologies, by way of developing a model of these ideologies. That work is to be further pursued in the book on social interests and social welfare referred to above.

In most parts of this Report the literature is used to aid in formulating questions and problems or in conceptualization. Throughout, however, I have been wary of laying borrowed conceptualizations on the data. Instead I have made extensive use of the open coding methods of grounded theory to *induce* concepts and principles from this data. These are then compared with the concepts and principles promulgated by others, such as neoconservative critics and various defenders of liberal social welfare provisions. Though I don't go as far as George Bernard Shaw, who asserted that "eading rots the mind," I do hold that theory building should be something more than a reworking of the thoughts of several dozen previous authors.

Some readers may be bothered by my ignoring the standard way of proceeding: a review of literature from which to deduce one's questions for enquiry. I have ignored this formula because I believe that it is based on a false analogy to research in the highly developed sciences. There the question is usually one of verifying well-established relationships. The variables are much more likely to be known. In a field such as public opinion research on social welfare issues we don't even know what the variables are. To limit ourselves to those variables suggested by previous research can be a serious mistake. It is much more important to use original data as a source of concepts, variables, and research questions.

The central problem addressed in Part II is the meaning of social programs to Canadians. Knowing how important (or unimportant) these programs are to our respondents, we are in a good position to understand the valuations that we ask them to make about the programs. But meanings themselves, as we suggest in Chapters 2 to 4, have at least three meanings. These can be described as *semantic or definitional, evaluative, and indicative of import or significance*. We pursue each of these aspects of "meanings" in separate chapters.

Chapter 2, on semantic meanings, documents in considerable detail the point that the Canadian public, judging by our results, is far closer in its thinking to the European model of social welfare than the American. By the European model the social services are for everyone, and by the American model they are for the allegedly small minority of the population who have failed to provide for themselves.

That the Canadian view differs from this is stunningly reinforced in Chapter 3, on the import or significance of social programs, as the public experiences them. This chapter provides some statistics showing that the social programs not only reach the whole population but are of major significance to the vast majority.

Chapter 4 shows that the *evaluations* placed on encounters with the social programs by the public are overwhelmingly positive, but also that there are widespread concerns about the inadequacy of administration of the social programs. The latter point is further documented in slightly different contexts in Chapter 8, on support for social programs, and Chapter 9, which deals with the future directions for these programs as seen by the public. In Chapter 11, on policy implications, the administrators of social programs are invited to take account of *a general uneasiness in the public about the way programs are set up and delivered.*

Part III, "Social Welfare Issues and Campaigns in Canada," is, like Part II, concerned with the context in which our respondents are making their judgments about social programs, but takes a different tack. The central problem here is: *to what extent have would-be shapers of public opinion succeeded in setting the agenda for public evaluations of the social programs?* Hardly at all, it appears from our data.

A particularly interesting case is the media campaign of the neoconservative "think tanks" aimed at rolling back the welfare state. In Chapter 6, I lay out the planks in their platform and in Chapter 8 use these as a framework for analyzing the respondents' ratings of their support for a list of programs. I find little resemblance of the neoconservative and respondents' ways of thinking. This is in spite of the elaborate campaigns of the Fraser Institute described by Beverley Scott in Chapter 7.

The same point holds for contributors to the newspapers, whose work is compiled by Chris McNiven in Chapter 5. Contributors to the papers are, by these data, most often concerned with particular programs about which they have a case to make, either for or against. Reading this chapter, one is impressed by the sophistication and detail of their arguments. These contributions are also notable for the degree of insider knowledge they display about social service management, *but their arguments seem largely to have escaped the general public.* They seldom appear in the comments of our respondents as to where they would take the social programs in the future. These *contributors to the Press seem to be talking mostly to themselves.* The same can be said for the proponents and opponents of social charters. As far as the survey respondents are concerned, the social charter movement, which Beverley Scott describes in a companion paper,[3] has apparently disappeared without a trace.

A number of conclusions can be drawn from the foregoing observations on social welfare campaigns. One is that *the public is much less ideological and much more pragmatic than those who argue for and against particular causes.* Thus, the public is in favour of welfare programs but also insists that they be set so as to avoid undermining the principle of responsibility for one's own problems. Likewise, pragmatism rather than ideology appears to govern the public's thinking about how programs should be funded.

The second conclusion that emerges from this is that *we must be leery of drawing inferences about trends in public opinion merely by looking at what gets into the media.* Social welfare experts and media people may have relied too much on this source, without realizing that those whose writings appear in the Press are usually talking to one another and talking past the general public. Obviously, this bears further enquiry.

The conclusions of Part IV, "The Public's Views of Social Programs," are fairly straightforward, and need little comment here. The public clearly expects government to continue to strive towards the goals of the welfare state and is not about to let government off the hook for this. At the time, the public may be willing to acquiesce to cuts in the social programs, but only because the public has been persuaded by the government itself that there is no alternative. *It behooves those who believe otherwise to make a stronger case for their views. Certainly, leadership from the social welfare community, in the form of a stronger defence of social programs and a focus on unmet needs, is called for.*

A note on validity: I have relied principally on a strategy of collecting data by differently styled items and by different methods (e.g., focus group versus individual interviews) and looking to see whether the results are consistent. This is the best available method for avoiding the risk of producing results that are artifacts of the way in which one posed the question to respondents. In this case, the pattern of findings proved to be the same regardless of the method of data collection. I have included data samples in enough detail to enable readers to judge this issue for themselves.

Finally, this is the place to acknowledge that this study would not have been possible without the contributions of:

David Thornton and *Sandra Chatterton* of the National Welfare Grants Program of Health and Welfare Canada, who provided consistent interest and support throughout the project.

Jacqueline Alex, who did excellent work on questionnaire coding, database construction, and project administration in the formative stages of the study.

Harold Goodwin, who chaired focus groups, helped keep finances in order, looked after a thousand administrative details, and used his social work skills to mediate quarrels when our work threatened to become science friction.

Linda Fletcher-Gordon, who directed field operations and showed a great capacity to keep things moving

Chris McNiven, who co-chaired focus groups and also struggled for two years with piles of press clippings, finally turning them into the useful account given in Chapter 5.

Beverley Scott, the thoroughness of whose library research is evident in Chapter 7.

Rosalee Tizya and *Stan de Mello,* who successfully negotiated participation in our study by First Nations groups.

Frank Tester and *Nancy Pollak,* who conceptualized and composed the companion report to this one, the Workbook for community groups.

John Crane
1 September 1993

Part I:
Introduction

1
The Directions for Social Welfare Project

1.1 Overview

The Directions for Social Welfare Project is the first of a proposed series of regional studies in Canada (to be followed by a national study) on the public's views of directions for social welfare provision. It is a consultation, primarily by means of in-depth interviews (2.5 hours in length on average) with samples of heads of household in Vancouver and Abbotsford and members of organizations involved with social welfare issues. Focus groups were also extensively employed, and a file of media materials on welfare issues was analyzed. Data collection was carried out in October and November 1991, and a second, smaller wave in April 1992.

Two hundred and ten persons took part in the study. The households are a probability sample that passed stringent tests of representativeness. The organization samples were chosen to represent groups such as the Fraser Institute that advocate cuts in social programs; others, such as welfare clients' advocacy groups that are attempting to strengthen social programs or stave off further cuts; and First Nations groups that are calling for a revamping of social programs.

Findings deal with the meanings of the social services to the respondents, respondents' support for the "welfare state," and directions in which they want take social welfare in Canada.

The principal policy implication of the study seems to be that the public is deeply concerned about the erosion taking place in the social services, and especially that the real, enormous costs of this erosion are being overlooked in the haste with which governments are seeking to offload or unload responsibilities for social services. This theme is pursued in Chapter 9, on future directions, and Chapter 11, on social policy implications.

This chapter presents the research question and the plan of the study. Study design, data collection, sampling and data analysis methods are outlined in detail. Some technical aspects of sampling and estimation of reliability, and of the factorial design and the approaches taken to validity, are presented in supplementary unpublished papers.

1.2 Backdrop

The decade of the 1980s was a hard journey for the social services in Canada, marked by a shift to the political right in Ottawa and in several provinces; a fiscal crisis of unprecedented dimensions; deep cuts in social service funding, leading to predictable crises in administration and service delivery; a national health care system in jeopardy; a steady erosion in real median family income; diminished career prospects for the young; a crisis of national identity; and a steep decline in public confidence in the ability of government to cope effectively even with its basic tasks, much less this avalanche of crises. Loss of confidence in government was accompanied by declining faith in the efficacy and trustworthiness of professionals of various kinds.

The problem for enquiry in this paper is this: in the turbulent environment I have described, how well has the social consensus in Canada, by which liberals and conservatives agreed on the necessity of active government intervention to secure broad social goals, survived? Do the shifts to the political right and, in particular, to governments committed to neoconservative policies more radical than those of traditional conservatism indicate that Canadians have begun to move away from the social consensus, towards the neoconservative social credo?

The *neoconservative* outlook, which we explore in some detail in this Report, not only challenges the social consensus but writes it off as an invention of rumpled academic theorists and liberal politicians bemused by their own theories. According to the neoconservatives, these theories, besides being mistaken, were from the beginning in conflict with popular wisdom. The neoconservatives articulated a vision of popular wisdom that, oddly enough, closely resembles the neoconservative social credo. Not satisfied with that, they embarked, as we show in Chapters 6 and 7, on a high-powered campaign to reorient both academia and the general public away from the social consensus and towards a business-oriented culture, with an individualistic perspective on social needs. In the process they mounted a massive effort to discredit the liberal social consensus.

Thus, any study such as this one that attempts to survey the Canadian public's contemporary views of the welfare state needs to take account of this neoconservative onslaught. There is no way, obviously, to isolate the effects of the campaign from the effects of developments outlined in the first paragraph of this section. What can be done is to compare data on the public's judgments of social programs with basic elements of the neoconservative credo and with contrasting proponents' views. From these comparisons one can infer at least how consistent the public's appraisals of social programs are with the neoconservative and proponents' views of the social services, respectively.

Chapters 6 and 7 present accounts of the neoconservative and proponents' views of social programs, as well as the neoconservative campaign against these programs, in enough detail to permit me to identify several key issues on which these two viewpoints are sharply divided. The data can then be analyzed to display the public's views on each of these issues, as revealed in our data. I can then draw inferences on the following more general questions: To what extent, in light of the data, does the public view reflect the specific neoconservative theory of public opinion ("popular wisdom") concerning a varied sample of broad-scale social programs? To what extent does the public view resemble the views of the proponents of these programs?

1.3 Topic, Terminology

1.3.1 Topic

The present study is of the public's views of provision for social welfare in Canada. The key term here is *views*. This is a study not of programs, policies, or program policies but of persons and their perceptions and judgments of these programs and policies. This is reflected in the conceptual scheme for the project as a whole, organized around views as dependent variable.[1]

We have surveyed the public's support for a wide variety of programs[2] to test for the effects of these variables on the public's judgments, but our study is concerned not with programs as such, nor with program policies, a comprehensive definition of social welfare, or a search for the meaning of social welfare in some ultimate sense.[3] Our subject, rather, is the public's views, compared to some social welfare ideologies that have had an important influence on social policies in Canada.[4]

1.3.2 Selection of Programs

We are constrained to set boundaries for our topic that make sense to the respondents and can be explored within a single interview, even though professionals in social service management or policy might prefer to use different boundaries. With these points in mind, we obtained data on the public's support for or opposition to cash income transfers; a varied sample of income transfers in kind; contributory pensions; occupational safety and compensation for injuries; immigrant services; physical rehabilitation services; tax benefits for low-income groups, for small business for investment purposes, and for private pension plans; affirmative action policies; counselling for a list of social and behavioural problems; and foreign aid policies. We judge this to be an adequate sample of programs with which to compare the public's views with those of neoconservatives and proponents.[5]

To keep the survey within manageable limits, we have made no attempt to survey the public's views concerning national defense policies as well most aspects of macro fiscal and economic policy (e.g., interest rate policies), immigration policies, and environmental policies. Arguably, each of these is in part social policy and indirectly affects the public's views on social policy issues. Although it is hardly practical to include them in the survey, we will, through several library studies and our newspaper file, be able to take account of the economic context of social policy making and opinion formation in Canada.

1.3.3 Terminology

Again, we are constrained to use terms that are no mystery to our respondents, though these are not necessarily the ones favoured by welfare policy analysts. After experimenting in our pretest with *social welfare* and with *social welfare provision,* we settled on *social services* as the broad catch-all term with which our respondents were best able to work. We included under this rubric not only the personal social services but also aspects of tax policy, human rights policies, and social security, and a range of income transfers in cash and in kind.

1.4 Variables

The pivotal variables for our study are those that attempt to elicit respondents' support for or opposition to these broad-scale public sector social services and their ideas concerning the allocation of responsibilities for funding for these services across the public and private sectors. No less important, we must place these judgments in the context of related views, especially the meanings of the social services to Canadians, their patterns of use of services, and their appraisals of the outcomes of these encounters. We must also view their support for programs in light of their varying degrees of dependence on the public sector social security system, as opposed to private systems of care.

1.5 Research Design

The research design of the study is a complex one, featuring, as I have noted, two models of data analysis, one qualitative and the other quantitative, used in tandem; three main types of samples (documentary, household, and organization membership); three main types of knowledge-building goals (exploratory-formulative, descriptive, explanatory); and a mix of data collection methods (interview, focus group, document analysis) and analytic methods (cluster analyses, regression analyses, grounded theory coding). The reason for these variations is the well-known principle that one should avoid putting all of one's eggs into one methodological basket: by using a mix of methods, we reduce the risk that our findings are an artifact of the method we have chosen. The complete design is displayed in Table 1.1. A detailed account of this design is available from the authors.[6]

1.6 Data

1.6.1 Sources of Data

1 Interviews with samples of randomly chosen heads of household (male or female) in the Lower Mainland and Fraser Valley areas of British Columbia.
2 Interviews with samples of members of professional, social services, and social action and development groups. The sampling method involved a random choice of participants from those who responded to an invitation to take part in either a focus group or an interview.
3 Samples of documents of various kinds, such as briefs, published and unpublished policy writings, and policy statements produced by members of organizations active on social welfare issues.

Table 1.1

A Comparative Design for Study of Social Welfare Ideologies

Theory	Models	Sampling Units	Patterning of Observations	Analysis
Construct of Ideology[1]	Causal[2]	• Households • Organization members	• Factorial experiment • Descriptive survey	• Ordinary least-squares • Hierarchical grouping
	Dramatistic[3]	• Organization members • First Nations • Policy science • Writings • Newspaper file • Households	• Exploratory • Formulative	• Grounded theory coding

Notes:

1 P. Diesing, *Science and Ideology in the Policy Sciences* (New York: Aldine, 1982); J. Schumpeter, "Science and Ideology," *American Economic Review* (1949) 39(2):345-59; K. Mannheim, *Ideology and Utopia,* tr. L. Wirth and E. Shils (New York: Harcourt, Brace and World, 1936).

2 P.H. Rossi and S.L. Nock (eds.), *Measuring Social Judgments: The Factorial Survey Approach* (Beverly Hills, CA: Sage, 1982).

3 K. Burke, *A Grammar of Motives* (New York: Prentice Hall, 1945); J. Gusfield, "The Literary Rhetoric of Science," *American Sociological Review* 41(1):16–33; Northop Frye, *Anatomy of Criticism* (Princeton, NJ: Princeton University Press, 1957); B. Glaser and A. Strauss, *The Discovery of Grounded Theory* (Chicago: Aldine, 1968).

1.6.2 Methods of Data Collection

1 In-depth interviews with heads of household and organization members, with an average duration of 2.5 hours. Open-ended questions were used extensively to provide a framework for interpreting replies to closed-ended questions. Questions using a variety of formats were employed to check on the effects of question wording.

2 Focus groups that were formed from professional, social service, and advocacy groups taking part in the study. The agendas were based on key questions of the household survey. Verbatim transcripts were kept, and subsequently analyzed using grounded theory methodology.

3 Documentary data retrieval and storage. A computer database, employing the WordPerfect 5.1 Database system, was devised, and some 1700 items were entered. The use of this file is described further in Chapter 5. See also section 1.6.6 below.

1.6.3 Interview Guide

The interview guide was organized according to the main study topics, as follows:

- the *meaning* of social welfare to the different groups represented in the sample, and whom they see as benefiting or not benefiting from social welfare programs according to these meanings;
- their *awareness of and familiarity with* Canadian social welfare programs and their appraisals of the impact of these programs on their lives;
- the *relative priorities*, given limited resources, that they feel should be assigned to social welfare programs addressed to different problem areas and beneficiaries;
- their views concerning the *distribution of responsibility for the initiation, funding and delivery of social welfare* across different sectors of Canadian society (for example, the voluntary sector, the private and market sector, government, and individuals and families) and variables they see as important in determining these allocations, as well as the rationales that they give for their preferences.

1.6.4 Items

Within each section of the guide, a mix of different items was employed, as described above. The guide was extensively pretested on samples of social service professionals and on random samples of households in Vancouver and Abbotsford, B.C. Methodological strategy is further discussed in the preface, and a copy of the complete guide is available from the authors. As items from the guide are used in the analysis, they are reproduced below in full.

1.7 Databases

1.7.1 Respondents' Database
In the household survey branch of this study, 128 respondents in Vancouver and Abbotsford were sampled. Of these, 106 were heads of households and 22 were members of business, consumer, women's, and professional associations. Household samples were drawn randomly from the City Directories and the organization sample from a list constructed to represent diverse points of view on social programs.

Rate of interview acceptance was two-thirds. Data were compiled on reasons for refusal, which were primarily related to problems in making time for the interviews rather than the subject matter of the interview. On gender, income, age, and occupation, our household samples proved to be within a 95% confidence interval for the population parameters which we estimated from the City Planning data. Technical details of the sampling method are described in a paper available from the authors.[7]

Sample size for the pilot study was set so as to fix Type 1 error at .05 and Type 2 error at approximately .04 for a difference of medium size as measured by Cohen's Index. The substantive hypotheses tested were that a majority of respondents supported and that a minority of respondents opposed each social program and similarly favoured or opposed taxes, if necessary to maintain each program. Since we have three categories (oppose, mixed, and favour), we have the degrees of freedom needed to test hypotheses about both support and opposition.

In accordance with standard hypothesis-testing procedures, these hypotheses were tested against a null hypothesis of a 50% split in opinion.[8] A summary of the results of these tests is given in Chapter 8 of this Report. The effect of our decisions regarding Type 1 and Type 2 error is to demand a substantial departure from a 50:50 split in the data (a split of at least 65:35) before rejecting the null hypothesis. This is a conservative standard (conservative in a statistical rather than a political sense), which I introduced in order to help protect against any "liberal" bias in the findings. We are in effect demanding that majorities be large in order for support or opposition to be accepted as greater than could plausibly be accounted for by chance.

1.7.2 Vignettes Database

In accordance with the factorial design,[9] respondents were presented with sets of vignettes, each one describing a particular instance of a social service benefit. The following is a sample vignette:

Sample Vignette

Computer-Generated from the Schedule of Variables

Male

Age 38

Married

5 dependents

Landed immigrant from Britain

Has a university degree

Engineer

Physically fit, in good health

Is on probation for dangerous driving

Has been steadily employed

Owns a small business in office services.
Writes off a percentage of lease car, clothing, equipment, and office expenses to reduce income tax payable. This benefit is paid for by tax exemptions.

Included in this vignette are 11 variables, such as gender, marital status, immigrant status, education, health, personal problems, occupation, and benefits received. Based on the information included in the vignette, we asked the respondents to rate the degree to which they were in favour of or opposed to the service described in the vignette.[10] Each respondent was presented with a package of 15 vignettes; on average, they completed between 13 and 14. The result was a total sample of 1700 vignettes. In the analyses reported here, the total sample was sorted by the 25 social programs.

In accordance with standard procedures of factorial design, the values of the variables making up each vignette were determined randomly, subject to several restrictions, e.g., professionals must have university degrees. Under these circumstances the number of observations for analysis becomes the number of vignettes.[11] We are able to use procedures such as ordinary least squares to estimate the effects on the ratings of support or opposition of different values of the variables contained in the vignette.

Probabilities of social programs appearing in the vignettes, which were set in advance,[12] were varied in several cases to take account of greater and more varied populations served by some of the programs compared to others. Thus counselling, which is applied to a wide variety of problems and populations, was assigned a relatively high probability (.09) compared to a legal suit on behalf of a Métis community (.025).

These probabilities were also affected by the restrictions introduced in the computer generation of the vignettes. For example, if the program were affirmative action on behalf of a Métis community, the variable "ethnicity" had to be fixed as Métis. The effect of these modifications is to reduce the sample sizes generated for the latter program. The resulting variations in sample sizes, when the findings are sorted by program, are shown in the tabulations displayed in Chapter 8.

1.7.3 Survey Items

The key items of the survey, dealing with support for the social services, are reproduced here. Other items are presented along with relevant findings in subsequent chapters.

The first of these items used brief program descriptions rather than program labels, as we felt that the labels might be unfamiliar to many. The following is an example of the phrasing of a program description: *"This program provides translation services, information and referrals for immigrants."* These descriptions were summarized from published directories of programs. The question was in each case presented in the following form:[15]

Would you support or oppose this service?

1	2	3	4	5	6	7
Strongly Oppose			Mixed: Favour and Oppose			Strongly Favour

The following question was one of the series of questions asked about each vignette:

Based on the information provided in the vignette, please tell me which answer expresses your opinion.

How strongly are you in favour of or opposed to this program/service?

1	2	3	4	5	6	7
Strongly Oppose			Mixed: Favour and Oppose			Strongly Favour

The question concerning willingness to pay increased taxes was presented in the following form:

If funding the service should call for an increase in tax rates, how strongly would you favour or oppose this increase?

The rating scale employed here was the same one employed for the question on support:

Based on the information provided in the vignette, please tell me which answer expresses your opinion.

How strongly would you favour or oppose this tax increase?

1	2	3	4	5	6	7
Strongly Oppose			Mixed: Favour and Oppose			Strongly Favour

Along with each vignette, we included the question:

If you are in favour of this program/service, how should it be paid for? (You may check more than one: some items may not apply).

This was followed by a list of funding methods, including the following:

... taxes; user fees; lotteries; charitable donations; corporate contributions; contributions from employees; other.

1.7.4 Focus Groups Database

This Report makes use of data from five focus groups that were conducted between November 1991 and April 1992. These groups had, on average, five participants. Represented in the groups were consumer and advocacy groups concerned with environmental issues, poverty, immigration and multicultural issues, immigrant women, women's health issues, mental patients, seniors, and the disabled. Also represented were a chamber of commerce, a downtown business group, a service club, a church group, community centres, food banks, a social policy and research agency, and two social work professional organizations. This sample was drawn from a more comprehensive list constructed to represent as fully as possible the range of citizen interest in social welfare issues. The sampling was for variation, and the groups were organized to bring together different points of view in order to stimulate challenges to and defense of contrasting positions. In this we were only partially successful, as it proved to be difficult to control the mix of participants available for a particular meeting. We were successful, however, in bringing out a range of perspectives on Canada's social programs.

1.7.5 Focus Group Topics

This Report makes use of data generated by the focus groups. An illustrative agenda item in these groups was as follows:[14]

As a taxpayer, you contribute, or could be expected to contribute, to a number of social programs and services, such as those included on the attached list. For each one, indicate whether you are satisfied or dissatisfied to have your contributions used in this way, and state briefly the reasons for your preferences.

If you are not fully satisfied in paying taxes for a particular program or service, how do you think this program or service should be funded? Specify and give reasons for your preferences.

Who should be eligible to receive benefits from each of these programs or services? Why?

The remaining agenda items are reproduced in subsequent chapters. The focus group data were analyzed for concerns about the social services in Canada today, and these concerns were grouped into principal themes that are presented in Chapters 8 and 9. These themes were then compared with the views of neoconservative critics and proponents of social programs, respectively.

1.7.6 Documentary Databases

Initially we had hoped to collect data from several media. It soon became apparent that this was beyond our resources for this part of the study. We decided, therefore, to concentrate our sampling on the establishment press, the newspapers with the broadest circulation. This would give access to the social welfare issues being placed before the Canadian public at the time of our survey. With this in mind we chose the *Globe and Mail*, the *Financial Post*, the *Vancouver Sun*, the *Vancouver Province*, *Maclean's*, *Saturday Night*, and a small sample of literature published by the B.C. labour unions and by social welfare organizations and think tanks. The *Globe and Mail* was selected because it provides a fairly comprehensive cross-section of national and international news and points of view. The two local papers addressed issues that are related more specifically to B.C. Items from the *Financial Post* were seen as providing economic and policy views that differ from views expressed by labour.

Within these various sources, items have been collected from editorials, commentaries, general news items, columns and letters to the editor. Further details of method are presented in Chapter 5.

Two additional documentary studies were conducted. The first was based on documents supplied by the Fraser Institute (see Chapter 6), and the second was based on a collection of published and unpublished materials on the Social Charter movement in Canada.

1.8 Model Development

A first stage in analyzing the data of our study is to explore, describe, and classify our respondents' judgments concerning programs and policies, and to compare these with the trends noted in our documentary materials. The present Report is primarily concerned with this first stage. Beyond this, however, there is a need to explore the ideological structures that underlie these judgments. The present Report makes a beginning on this task, by working out a conceptual model for the next stage of the enquiry.

I began this process by examining recent work on political ideologies in Canadian society, particularly the work of Patricia Marchak.[15] This work is about as close to our concerns as theory of ideology gets.

Marchak's two dimensions of political ideology, the *individualist-collec-tivist* and *egalitarian-elitist,* and her resulting set of 10 ideological systems (e.g., social democratic, socialist, neoconservative, corporatist), are helpful but much too general for our purposes. The same is true for Mishra's generally excellent work on the social welfare ideologies of the new right and the social corporatists.[16] The assorted European work on ideologies, from Marxists and Neo-Marxists, structuralists and post-structuralists, and followers of Foucault, Heidegger, et al., is even further removed from the social worlds in which we wish to work. *The grounded theorists are on the right track, I believe, in insisting on the need to induce substantive theories from data before trying to develop new formal theories.*

Beginning with this latter assumption, my objective is to work out a theoretical model of "social welfare ideologies" that can be continuously grounded in observations as it is developed. I have begun with the work of Diesing,[17] who proposes a general construct of ideology as "how the world looks like from a given social location." My model building is an elaboration of Diesing's construct along two lines. The first is a quantitative model of social welfare functions *à la* Welfare Economics. The second is a qualitative dramatistic model incorporating ideas from Northrop Frye, Gusfield, and the grounded theorists. This model is presented in Chapter 12.

In the Part II of this Report, I turn to our first major topic: the meanings of the social services to Canadians.

Part II:
The Meanings of the Social Services to Canadians

2
Meanings of the Term "Social Services"

2.1 Problem

To understand the judgments we are asking the public to make concerning directions for social welfare in Canada, we must first enquire into the meanings of Canadian social programs to our respondents. "Meanings" itself has three meanings:

1 The first meaning of "meaning" is *lexical*, or *referential*: what our respondents understand by the term "social services." This is the subject of the present chapter.
2 *Significance* or *import*: what the social services mean to our respondents in their everyday lives. This is the topic of Chapter 3, in which I focus on the degree of impact, regardless of whether it is good or bad, and also on the dependence of the public on public sector pension programs.
3 *Evaluation*: how people evaluate the impacts of the social services (Osgood's work on how people understand concepts[1] showed that there is always a strong evaluative element in these understandings). In Chapter 4, I elaborate on this aspect of the meanings of social services, looking at both the evaluations of specific encounters with the social services and more general views of their effects.

2.2 Method

2.2.1 Data

The data on which this chapter is based are drawn from the interview sample and focus group databases described in Chapter 1. From the interview sample, the data presented herein consists of 124 responses to the following open-ended question: "What does the term 'social services' mean to you?" In our first pretest, we used "social welfare" rather "social services," but found that a number of respondents understood the former phrasing to be a question about Income Assistance. As the term "social services" involved no evident misunderstanding and as respondents were comfortable with it, we used this term in the final edition of the interview guide.

The same question was posed for discussion in the six First Nations focus groups and the five focus groups representing community and professional organizations. In this chapter, I employ a sample of data from the latter set of focus groups.

The data presented here are from the interview sample unless otherwise labelled. The survey data are verbatim, and the focus groups data are summaries prepared by Harold Goodwin. Each of these summaries is followed by a brief indication of the focus group membership.

2.2.2 Coding Method

1   The data were examined, line by line, to identify *"dimensions of meaning"*: the set of concepts by which the respondents organize their views of the social services.
2   Whenever a word, phrase, or longer passage was identified describing some attribute of the social services, a *"code"* or category name was attached to the passage. In a number of cases, the newly identified concept was seen to be a subcategory of a previously identified concept and was so labelled.
3   This process was continued until no new categories emerged.

2.3 Codes

The line-by-line coding yielded three levels of categories, or codes, displayed in Table 2.1. In the following sections, these codes are presented together with the data from which they were derived.

2.4 Scope of the Social Services

2.4.1 For Whom Services Are Provided

In her new book, *The Wealthy Banker's Wife,* Linda McQuaig draws an important distinction between American and European approaches to social provision:

> In the U.S.-style model, the well-being of the citizenry is largely left up to the private marketplace. This approach is rooted in the notion

that people function best under the discipline of the market, where the need to survive drives them to work hard ... The state should intervene only where it is necessary to protect those who are simply too weak or too vulnerable to make it on their own.

... To the Europeans, however, the concept of welfare is linked to the broader concept of "social welfare," and implies a set of social rights and responsibilities ... Society is seen as an interconnected community where everyone contributes to the communal purse and everyone benefits from it. In this sense, everyone is part of the welfare state.[2]

Table 2.1

Categories of Meaning of the Term "Social Services"

Scope of the Social Service
For Whom Are Services Provided?

- For the entire population
- For the needy

Who is Reponsible for Providing Services?

- Government
- Private groups or individuals

What Services Are Provided?

- Welfare
- Comprehensive network of services

Efficacy of the Social Services
Adequacy of Provision

- Provision is adequate.
- Provision is inadequate.

Competence of Administration

- Administration is competent.
- Administration is incompetent.

McQuaig worries that Canada's welfare state, originally set up along European lines, seems to be moving towards the American model.

It turns out that the distinction McQuaig is making between the European and American approaches is the major theme in our data on meanings of the term "social services." The clearly preponderant view is that "social services are for the entire population," but a number of responses identify social services with "welfare" in the American sense of the word as discussed by McQuaig.

In Section 2.4.1.1, the former view is shown, and in 2.4.2.1, the latter view. Where the data are taken from focus group summaries, this is noted. Otherwise, all comments are from the interview sample.

2.4.1.1 For the Entire Population

Help the people. Anyone that needs help. Is pretty general.

It means I can get health care or if I'm in dire straits, I can get help.

In terms of the notion of breadth or re narrowness in the definition of social services, we've often tried to separate out what is referred to as the economic and the social, and I'm not sure we can do that any more. Neat divisions between the social and economic no longer exist. Clearly, the rich benefit and the poor get the scraps. Need to look at services not just in an absolute form but also in a relative sense in terms of pay-off. *(Focus group: social service board members and professionals)*

One also has to raise the issue of boundaries when one is defining the term social service as social programs provided by government are for the benefit of all Canadians. The connection between social well-being and economic well-being is now interwoven in our society and in all industrialized societies. *(Focus group: social service board members and professionals)*

To provide service and care for the whole population without discriminating. Specifically, counselling, financial aid, for example: single moms and disability insurance.

Social services means to me a citizen's right to health, income and educational services. Add to that food, clothes and shelter and a protection blanket which provides that when a person hasn't got a job and no other source of revenue. Social services provides a community or a society with the means to have some equatability in terms of what we need to survive.

Government or provincial help to individuals who need help.

Taking care of people's health. Taking care of people who are battered and abused. Welfare, children abused by parents. Making sure everything is running properly and if not then filling in the gaps. *(Focus group composed of seniors)*

Looking after social concerns of individuals and communities: health, education, safe place to live, adequate housing. Services organizations giving people places to socialize. Everyone needs, all facets of living need these services, a sense of security for people.

Supplying people with services they need. For example, money, physical, psychological. *(Focus group composed of seniors)*

Means looking after the welfare of the general public. Medical, drug addiction, social welfare. The government itself is social welfare. They are to look after all society.

Peace, shelter, education, food, income, a stable ecological system, sustainable resources, social gestures, and equity. Social services is a process of enabling people to increase control over determinants of their lives, and implicit in the idea of promotion of the social services is the empowerment of individuals and communities. *(Focus group: social service professionals and board members)*

It's a social services provided by the government to society as a reflection of what society is. It takes many forms, social services can fall into as many categories as you have categories in society. It's not necessarily relief or welfare based. Promotion as well as support. Not just picking up people when they have fallen. CMHC is a social service, not designed to bail people out.

Providing help to those who need it. No consideration to income, social status, financial circumstances, including health and education. There is a trained group of professionals who know the problems of individuals/groups that there information should be sufficient to allocate the service. Part of that service is also income supplementation. There should be guaranteed adequate income to everyone, removing welfare from social services.

Social services is a service to everybody, including poor people.

It encompasses all of the programs provided by public agencies to the public at large.

Meeting the social needs of the particular community you are dealing with.

A safety net for people who need government help. They cannot help themselves. It also provides a base levels of services or assistance to everyone.

A safety net for people in need that is very narrow. It covers more, it covers medicare, UIC, pension, and CPP expands it beyond the safety net.

In an advanced society to see people have needs met: medicare, housing, decent income for proper food, and clothing.

It is for the benefit of all citizens to assist them in a better quality of life.

Services for the public including all classes, accessible to everyone, free on a sliding scale.

Broad/philosophical sense. The way we care for each other, private and public, including funding in a private and public manner.

Programs that the government, provincial or federal, assist people in ways that are needed.

Things to help people. Services.

A service that the government of city offers everyone, rich or poor. Everyone has the right to use it.

All the support to assist with people's social well being rather than vocational or educational support, e.g., family support, housing in vocational context. It is only to a lesser extent, e.g., providing in a financial sense.

Services that are here for the people and support them.

"So broad"/welfare. People needing help or assistance of some kind. Doesn't have to be financial, could be emotional.

Help people help themselves. Community support as well as government. Who uses it? Single parents, elderly, immigrants. Volunteer programming.

Services that are available to you that you can use if someone refuses you, i.e., MSP and homecare services, hospital, standard medical. They may not all be paid for by government exclusively.

Means where the state provides a variety of service to those in need. Ranging from UI, counselling, health, etc.

Assistance where needed for problems. When you needed help the appropriate services would help you. If you know where to go. You just have to ask a lot of questions, a lot of it is by guess and by golly.

Providing people in general with the support and counselling to help develop and overcome life's problems. There is a prevailing opinion in Canada that the provision of social services is costly, but in the long run, the money spent will be worth its cost many fold. It has the potential of decreasing criminality, unemployment, underachievement. It can help people to help themselves.

Access to housing, on a personal level. Money that allowed for two sons' illnesses, i.e, handicap pension. The link between government and community. Living conditions generally for anyone in need.

Means services provided through government organization to help people in need.

Services that a community provides to people who need assistance in areas such as jobs, education, medical, etc.

2.4.1.2 For the Needy

The major motif of this section is that the social services are a safety net for persons in need. In most of these comments, "persons in need" refers to a group apart, in some way: the poor, the disadvantaged, the elderly. Other comments are phrased in such a way as to leave it open as to who might be included – almost anyone might be in need. But these comments fall short of claiming explicitly that services are for the whole population. In the large majority of these comments, social services are intended to protect the "weak" and "vulnerable."

In most of the comments, the weak and the vulnerable are seen as victims of circumstances, not simply, as in the pure American model, victims of their own character weaknesses.

Services that are rendered to canadian people who need extra income, have to retire early, UIC ... mixed feelings but like to live in this country where there is compassion.

Service to help people in need. People who have no other recourse.

For me, social services has meant societal support for vulnerable members: the young. *(Seniors focus group)*

Assisting those who don't have the ability to pay for the expenses of daily living. One of my cheques comes from the government. Medicare different, only available to young people.

Encompasses quite a lot. Helping poor and destitute, single mothers.

Helping the needy. I worked in a hospital so some of the examples are drug addicts, alcohol, family problems. Need some social workers to help clear the situation to help them understand that arguments don't solve anything. Also, people with mental illness, depression. Lately it seems to be a problem. I have had lots of calls form people who just need to talk. I am not a social worker but I do what I can.

Services to people who are poor and don't have sufficient means. Services for people who need some help from society.

Support services to people in need. Mostly dysfunctional families in the community. Crisis intervention as opposed to preventative services.

Help the people who need help. Mostly financially, welfare cheques, and emotionally, suicide prevention.

It means welfare, UIC, and benefits which are provided to the needy. It means that if you need help with something, like finding a place to live, you need money the government will help you out.

It's for people ... single moms on low income, people who can't find jobs or, people with disability, or old age.

Word that comes to mind is welfare. I think it's good for people who are needy, to help them on their feet. Some people probably stay on too long and latch onto the system and don't find a job. It should just be for the interim.

There's support services that are provided to the public when people are in some kind of dire straights. I suppose they couldn't get on with their lives effectively if these services were not there to get them over the hump. I'm a nurse so I have an idea of how social services works. And because of that I would have to say there are greater number of people needing social services than there are social services people. There's too much work and not enough people to do the work. There's a lot of people who need social services but we have been conditioned in our society to let people who are in the least bit of difficulty to turn to the government for a handout. The system doesn't promote self-motivation sometimes. It's too easy, people get stuck in the system sometimes.

Care for those who have fallen on some form of misfortune.

Government assistance for those who can't afford necessities.

A network of services to protect people in bad circumstances. Hopefully short-term. To prevent suffering that took place during the depression when there was nothing to fall back on.

Financial assistance for people unable to make their own living. Help themselves, includes transportation, clothing, medical assistance, physical and mental on a continual basis.

Basically a support network for people unable to provide for themselves one way or another.

Safety net if you fall on hard times through illness or etc.

Usually think needy people out there, whether fallen on hard times or a single mother whose husband left her. Social services provides assistance for her.

It's a help for those who need it. Not for any length of time but for a time of need. Of course some workers seem like they're giving money out of their own pockets.

It reminds me of the old welfare system. It's a good thing for those who really need it. There are many abuses that go on. I don't always agree with their policies, they should send more people to school. I know a lot of women on welfare who want to go to school but if they went they would be cut off. They should go to school to get off welfare.

It means helping people in need. Providing for the less fortunate.

Services that provide support to people in need and services that prevent people from becoming at risk.

Public safety net, i.e., for disabled persons, mentally, emotionally, and physically, single parent, unemployable – i.e., the administrative needs of these people.

2.4.2 Who Is Primarily Responsible for Providing Services?
This was a minor theme in the data. Apparently few respondents saw it as an issue requiring comment. *Most comments implicitly assumed that government is the major provider of social services.*

2.4.2.1 Government

It [government] has the scope to go into any area where there is a need, i.e., AIDS program, etc. The byproduct of the century where change was more rapid than in many previous ages. Government has both the right and should have the responsibility to address issues such as needle exchange programs, prostitution, drug addiction as a social program, lifestyle counselling, teaching is a further extension of this services that could benefit the greater society and the individual. Follow-up to wife battering, child abuse, substance abuse, and the root cause of these issues. Respondent feels that the social service issues are now so broad and pervasive. (Education??, immigration, criminality) that funding allocation of responsibility for policy making (i.e., immigration where problems are race related) make it difficult for respondent to see where the boundaries are between vastly different departments (unemployment and early retirement) and how they can effectively collaborate and augment problems whose roots are not easily seen as social service related. An example of this could be a collapsed economies victim such as a woman on the poverty line, the elderly, the children.

A range of services that governments provide for individuals in need. Some are provided universally, e.g. UIC, worker's compensation, and medical.

Government body. Provides services to people who need help. Government bureaucracy.

2.4.2.2 Private Groups or Individuals

Only three respondents mentioned private provision as major source of social service programs. Had the questions been in the form of closed items (with fixed-response options), it is likely that many respondents would have checked private sources of provision as a part of the overall pattern of services. The open-ended question we employed has the advantage of eliciting spontaneous responses – what is uppermost in the minds of the interviewees. "Government" is what they think of when asked who is primarily responsible for providing social services.

The three responses referring by implication to private provision are as follows:

Social services means a lot more than it used to. Twenty years ago, social services meant welfare, and there was a stigma to it. Now it encompasses a much broader set of services without as much stigma. It's a business. It started out as a social service and it has become a business. Are we becoming such a big business that we're being overburdened with it? Everybody's getting on the bandwagon and providing a social service because it's the right thing to do. Are we broadening our focus too much and providing things that maybe we shouldn't be providing but may be more appropriately provided in a different milieu? *(Focus group of small business entrepreneurs and professionals)*

A group of people interested in the well-being of the people in their community. Offer social services to people who need it and/or cannot provide it for themselves. Anyone needs to be able to accept, inform, receive guidance.

Services provided by government agencies or volunteer agencies (non-government agencies) or charitable organizations who work for the benefit of people, society, or targeted groups (e.g., groups for unemployed people, paid action groups, and service groups e.g., Lions club).

2.4.3 What Services Are Provided
Another way in which the respondents expressed their ideas about the scope of the social services is to emphasize the types of services provided, rather than the persons and problems with which the services are concerned. Obviously, these two ways of defining the social services overlap. For those who chose to emphasize kinds of services, the response is to name an inclusive category such as "services provided by the government," referring to a comprehensive network or giving an omnibus list of examples. A much smaller number of respondents identified the social services with "welfare" in its American meaning, à la McQuaig, as shown in the following section.

2.4.3.1 Welfare

Financial aid for both short-term and long term goals for the poverty-stricken.

Services that are rendered to canadian people who need extra income, have to retire early, on UIC. Mixed feelings, but like to live in this country where there is compassion.

Primarily an agency to assist people in need and to explain what assistance is available.

It means welfare, UI and benefits that are provided to the needy.

Financial assistance to people unable to make their own living. Including transportation and clothing, medical assistance, physical or mental, on a continuing basis.

Welfare, social workers, assistance.

Pension. Very comforting. Need it to survive. Some countries don't have any.

Welfare, basically, that's it. Government aid.

System provided by state to provide basic necessities for those unable to fend for themselves.

2.4.3.2 Comprehensive Network of Services
The majority viewpoint is presented in this section:

A network of support agencies to support people with mental, emotional, and physical handicaps. Specific agencies such as alcohol and drug programs, mental health services and agencies, hospital services, MSS. Supports structure of society that provides bottom line care beyond which people can fill, i.e., housing. We are a wealthy country and, therefore, we can support each other to get back up or carry on.

The provision of information and housing, health care and essential needs of the society.

Services from the government advantages, libraries, medicare.

A country's ability to meet people's needs. Example, low income individuals, medicare, immigrants, family court services.

Services that the government offers to the public, be it paid for or subsidized.

A body of organizations that can assist a person with a problem or feel they're interested in pursuing.

First acquaintance welfare provisions and child protection. Beyond that, any type of helping service in both institutions and community settings, i.e., hospitals.

Welfare and all that, health and welfare.

Unemployment insurance, welfare, support services, women, married and unmarried.

Services provided by the government for the welfare of people. Includes money and services.

Anything that can help people who are sick or financially in need. People to talk to, also social services help when someone dies. They provide someone to talk to. They did when my husband died.

Services offered by the government for the people for the general public.

Services that are rendered to canadian people who need extra income, have to retire early, UIC. Mixed feelings but like to live in this country where there is compassion.

The welfare of citizens at large. Example, health, UIC, CPP.

A variety of things. Helping people not able to help themselves. Some people tend to use it as a crutch. Essential services. There is no monetary label. Some can fall through the crack.

What government can give. Services government can provide. Medical coverage, housing.

Assisting those who don't have the ability to pay for the expenses of daily living. One of my cheques comes from the government. Response to prompt "what are some of the parts of social services": Medicare different, only available to young people.

Benefits available to all citizens. Benefits come from the government.

Providing necessary services to the citizenry. Services that are regarded as being essential. It is a wide-ranging term. It is not open-ended.

Social programs supplied by government. Example, UIC, family allowance, medicare. That's all I know.

Publicly provided services that are available universally. Providing for people in society who are unable to provide for themselves, temporarily or over the long term. These services are best provided on a [universal] basis versus on a hit and miss basis.

Government body that provides services to people that need help. Government bureaucracy.

Has to do with the well-being of each community. To take care of people in need. Example, welfare and recreation, community centres.

Services offered to the public administered by the provincial government, i.e., health, housing, and financial support.

All services that are for the well-being of the people in a country. All services including health, social work, UIC, welfare. It is pretty broad ranging. Anything to do with the elderly, disabled, etc.

A range of services the government provides for individuals in need. Some are provided universally, UI, worker's comp, medical.

I guess any kind of service that is provided to people rather than citizens by a government body. I don't interpret it as welfare, I think it's good for everybody. It should be good for everybody and not necessarily something that comes free. I guess it's a service aid in whatever particular need you have to ensure the very best of that particular circumstance – be offered to whoever is using it.

Are what the government provides to the people as opposed to putting up more military bases. This is stuff that people use.

Government paid program for the public in general. Most of them are essential and for the most part they are good.

It's a social service provided to the society by the government as a reflection of what the society is. It takes many forms, social services can fall into as many categories as you have categories in a society. It's not necessarily welfare based. Promotion as well as support. Not just picking up people when they have fallen. CMHC is a social service not designed to bail people out.

It encompasses all of the programs provided by public agencies to the public at large.

A network of support agencies to support people with mental, physical, emotional, behavioral handicaps. Specific agencies such as A and D programming, mental health agencies, hospital services, MSS. Support structure of society that provides bottom line care beyond which people can fill, i.e., housing. We are a wealthy country therefore we can support each other to get back up or carry on.

Services provided to members of society.

Meeting the social needs of the particular community you are dealing with.

Broad/philosophical sense. The way we care for each other, private and public, including funding in a private and public manner.

Generally, broadly. In respondent's view, the whole range of income security, such as old age security as well as the more personal social service programs. Family and children services, seniors, and more specialized treatment programs, sexual violence, sexual abuse treatment, family violence. The broad ranges versus welfare only. Any service that has to do with the way of being of any person who lives in Canada, including immigrants.

Programs that the government, provincial or federal, to assist people in ways that are needed.

Services such as welfare system, UI, rehabilitation programs, family support services, medical. Where provincial services don't cover for individuals losing their job and need an income. Welfare for people who are unable to work for some reason as they may be single parents, have some addictions, etc.

All the support to assist with people's social well-being rather than vocational or educational support. ie. family support, housing in vocational context. It is only to a lesser extent, i.e., providing in a financial sense.

The services provided by the government through tax sources. example, for the very young the very old, the rich, the mentally ill.

Services that are available to her that she can use when someone refuses her. She recommends the services: MSP, homecare service, hospital, standard medicare, cancer clinic, pharmaceutical support, therapies, glasses. They may not all be paid for by the government exclusively.

Government or some sort of institutions providing services. No users don't have to pay, i.e., financial, educational counselling.

The individual no longer lives in a close community where the individual can control what happens in his life. Extended families no longer exist. The social ills are often are so distant from what was originally perceived that damage control has to be put into action in the form of additionally social services, programs, including thousands of dollars. An area that crosses over in respondent's view to medical services, day care, counselling ... anything that is provided by government (funding programs) for the general well being of the population/the country. It may be also immigrant services, job counselling, retraining ... anything that the government puts funds into that is not strictly economic development, education.

Group of programs for providing various social services (medical, social, family, elderly, disabled, or in need) persons to assist them in a number of social ways. Example, childcare, counselling, legal, housing, employment, etc.

2.5 Efficacy of the Social Services

This topic emerged as a secondary theme. Most respondents made no comment about it. In the minority of comments that do mention this topic, the principal concern is doubt about the administrative efficacy of the social services that we presently have in Canada. A small number of respondents dealt with the adequacy or inadequacy of provision for the social services. Most of this latter comment is negative in tone, referring either to abuses of the services or the limitations of policies, such as the failure to give welfare clients an opportunity to get further education or training. Relatively few comments referred directly to the adequacy of provision, but a number of respondents pointed with pride to Canada's generous provision compared to that of other countries.

Both adequacy and efficacy emerge in Chapter 4 as major themes when the respondents were focused on their own encounters with the social services.

2.5.1 Adequacy of Provision

2.5.1.1 Provision Is Adequate

Implies that our government provides to the people (service) through taxes (income), something that we have an active role in – Health care, UI, welfare, shelter to battered women, adoption service. Proud of the social services that Canada has compared to other parts of the world, ie. Germany, US.

It is for the general benefit of those with limited means. I feel really good about it.

Looking after social concerns of individuals and communities. Health/Education, safe place to live, adequate housing, service organization gives people places to socialize, everyone needs, all facets of life, sense of security for people.

2.5.1.2 Provision Is Inadequate

Providing people with services in the community to improve their lives. I feel pretty strong about services to the mentally handicapped. I see a lot of homeless people. I see a lot of these people in my work, they become deinstitutionalized and there is no support services for them. It's a catch twenty-two. To get on welfare you have to have an address and to get a place you have to look respectable. Something needs to be done for these people.

It means UIC, health benefits. It also means abuse of it. We see a lot of this in Abbotsford. I've paid into UIC for forty-two years and hate to see it abused. The cost keeps going up. There needs to be control, if they're healthy and can work they should not get benefits. If it (costs) keeps climbing, something has to change.

There's support services that are provided to the public when people are in some kind of dire straits. I suppose they couldn't get on with their lives effectively if these services were not there to get them over the hump. I'm a nurse so I have an idea of how social services works. And because of that I would have to say there are greater number of people needing social services then there are social services people. There's too much work and not enough people to do the work. There's a lot of people who need social services but we have been conditioned in our society to let people who are in the least bit of difficulty to turn to the government for a handout. The system doesn't promote self-motivation sometimes. It's too easy, people get stuck in the system sometimes.

It reminds me of the old welfare system, it's a good thing for those who really need it. They're many abuses that go on. I don't always agree with their policies. They should send more people to school. I know a lot of women on welfare who want to go school. If they went to school they would be cut off. They should go to school to get off welfare.

It is a necessary program but doesn't do what it says, it helps people but not enough.

2.5.2 Competence of Administration

2.5.2.1 Administration Is Competent
The major theme in the data on competence of administration is doubt or uneasiness. The few positive comments about this grew out of favourable personal experiences as reflected in the following example:

I had a major operation at UBC. That and other services I've had were excellent. I feel really good about it.

2.5.2.2 Administration Is Incompetent
From the data to be presented in this section, and in more detail in Chapter 4, it seems to be a fair inference that there is substantial doubt in the public's mind about the competence of the administration of the social services. This is reflected in the following comments (see also Chapter 6, section 2.3):

What it should mean, helping individuals, organizations, families with financial, medical, and supportive assistance. In reality we tend to get away from the basic principles of social service. We have tried to be everything to everybody. By doing this we are duplicating services in many instances. Several organizations looking after the same area. Buck gets passed from one organization to another and the individual gets lost.

Set up to help the general public. I disagree with a lot of the ways they are set up. They are spineless. If the client screams loud enough they get what they want. The client knows more about it then the employees. It should be scrutinized. Some people definitely need help but the bus only goes so far. They use a "CYA" policy = cover your ass, provincially and federally as long as they are right they don't care.

Safety net without the responsibility of understanding the people that require the need. I used to work on the street, now I need a degree to work. People need people that can understand. It scares people away when you have to go to an office. Easier to have a community worker to meet people where they are.

The services are not necessarily understood and accessed by the general public and/or family of individual and the person in great need. Public administrators ... they sit in their offices and wait for people to come to them. It is a more and more important link to society. If social services were on top of things properly they could prevent a lot of unnecessary costs by providing support when most crucially needed.

The provision of assistance to people who are in a state of need. Need varies from financial to emotional. This service system fails to deal with either one well.

2.6 Conclusions
1 The meaning of "social services" to the respondents, as reflected in their comments, appears much closer to the European model than to the American (on these two models see McQuaig's remarks, quoted in section 2.1). Social programs are seen as designed for everyone, not just the welfare poor.
2 The interpretation of the meaning of this observation, however, especially its relationship to data presented later (Chapter 8) on support for social programs, is complicated. Policy analysts from right, left, and centre have assumed that support for comprehensive social security, or the welfare state, is enhanced when everyone is seen to benefit from social programs. This is one of the main justifications advanced for universal social programs: everyone's interest is served by them, and the all-important middle class is more willing to see tax monies go to the poor if they see themselves as benefiting as well from social programs.
3 From this formulation it would appear that since support for social programs is enhanced by knowledge that one's own interest is

served by them, people will give greater support to programs from which they themselves directly benefit. However, data presented in subsequent chapters show at best a weak relationship between support for particular social programs and prospects of benefiting directly from these programs. Thus the well-off are hardly more enthusiastic, as shown in our data, for tax exemptions for investments than are the low-income respondents. This is a typical finding, as revealed in a recent excellent summary of research:

> A spate of recent studies challenge the proposition that self-interest is the underlying source of policy preferences. These studies show that in a wide variety of domains, including racial and gender issues, government spending, foreign policy and social welfare programs, people who seemingly are affected by proposals in different ways do not differ in their views. Moreover, when conflicting opinions are related to differences in the personal impact of a policy, self-interest plays a minor causal role, accounting for relatively little of the observed variation in preference.[3]

4 In the light of these data (and our own findings presented in Chapters 8 and 9), the most plausible interpretation of the relationship between self-interest and public support for social programs is to define self-interest broadly as identification with the community or the nation (or beyond). This broader identification is reflected in many of the comments of the respondents quoted in Chapters 8 and 9.

3
Encounters with the Social Services

3.1 Problem

This chapter is concerned with the following problem: *how significant are social programs in the lives of Canadians?* Thus, how real to our survey respondents are the questions we are putting to them on directions for the social services in Canada? Not surprisingly, people take seriously questions about topics that are important to them in their daily lives. If social programs are important to our respondents, we can give more weight to their views about the programs (and put more trust in their validity!) than if these respondents were merely giving us polite responses.

Most important, knowing what social programs have meant to the public, we are in a much better position to understand how they evaluate these programs and why they take the positions that they do on present and future directions for the social services.

3.2 Guiding Questions

To obtain data on the significance of social programs in the lives of our respondents, we devised survey questions to tap into the following topics:

1 How *familiar* are the respondents with social programs currently in effect in Canada?
2 How and to what extent have the respondents become *involved* with these programs?
3 We hear a good deal these days about the inadequacies of universal pension plans such as Canada Pension and Old Age Security Pension. *To what degree do our respondents count on these plans*

to support them in their retirement years, and to what degree have they moved away from such plans into private pension schemes? This tells us whether our respondents are looking at government pension plans as customers of such plans or as outsiders.

4   What *assessments* do they make concerning the impacts on their lives of their encounters with social programs? Have these impacts been essentially nil? Appreciable? Major?

5   How do they *evaluate* these impacts? Along what lines? Favourably or otherwise? This topic is taken up in detail in the next chapter.

3.3 Data

3.3.1 Sample of Social Programs

We composed a list of social programs about which to obtain our respondents' views. Our list includes the varied types of programs one would expect to find in a society with a comprehensive social security system. After testing a preliminary list with several consultants and in a pretest study, we included the following social programs:

Income Assistance	Immigrant Services
Family Allowances	Child Protection Services
Unemployment Insurance	Mental Health Services
Canada Pension Plan	Public Health Services
Quebec Pension Plan	Hospitals
Old Age Security	Nursing Homes
Survivor's Allowance	Pharmacare
War Veteran's Disability	Home Support Services
Pension	Student Loans
Workers' Compensation	Disability Tax Credit
Medical Services Plan	Child Tax Deduction
ESL Classes	Investment Incentive
Employment Training	Deductions
Programs	Registered Retirement Savings
Subsidized Housing	Plans
Residential Tenancy Branch	Capital Gains Tax Allowance
Affirmative Action Programs	Tax Deduction For Exploration
Victim's Assistance	and Development Expenses[1]
Day Care	

3.3.2 Survey Questions

The findings reported herein are based on three items of the household survey, reading as follows:

Here are two cards. One contains a number of short descriptive statements. I will read you a list of programs or services and if any of these statements describes your involvement with that program, please tell me which number applies. There may be more than one statement which applies to you.

In addition, by referring to the numbers on the second card, please indicate what effect the experience had on your life.

The "short descriptive statements" on one of the cards read as follows:

1 = I have never heard of this program/service.
2 = I have heard or read about this program/service.
3 = I know others who may have used it.
4 = I or someone in my immediate family, have used it during the past 12 months.
5 = I have served as a volunteer for this program/service.
6 = I have been employed by this program/service. (If so, please indicate the position you held.)

The second card, dealing with the effect on the social service use on the respondent's life, reads as follows:

Effect on your life (either good or bad):
1 = nil
2 = some
3 = average
4 = major

These questions were followed by an open-ended question dealing with the impacts of the social service encounters on the respondent's life. This topic is taken up in detail in Chapter 4.

3.4 Findings

3.4.1 Familiarity With Social Programs

One person recognized only 9 of the 32 social programs. At the other end of the scale was a person who recognized 31. The remainder of the respondents were evenly divided between these two points. The median number of programs recognized – the number below which half the respondents fell – was 19.

Since one would not expect detailed recollection of program names from persons who were not directly involved with the programs, these data look reasonable. The numbers of programs recalled are neither so small as to create worries about the respondents connection to the subject of the survey nor so large as to suggest that the persons interviewed were significantly inflating their knowledge of social programs.

3.4.2 Use of the Social Services

It should be kept in mind here that *our study is of self-perceived impacts on families,* a different project from measuring program utilization. For the latter, one standardizes the word "family" or "household" to make comparable the units being counted. To study self-perceived use and impacts, we leave the definition of these units to the subjects themselves. What matters here is the group of persons whom our respondents think of as their families.

In some cases respondents included more than one household in the "immediate family," and this should be kept in mind when reading the following statistics. Reported use of the social services is in the 12-month period prior to the interview, as recalled by the person interviewed. We used the open-ended questions on impacts to check on the accuracy of the respondent's recall of the services given under each example of reported use and on the timing of the service. No discrepancies were found. Nevertheless, the recollections of whether services occurred in the previous 12 months or before are probably only approximate.

The findings on self-reported use of our list of social services during the previous 12 months are as follows:

- 98.4% of the sample reported use of at least one of the programs on the list.
- 50% of the sample reported use of between two and six of the programs.

- Nearly 50% of the sample reported use of more than six of the programs.
- If we omit the large universal programs of Pharmacare, Canada Pension Plan, Old Age Security, Medical Services Plan, as well as hospitals, we find that 72% of the sample have used at least 1 of the remaining programs on the list, 58% of the sample have used 2 of these programs, and 42% have used between 2 and 11 programs.
- A sample of findings on reported use of individual programs is: Income Assistance, 21% (about the same as the census estimates of the percentage of low-income families); Unemployment Insurance, 26%; Workers' Compensation, 15%; ESL classes, 7%; Employment Training, 15%; Subsidized Housing, 9%; Residential Tenancy Branch, 4%.

Thus the data show that use is not confined to the large and familiar programs with universal coverage, but is also extensive in the programs that are not set up on a universal basis.

3.4.3 Reliance on Government Pension Plans

For each of our respondents, we prepared a profile of retirement plans consisting of items that the respondent checked from the following list of sources of retirement income: RRSP, Employers' Retirement Pension Plan, Life Insurance, Investment Dividends, Canada Pension Plan, Inheritance, Cashing Savings Bonds, Selling Rental Property to Obtain Cash, Selling Family Home, Selling Stocks/Bonds, and Other. Respondents already retired checked those items that are their sources of retirement income.

To analyze the resulting data, we employed a computer program that is able to identify similar and contrasting profiles of retirement plans, and sort the sample of respondents into two groups based on the similarity of their profiles. These groups were formed according to the following rules: the profiles in each group should not only be as similar as possible, but should also be as dissimilar as possible from the profiles in the other group.

Working according to these rules, the computer program produced two groups, the first having 89 members and the second, 36. The proportions of these two groups that checked each item on the list of sources of retirement income are shown in Table 3.1.

From these data it appears that only a small proportion of Group 1, with 89 members, has significant sources of retirement income other

Table 3.1

Computer-Generated Profiles of Retirement Plans

	Proportions Checking Each Source	
Sources of Retirement Income	Group 1 (Size = 89)	Group 2 (Size = 36)
RRSP	.45	.89
Employer's Retirement Plan	.39	.69
Life Insurance	.32	.53
Dividends from Investments	.10	.69
Canada Pension Plan	.80	.97
Inheritance	.15	.36
Cashing Savings Bonds	.18	.61
Selling Rental Property	.00	.38
Selling Family Home	.24	.61
Selling Stocks/Bonds	.01	.72

than government pensions. Group 2, with fewer respondents (36), also includes these government pensions in its retirement plans but obviously has other significant sources of income.

The message of these data is similar to that of the data on use of social programs. Both sets of data indicate that social programs continue to play a major role in the lives of our respondents. In the following section I look at how the respondents rate the impact of these social programs on their lives.

3.4.4 Impacts
The findings on impacts of the encounters with the social services during the previous 12 months as experienced by the consumers of these services are as follows:

- 97% of the sample reported that encounters during the previous 12 months with one or more of the services on our list had at least some impact on their lives.
- 77% of the sample rated at least one of these encounters as having a major impact on their lives.
- About 40% of the sample gave this same rating of major impact to two to four encounters.

- About 13% of the sample gave this same rating of major impact to six to eight encounters.

These data call into question the premise of much of the literature on "targeting" of social services, that the social services are aimed only at the severely disadvantaged members of society.

3.5 Conclusions

1 We hear so much these days about retrenchment of the social services that *it is easy to overlook the enormous role that these services continue to play in the lives of Canadians.* The data of this chapter are a useful reminder of this role.

2 The data on "use" and "impacts" remind us, as well, that the term "those in need" includes the entire population. These data seem to support the claims of the original proponents of comprehensive social security schemes that the benefits would not be confined to the "needy" as conventionally defined.

3 In the light of findings like those in this chapter, it is easier to see why efforts over the last 15 years of governments committed to rolling back the social services have had limited success.

4 One prerequisite of a successful survey is to avoid asking people about matters with which they have little experience and in which they have no real stake. The data of this chapter indicate that this error was clearly avoided in the present study.

5 In the next chapter, based on the open-ended questions on impacts of encounters with the social services, I explore the question of meanings of the social services to the public at greater depth. I am particularly interested in how our respondents evaluate these encounters and the programs on which they were based.

4

Impacts, Good and Bad, of the Social Services on the Lives of Canadians: Survey Results

4.1 Problem

In the preceding chapter, I have summarized the quantitative data on our respondents' use of social programs and their ratings of the impacts that these encounters have had on their lives. In this chapter, I explore these impacts in greater detail, using the open-ended comments that were obtained along with the ratings.

The problem with which I am concerned is the same as in other chapters: I am looking for *evidence of the respondents' support for and opposition to broad-scale public sector social programs, and the grounds that they offer for their opinions.* In this chapter we have the opportunity to look at these opinions in the light of the respondents' direct experiences with social programs. These opinions can later be compared with the more abstract and general judgments that we obtain in subsequent chapters.

4.2 Guiding Questions

One important worry these days about the social services is that they are no longer serving, if they ever did, the purposes that they were intended to serve. The data employed in this chapter enable us to re-examine this concern. More specifically, I ask: how do the impacts of encounters with the social programs, as seen by "consumers" of the services, compare with some of the basic aims of a comprehensive social security system to provide, among other things:

- a basic minimum income for all;
- a safety net against loss of income from disability, catastrophic illness or unemployment;
- an adequate system of personal social services?

To get at these questions, I first analyze the data to show the detailed "dimensions of impact": the aspects of the lives of the respondents that they see as most affected by social programs.

Following this, I look at the observations made by these respondents on operations of the social programs: in the eyes of our respondents, how do these programs work in practice? How does practice compare with intentions and, where the fit is imperfect, what should be done?

Finally, I compare the "dimensions of impact" with the classic social security aims listed above.

4.3 Data Analysis

4.3.1 Coding Method

1   The data were examined, line by line, to identify "dimensions of evaluation": the frames of reference by which the respondents evaluate their encounters with the social services. Whenever a word, phrase, or longer passage was identified containing some form of evaluation of the social service encounters, a "code" that labelled the category of evaluation was attached to the passage. The result of this process was the following set of categories, and under each category a set of subcategories:

- *Dimensions of impact*: values supported or promoted in individual lives. Subcategories include: survival past a major life-crisis; economic security; improved opportunities for self-help in order to better oneself; enhanced self-esteem; strengthened family relationships; crisis management leading to a "turning point" in a person's life.
- *Principles*: e.g., arguments for or challenges to program aims, or need, based on principles such as the principle of stimulating the economy by means of investment incentives to business or levelling out income inequalities by providing tax deductions based on income levels. The complete set of principles is presented below as subcategories.
- *Realities of program operations*: positive or negative views of the way programs operate. Subcategories include, for example, showing proper respect for clients; demonstrating efficiency or effectiveness.

2 I then sampled comments classified under each of these subcategories for inclusion in this Report. Sampling was "for variation,"
   as I shall further explain.

4.3.2 Sampling the Database

The survey interviews received a total of 659 comments on the services, with a total length of over 70 single-spaced pages. Although I
would have preferred to include all of these in this Report, this was
hardly practical. The alternatives were to summarize or to sample the
comments. Summarizing would have allowed every comment to be
reflected, but would have lost the original wording, a loss that I
decided I could not afford. Therefore I have sampled the comments,
employing the following rationale and method:

1 *Sampling rationale*: sample for variation, endeavouring to include
   the full range of positive and negative comments. This is plainly a
   judgment call. If there is bias, it is "overcompensatory." Here, as in
   the analyses reported in Chapter 8, I was anxious to avoid a "liberal" bias in the interpretations. Therefore, I have made sure that
   any "neoconservative" comments found in the data are included,
   even though the number of these comments is small.

   I must mention here a second possible "bias" in the data, not
   unrelated to the first: proportionately more critical than favourable
   comments from whatever direction have been included. My rationale for this is simply that critical comments lead to program
   development and change more often than laudatory comments.

2 *Sampling method*: classify the comments under each of the rubrics
   presented above (e.g., comments that support or challenge program aims); select from each category comments representing
   favourable, mixed, and unfavourable points of view. Again, this
   represents a series of judgment calls, but necessary ones.

4.4 Findings

After the data were grouped into the three broad categories listed
above, line-by-line coding was employed to extract subcategories.
These are presented in the form of statements, either declarative or
imperative in mood. Each of the subcategories is followed by examples quoted verbatim.

4.4.1 Impacts

4.4.1.1 It Enabled Me to Survive

Income Assistance: Example 16 – Kept the person alive, but quickly found a job. Good.

Income Assistance: Example 17 – Sister on welfare. Single mother, unable to work while taking care of my nephew. Without it wouldn't be able to survive. Good for sister.

Family Allowance: Example 11 – People below poverty line depend on these funds arriving on time. I'm living borderline. I spend $100 a month more than I take in. People on welfare use the system to make up the extra $100.00. You have to. Some people are too proud to go to food banks. $33 a month goes nowhere. Not enough.

4.4.1.2 Without It I Would Have Been Impoverished

Veteran's War Pension: Example 78 – Helps pay for glasses, teeth, and medical service payments. Depends on income – it's major to me – helps have better standard of living. We all get old you know, never say you won't help those old guys.

Medical Services Plan: Example 47 – The funding has had major impact because I'm diabetic. I've spent a lot of money on medicines. The tax system allows deductions so it's had a positive, major impact on me.

Subsidized Housing: Example 4 – A necessary benefit to the poverty stricken; reduces stress in allowing available income to stretch further.

Pharmacare: Example 81 – Major effect on our life. Use it when require drugs. If didn't have benefit, would have to do without other things in life. One prescription costs $118.

Pharmacare: Example 88 – Grandmother – Multiple medicines. If she had to pay it would be a significant impact on money she would have for food and housing. Elderly have made their contribution to society, they deserve it.

4.4.1.3 Helped to Keep Our Family Together

Example 63 – Once my brother-in-law passed on – she never worked a day in her life. She's 50 something and has her family to raise. That's been the only money. It's had a major effect on kids, they've had to rally around and help. We've all supported each other.

Disability Tax Credit: Example 110 – Major difference to their family – (taking it for sons' condition) allowed family to stay in their home – and also to continue doing as much for their son as they've been accustomed to doing.

4.4.1.4 Enabled Me to Be Independent, Help Myself

Employment Training: Example 93 – Son-in-law has gone through it (to that time, he's had no training – in and out of work regularly). The program assisted him to good training (heavy equipment operating) and was able to get steady, well-paid employment. Considerably assisting in stability.

Subsidized Housing: Example 85 – 1977 bought AHOP house (Assisted Home Ownership Plan). Had to build within a certain stipulation (e.g., not mansion). Govt subsidized a percentage of mortgage, e.g., knocked 2% off interest rate. Had to pay back after five year term. This gave a break at the beginning to get into home owner market – deferring income – not a gift. Wouldn't be in home have now without help with first home.

Day Care: Example 19 – Sister able to go to employment training because of it. Very good effect.

4.4.1.5 Program Meets an Important Need That Would Otherwise Be Unmet

Unemployment Insurance: Example 83 – My husband is a heavy duty mechanic and gets laid off quite often. He relies on UI. With the economy so up and down he has a hard time getting on full time. It's been a little slow getting cards back. Generally – good.

Unemployment Insurance: Example 93 – Have received it in past – and found it a tremendous assistance at the time. As a whole, it is run well and appears reasonable in both employer and employee contribution.

4.4.1.6 Has Positive Effects on Society or Economy

Employment Training: Example 129 – In highly technical and changing industry/technology such as film – these kinds of programs can provide retraining and professional skill to enable Canada to compete globally. Respondent feels this is also true with the number of careers the average person may need in a lifetime. This is particularly the case with women. To learn skills they haven't been exposed to in new technology and/or because of the way they were raised. As well, to provide confidence for those out of the workforce for prolonged periods of time. Similarly, for those becoming [frustrated] with redundancy in entrepreneur jobs that are disappearing because of advanced technology.

4.4.1.7 Helps Protect Us from Failures of Public Provision

Home Support Services: Example 2 – As your retirement programs, pension, and other resources are diminishing in proportion to living costs, it is very necessary to get this type of assistance for the elderly.

RRSPs: Example 67 – It is necessary. The social service net can only support so much. As part of the "post-war baby generation" I will have to help support myself in retirement. The deduction is very fair.

4.4.2 Principles

4.4.2.1 Social Programs Must Reach Those Who Need Them, Should Not Benefit Only Middle- and Upper-Income Groups

Investment Tax Incentives: Example 2 – Any company that has profit for three consecutive years should have to pay a sizeable tax and not carry a liability on year after year. Otherwise benefits are going to business that are badly needed elsewhere in the system.

Home Support Services: Example 2 – As your retirement programs, pension, and other resources are diminishing in proportion to living costs, it is very necessary to get this type of assistance for the elderly.

Capital Gains Allowance: Example 6 – Short-term benefit. Eventually we'll have to pay the piper. Again, though, only those who have the money can take advantage of it. Lower income people are caught in the crack.

Employment Training Programs: Example 94 – Can be a very effective method of bringing people back into the job market – there needs to be a better screening process of screening on the eligibility of potential clients. More information needs to be shared, as they relate to employment success with the potential employer. Programs are somewhat self-perpetuating, as the programs using it want to be "seen" as successful – however, there is a need to better measure criteria of successes: often the employment training program itself becomes the job creation program, ie. the need is always there – and the need for training do not translate into the best training programs. Many times govt agencies allocate funding before assessing the real need to individuals/groups and other organizations design programs to access the money.

4.4.2.2 We Must Retain or Even Extend the Principle of Universality

Public Health Services: Example 129 – An example of service that should be universal is immunization provided to 15 year old. Again feels that universal provision is vital because of all these new outbreaks. Baby clinics provided at local schools a wonderful way to reach out in the neighbourhoods to even those who have no transportation ....

Medical Services Plan: Example 91 – Essential and good; opposed to the premiums as they restrict access – knows several people who do not have it. Premium assistance is good, but a lot of people are not aware of its existence and complicated application. Dental care should be part of medical services – too many people do not use dentists.

Medical Services Plan: Example 110 – Absolutely wonderful with their needs. Feels it's a must to keep for Canada – wishes there was a dental plan, even though husband has a bit of a coverage from [work]. She feels that it is basic to our lives. Spouse has just gone through 7 months of testing for a disability that is treatable. One son has been in Riverview since last July – in research section. Family would have been wiped out, if MSP not there.

Medical Services Plan: Example 51 – I lived in the States 28 years. Was in hospital 3 days and got bill for $600. It would never happen. MSP is much superior to American. Best thing that ever happened to Canada. I'm against user fees. It would greatly affect the poor. If there was a $10 fee it's the difference of milk for kids vs. medical treatment. The service is good – my wife was in GF Strong for 6 weeks – great help – no cost to us. My $50 today will go as a donation to GF Strong.

4.4.2.3 We Must Invest in Human Capital: Social Programs Are an Investment

Tax Deductions for Tuition: Example 59 – I think there needs to be greater subsidies from the state. There is an occurrence that education is becoming a luxury rather than available to everyone.

Student Loans: Example 127 – Education costs should be deductible dollar for dollar – free – some way to not have income to deduct it from. Again, it is money that will return to society.

Employment Training: Example 129 – In highly technical and changing industry/technology such as film – these kinds of programs can provide retraining and professional skill to enable Canada to compete globally. Respondent feels this is also true with the number of careers the average person may need in a life-time. This is particularly the case with women. To learn skills they haven't been exposed to in new technology and/or because of the way they were raised. As well, to provide confidence for those out of the workforce for prolonged periods of time. Similarly, for those becoming [frustrated] with redundancy in entrepreneur jobs that are disappearing because of advanced technology.

4.4.3 Realities of Program Operation

4.4.3.1 Program Is Inadequate to Need

Income Assistance: Example 77 – Because had four kids when left husband, one in a wheelchair, I was doing everything on my own (found out after could get car insurance paid for) (sold wedding rings). Once phoned welfare when sick and unable to drive sick son to appointment at hospital was told "Your problem" by worker. I had to sell furniture to make ends meet and needed ex-tra help for son in wheelchair – didn't get enough. One worker "He's your responsibility not ours."

Family Allowance: Example 74 – Not enough, when you have four kids. You wouldn't know if these were not your own children and you don't see what they go through.

Unemployment Insurance: Example 119 – In a way it's good – at least you can eat; too many things, such as rights, are not known. When you want to do something, such as studying, they consider the person as not free to look for work. The rules are unclear, re-strictions are rigid and narrowly defined, such as a minimum hours of study (25 hours a week). Some programs, such as sign language are not offered at that many hours per week.

4.4.3.2 Program Has Been Allowed to Deteriorate

Medical Services Plan: Example 81 – Charge a fee at emergency to eliminate back log of people who go in for snuffles and mosquito

bites. Some abuse it. Good friend died because didn't get attention (in papers). Medical staff and services are lacking. Need hospital in Abbotsford desperately. Feel wouldn't have member of
family go in without another family member to supervise what's
going on. Son a few years back haemorrhaged after operation and
Mr. R. caught it before any staff. Shortages cutbacks – Social Credit
did this, now nurses run off their feet. When I was in I saw people
go unfed who couldn't feed themselves.

Medical Services Plan: Example 124 – Are on a crisis point – closing beds, serious financial difficulties. A lot of unemployed medical personnel ready to work, but it's a catch 22 situation, no beds,
no patients, no work. The govt is eventually going to step in. The
elderly is already clogging up the system (e.g., homeless at age
58); there are no extended care in adequate supply. Extending
medical care into the community will be essential for a lot of very
good reasons, including the welfare and psychological well-being
of the elderly. However, their frailty doesn't make it possible to go
anywhere else.

Mental Health Services: Example 47 – I know a lot of mental patients who have had a negative impact because of deinstitutional-
ization. But not enough money was spent on them. The money
saved was not put towards helping them. They were put into the
community. There was a net service loss.

4.4.3.3 Only Middle- or High-Income Persons Can Take Advantage of It, Thus It Benefits Mainly Those Who Don't Need It

RRSPs: Example 109 – Important – but unfortunately only mid to
upper income can take advantage of it now. It is a very important
system, but is a disproportionate benefit – again to higher income – nothing for income redistribution. This has to be attend-
ed to.

Capital Gains Allowance: Example 6 – Short-term benefit.
Eventually we'll have to pay the piper. Again, though, only those
who have the money can take advantage of it. Lower income people are caught in the crack.

4.4.3.4 Robs You of Dignity, Self-Esteem

Unemployment Insurance: Example 26 – Wasn't really good experience. She got the impression she was a criminal – but she needed the service and paid into it. I couldn't have made it without UIC, but they made me feel I didn't need it. I was a new Canadian and maybe because of my ethnic background I didn't understand. It has helped lots of people – of course lots of people abuse it. There has been lots of improvement with that service.

Immigrant Services: Example 1 – Extremely negative. Lack of organization of the Immigration office to keep new immigrants informed of procedures/time periods, and their rights. Personnel seemed to operate under either very changing conditions (lack of education to keep informed and/or lack of knowledge of procedures). The so-called orderly system was totally at the expense of the immigrant's time. Economic costs considerable to recipient and was also threatening his relationship to his wife (uncertainty of her acceptance created a lot of strain in relationship and made it difficult to make plans for life together). For personal independence, extra risks had to be taken to financially and socially establish the necessary business connections. Procedures were dehumanizing.

4.4.3.5 Program Is Essential but Is Threatened

Student Loans: Example 129 – Respondent's view is negative – fears that the golden age of universal access is fast fading. We are moving back to the '20s philosophy. Education is not going to be made available to lower and middle income families as well as the really poor.

Medical Services Plan: Example 124 – Are on a crisis point – closing beds, serious financial difficulties. A lot of unemployed medical personnel ready to work, but it's a catch 22 situation, no beds, no patients, no work. The govt is eventually going to step in. The elderly is already clogging up the system (e.g., homeless at age 58); there are no extended care in adequate supply. Extending medical care into the community will be essential for a lot of very good reasons, including the welfare and psychological well-being of the elderly. However their frailty doesn't make it possible to go anywhere else.

Medical Services Plan: Example 7 – Knowing that you can get the service without having to pay for it when you need it is important. Feels that it is very fundamental to the services provided in Canada, but is concerned that thinking within government is that the services need to be changed and/or amended. Generally meaning a lowering of service, ie. lessening of freedom of access and the type of service provided to Canadians. Recognizes that there is a lot of abuses, but that need to be better organized, but not a lowering of service.

4.5 Conclusions

1 Impacts are primarily positive. Nevertheless, there are some negative impacts, which the respondents attribute mainly to inadequate provision or programs set up in such a way as to defeat their declared objectives. The former problem is reflected in comments on incomplete medical and dental coverage and the latter in comments about programs with rules that trap you forever in the social program and about overworked, harried staff who make you feel like a criminal.

2 There is also concern about abuses of some services, particularly Income Assistance, Medical Services, and Unemployment Insurance. These are seen as problems to be minimized by effective administration rather than reasons for opposing these programs. The only program about which doubts or reservations were expressed was Investment Tax Incentives. No one argued against a comprehensive system of social programs for Canada. As will be seen in later chapters, this is consistent with the quantitative results.

3 The verdict on whether the existing social services are meeting the basic goals originally proclaimed for the "Welfare State" is mixed:

- The thrust of many of the comments about impact of services is directly in line with these goals. This is seen in themes emerging from the data on impacts.
- There is virtually no questioning of the need for social programs, only of the adequacy, efficacy, or efficiency of some programs as currently administered.

- Given the chorus of grim warnings about deficits that we hear today, it is remarkable how little of this is reflected in the data.
- The respondents' accounts of impacts of social service encounters on their lives are too real and detailed to suggest that they were merely being pollyannish or polite. These comments might be dismissed as "testimonials," not to be taken seriously, except that they come from the very large majority of the sample, and thus escape the principal objection to testimonials, that they are selected.

4 The most important message of the data is a gloomy one. On the one hand the respondents see the social programs as desperately needed and efficacious. On the other hand they see the programs as eroding under their feet. This is particularly true of the mainstay programs of health services and pensions. There is a strong feeling of worry about these programs, with no convincing solutions in sight.

5 In view of the erosion of pension plans, one sees efforts to build retirement security through a variety of private pension schemes. At the same time, both the quantitative analysis presented in Chapter 3 and the comments of respondents strongly indicate that retirement security through private plans is becoming increasingly beyond the reach of the majority. No clear solution to this dilemma emerges.

I return to points 4 and 5 in Chapter 11, on social policy implications.

Part III:
Social Welfare Issues and Campaigns in Canada

5

Chris McNiven

Welfare Issues in the Establishment Press in Canada

5.1 Introduction

This chapter is an exploration of the views and comments about the provision of social welfare in Canada, expressed by various categories of press contributors whose writings appeared in the *Globe and Mail,* the *Vancouver Sun,* the *Vancouver Province, Maclean's, Saturday Night,* and a small sample of literature published by B.C. labour unions, social welfare organizations, and the feminist press between March 1991 and June 1993. A few documents collected before 1991 were also used.

The main objective of the press review was to gain a sense of the type and range of social welfare issues and perspectives that were addressed in a selected sample of the Canadian press during a period when Canada was undergoing major economic, social, and cultural changes.

Since the review covered only a limited number of articles, commentaries, editorials, and letters from a non-representative sample of contributors, we make no claim that the debates and the views identified and explored were representative of Canadian public opinion. But, in a study dealing with the views of the public, we believed that it was important to take account of the issues which were promoted and debated in the press, and of the fluctuations in the moods of the contributors. The findings enabled some comparison to be made between the views of these contributors and those of the household sample.

This chapter is divided into five sections: a description of the approach used to conduct the review, a brief exploration of background events which could have influenced the press contributors, an examination of the views of these contributors on the social security net and their views on the extended system of social programs, and a final section that includes a summary of the most relevant findings as well as some comments about trends and issues that were not addressed extensively by most of the contributors.

The data collected for the review were fairly extensive. In order to contain the material within the confines of a brief document only the major findings are described, and the detailed comments made by many contributors are not reproduced in this summary.

5.2 The Press Review

The conduct of the review was guided by questions raised to address the problem for inquiry in this project, as described in the Preface of this Report. In the press review it was impossible, of course, to ask specific questions or to select respondents and topics. Some contributors were well-known personalities but many letter writers did not provide any demographic information or clues about their background. Views and trends that seemed to be isolated or widespread could be identified but no precise levels of support for, or rejection of, a conservative or a liberal perspective could be calculated. It was not possible to probe and to elicit further information when comments were ambiguous, superficial, or based on inaccurate information, but it was possible to find statements that answered questions raised in the study. Contributors often gave reasons to explain their views and these reasons provided additional and useful insights into the notions of social welfare that were most prevalent in some circles in Canada between 1991 and 1993.

A wide-net approach was used to catch information that bore a relationship to the topics of interest to the study. Items that turned out to be too repetitive or not as relevant as had been first assumed were discarded. The items ranged in size from brief comments to lengthy articles; longer items were abstracted.

The press contributors included reporters writing general press releases, editors, syndicated columnists, commentators, article writers, experts representing different points of view in a field; members of organizations; politicians or their spokesperson, and members of the general public, the so- called ordinary Canadians.

Most of the relevant material available dealt with general social welfare issues, background material, and two fields of welfare: the basic social security net consisting of Family and Child Welfare, Health Care, and Income Security, and the extended system of programs and services consisting of Immigration, Human Rights, and other programs that had been added progressively to the initial net. Some material was also collected on crime and delinquency, the tax system, aid to business organizations and to voluntary organizations, and the Social Charter.

Table 5.1 indicates the number and sources of the items collected between 1991 and 1993.

Table 5.1

Breakdown of Number and Sources of Media Items
(Total Sources = 1733)

Topic	No.	Rep	Ed	Col	Pol	Com	Gen	Org
Background Material	264	21	29	12	30	92	27	53
Family and Child Welfare	195	12	9	11	20	10	48	85
Income Security	205	68	6	5	16	16	44	50
Housing	53	16	1	3	4	7	12	10
Health Care	257	33	10	7	48	21	36	102
Immigration	99	12	8	4	16	4	29	26
Human Rights	251	27	21	21	17	47	64	54
Crime and Delinquency	71	10	2	1	6	4	25	23
Foreign Aid	21	3	1	1	5	2	6	3
General Social Welfare Issues	317	34	11	23	78	28	58	85

Description of Source Codes:

No.	Total Number
Rep	Reporters
Ed	Editors
Col	Columnists
Pol	Politicians
Com	Commentators/Writers/Academic Experts
Gen	General Public
Org	Organizations

5.3 Background Factors

Between 1991 and 1993 events were occurring and situations were developing in Canada and elsewhere in the world which most likely influenced the views of many of the press contributors. Among the most important were:

- the grim state of the Canadian economy and its impact on the lives of Canadians;
- the second attempt, since 1987, to revise the Canadian constitution; and

- the growing awareness of the size of the federal and provincial debts and deficits, and of the massive social and cultural changes that had been taking place in the country for several decades.

Some of these changes had seemed to be too remote from the day-to-day experiences of a majority of people to warrant more than passing attention; but others, which previously had been considered to be quite positive and desirable, were suddenly perceived to be mixed blessings because they were occurring very rapidly and seemed to have the potential to destroy the quality of life people wanted to protect. Events occurring in other parts of the world had press contributors pondering about the fate of socialism, the future of capitalism, the appropriate role of the state, and the unpredictability of individual and collective behaviour.

The economic issues were explored extensively and intensively in editorials, commentaries, and articles, but some letter writers seemed less interested in abstract debates than they were in writing about their personal experiences and concerns. Opinions often were sharply divided. In May 1992, for instance, the federal Minister of Finance was arguing that Canadians had never been wealthier because the net worth of all Canadian households had increased from $1.8 billion at the end of 1990 to $1.9 billion at the end of 1991. But press contributors, whose incomes ranged from very low to fairly high, indicated that they did not share this interpretation of the situation. Their experience was that their standard of living had dropped between 1981 and 1991 and that they had increasing difficulties making ends meet.

At the same time, economic experts were sending strong warnings that worse was to be anticipated. Expressions of concern mounted and turned to anguish in 1992 as the level of unemployment remained quite high. The nature of the unemployment seemed to be particularly alarming, not only did it affect managers and experienced workers, but it also prevented young workers in the 16-to-25 age bracket from entering the work force. Moreover, by the end of 1992, civil servants, a category of workers who had always been protected from job insecurity, were starting to be affected by dismissals and salary cuts. Even more alarming was the rather glaring fact that large numbers of positions and jobs were vanishing permanently. Numerous pleas were addressed to the government to change the direction of its economic policies. But press contributors could not agree whether the shift should consist of an adoption of stronger neocon-servative economic theories or of some blend of neoliberal and neoso-cialist socioeconomic principles.

Different explanations were suggested to account for the problems facing the Canadian economy. The labour movement, for instance, at-tributed the permanent loss of thousands of jobs every year to the Free Trade Agreement and to the setting of a high interest rate, while members of business firms were more inclined to attribute the prob-lems to the inability of the Canadian work force to adapt rapidly enough to economic restructuring.

Other explanations included the influence of the American econ-omy, the erosion of traditional forms of government intervention to maintain demand and to stimulate the recovery from the series of re-cessions that had occurred since 1983, and the lack of appropriate educational and training programs for workers. By 1992, a growing number of contributors were tracing the situation back to interrelated and very complex factors that included the restructuring of the world economy, the consequences of the technological revolution that fol-lowed the Second World War, and the population explosion which was producing many more new workers every year than the interna-tional and national labour markets could absorb or would ever need.

Between the summer of 1991 and the fall of 1992, the constitu-tional revision saga unfolded relentlessly. The proposed constitutional accord included a clause referring to a commitment to the provision of a health care system, adequate social services and benefits, the pro-tection of the rights of workers to organize and bargain collectively, and the protection of the environment. The clause, however, was non-justiciable and the commitment limited to policy objectives rather than to the establishment of enforceable standards. It did not elicit overwhelming praise from supporters of the social services. The final constitutional proposal, known as the Charlottetown Accord, was rejected by a majority of Canadians when a non-binding referen-dum was held in October 1992. The government decided not to pro-ceed further and the constitutional process came to a halt. The cata-strophic crisis which supporters of the accord had predicted should the accord be rejected did not materialize. But the content of the ac-cord, and the approach used to encourage Canadians to endorse it, fostered a great deal of resentment and anger across the country. It revealed the existence, and probably increased the amount, of dis-unity between groups and regions in Canada. Many contributors indicated, however, that their views on various notions of social welfare had been either confirmed and strengthened or shaken and changed as a result of the numerous discussions that preceded the referendum.

In late 1992, after the debates on the constitutional revision had died down, the size of the national debt and the persistency of yearly deficits in government budgets moved to the forefront in the press reports and debates. The mood of contributors oscillated between anxiety and anger, between distrust of all politicians and experts and yearnings for leaders who somehow could convey hopes of a happy future, and between sympathy for the victims of the recession, unemployment, and economic restructuring and concerns for personal survival. Contributors tended to look for scapegoats. They blamed alternatively, or simultaneously, the proponents or the opponents of generous social programs and the supporters or critics of neoconservative theories. As taxpayers, they wanted to protect their incomes and investments from inflation, tax increases, and fluctuating interest rates. As persons at risk, they wanted to protect the social and health care programs they did, or would, depend upon to survive economically. In 1992, the deficit financing approach, which had been used in the past to resolve this problem of conflicting interest, no longer seemed to be an appropriate option to a majority of contributors. None of the political leaders and experts were trusted to be able to provide any reassuring and palatable plan which held obvious promise of getting the country out its economic mess. By 1993, the prevalent message found in the press was the awful necessity of having to make drastic sacrifices and to cut down to the bare bones. A key debate revolved around the selection of what was to be cut, and of whose bones were to be cut first or last, or left untouched. Political arguments, lobbying, and power struggles started to displace the abstract arguments of experts.

Although demographic and sociocultural changes are continual, most people notice them only at irregular intervals. Between 1991 and 1993, many contributors seemed to become more clearly aware of and more vocal about the implications of the changes that were occurring in Canada than they had been in previous years. Most often cited in the press were the following issues:

- the aging of the population and the economic and social costs associated with the phenomenon;

- the consequences of the Charter of Rights and Freedoms;
- the process of adaptation to the realities of a society that was becoming rapidly more multicultural and multiethnic;
- the contrasts between overpopulation in some parts of the world and the decline in population in others;
- the growth in the size and influence of the multinational economy;
- the end of the Cold War;
- the increasing number of outbreaks of violent ethnic and religious conflicts; and
- the terrifying spread of AIDS and of other diseases which modern medicine could not combat effectively.

Many contributors indicated, in a variety of ways, that while they still welcomed some types of changes, they also had increasing misgivings about many others. In 1992, they were yearning for stability, security, and a more cautious approach to the endorsement of rapid sociocultural changes. Workers felt that the demands placed on them to adjust to a new work culture, characterized by an extreme emphasis on competition, increased productivity, low job security, and acceptance of wage cuts, were damaging to their health and their family relationships, and were not improving the quality of their lives or the size of their wealth.

In 1993, the shrinking of the middle class in Canada could no longer be ignored. Many Canadians were beginning to believe that the shape of the socioeconomic structure of their country was changing from a pyramid to a small cube of wealthy people on the top of a large cube of low-income people, with a mass of expendable individuals no longer needed in their society and relegated to its at the bottom.

These background factors were not discrete. They, and others too complex to be presented in this summary, interacted, blended, reinforced one another, and created discomfort and disadvantages for many people, as well as satisfaction and advantages for some. A number of contributors noted that equality, justice, and genuine well-being seemed to be elements of the quality of life that had become more elusive, notwithstanding all the efforts to make them more real. Some articles contained interesting and plausible analyses of the phenomenon derived from an understanding of social psychology and historical experiences. An article by Mary Janigan "Mad as Hell," which appeared in June 1992 in *Maclean's,* reflected the major components of the mood of Canadians at the time. Janigan made references to three areas that elicited much concern on the part of the public: the widening gap between income expectations and take-home pay, the tax burden, and the erosion of the safety net. In early 1993, these concerns were still present but there were signs that contributors were very concerned also about the national debt.

In what appeared to be a paradox, the flood of information from politicians, community leaders and experts about the state of the economy, the general welfare of the nation, and other issues seemed to have left many members of the general public more confused and anxious than well informed and content. Much of the information could not be assimilated and understood fast enough and some was suspected of being inaccurate, distorted, and little more than propaganda to sell one or another questionable and bankrupt dogma.

5.4 The Views of the Contributors on the Social Security Net

A considerable amount of material was available on the Canadian welfare system. The material collected for this section dealt with programs and services which could be described as constituting the basic social security net: Family and Child Welfare, Income Support, Old Age Security, and Health Care. The data in each field was organized whenever possible in the following order: the events which seemed to have attracted the attention of the press to the field, the major issues that surfaced, the different points of view expressed by the press contributors, the debates and their outcomes.

5.4.1 Family and Child Welfare

In 1991 and 1992, the federal government continued to pursue the process it had started in previous years, and introduced further changes to the provision of family and child welfare services and benefits. This phase in the change process included the decision to postpone for an indeterminate period the establishment of a national day care service program, and the final replacement of the universal family allowances with two programs: an integrated system of child benefits for low-income families and a program to help children at risk of abuse and parental neglect. A major issue perceived by most contributors was whether these changes were a logical evolution toward a system that was more efficient fiscally as well as more relevant and effective, or whether the family and child welfare system was altered mostly to mark the final ending of the principle of universality and to promote the shift from a social security system to a neoconservative model of social welfare.

In the ensuing debates, a few proponents of the social service perspective and some Liberal and New Democrat politicians defended the notion of universality. They argued that universality protected people from demeaning needs or means tests, which had to be administered when programs were targeted, that it was a recognition of the collective commitment by all Canadians to the welfare of all children and families, and that it was therefore the cornerstone of the notion of social welfare as a right attached to citizenship, which had long been entrenched in Canada. They were a minority and they became silent fairly rapidly, probably because the main debate about the universality of family allowances had taken place earlier, when the initial steps to terminate the 1945 program had been implemented.

Conservative politicians and contributors who were known to be supporters of a neoconservative perspective strongly approved of the targeting approach when it was used to give benefits to those who were in genuine need and to protect children from neglectful or abusive parents. Representatives of low-income groups also supported the approach because they believed that it was more equitable to allocate a larger share of public revenues to the poor than to give the same benefits to every one. Some interesting speculations could be made about the near absence of complaints on the part of middle-income families who were to lose their benefits.

Almost all contributors seemed to support the notion of a selective program of child benefits with entitlement based on a declaration of means that could be easily administered. But several contributors indicated that they supported selectivity not as a principle but as a temporary measure only, because they believed that there were no longer enough resources available to continue to finance the former universal program during a period of economic recession without adding several billions more to the national debt.

There were no thorough debates about the logic, fairness, or validity of the choice of income lines established by the government to separate full beneficiaries from partial ones or from non-beneficiaries. Concerns were expressed, however, about the implications of a means test approach when the demarcation lines could be lowered administratively at any time and when no consideration needed to be given to the erosion of benefits resulting from inflation. Abruptly, or slowly, benefits could be withheld from all families but the very poor.

When the debates shifted from abstract discussions about principles and concepts of universality, selectivity, and means tests to discussions about the realities of the new programs, there were many more expressions of concern, including some from advocates of the poor and from low- to middle- income parents. The inequality of treatment between the families on welfare and the working poor worried many contributors, yet was praised by one Progressive Conservative politician. The level of benefits was also a cause of concern, particularly after it dawned on several contributors that under the new family benefit program many beneficiaries would not be getting more money than they had under the former allowance and taxation system. Although the federal Minister of Health and Welfare had openly and frankly stated that it was beyond his power to eliminate the problem of child poverty in Canada, there was a wave of disappointment and, in the case of a number of contributors, anger at what was beginning to be perceived as a "smoke and mirror" deception. A program that had been presented as an attempt to promote efficiency and fairness in the redistribution of public revenues seemed to be little more than a strategy to implement a political agenda.

The children-at-risk program elicited even more concerns and criticisms. As well as being perceived by some contributors as another example of the use of taxpayers' money to promote a neoconservative agenda, it was accused of neglecting the most pressing problem facing children at risk: poverty. Critics were of the opinion that the first order of priority in trying to help children was to provide adequate funding for income support programs. Several rather complex debates about the real or spurious aims of the new programs appeared in the press.

Debates about a national day care program flared up, off and on, between 1991 and 1993. They reflected a variety of underlying views about the roles and responsibilities considered to be appropriate for the government, families, parents, women, and men. Ideological, political, economic, and practical arguments were presented to support or oppose different points of views. Opponents argued that it would be impossible for the country to sustain the enormous cost of such a program, that taxpayers would rebel and foreign investors would object and take their investments elsewhere, and that the implementation of the program would constitute an attack on the traditions of Canadian federalism. Another argument stated that day care was not needed because mothers, having realized that day care was detrimental to the welfare of children and of the family, were increasingly choosing to stay home to care for their children.

Supporters argued that since many women had to go to work for wages and since all women had a right to be in the labour force if they wanted to, the provision of affordable and adequate day care services was a necessity and was as important as the provision of education. The supporters were of the opinion that child care was a responsibility to be shared by parents and society because both benefited from the procreation of children and the labour of women. A few contributors believed that the refusal to institute an universal day care system was a sexist message implying that progress toward gender equality had come to a halt in Canada.

Supporters did not indicate whether they would be prepared to pay higher taxes to finance a national day care program, but most seemed to favour an integrated system of funding arrangements whereby public revenues would be used to set up and maintain services, train staff, and subsidize families who could not pay the full and real cost of the services. They seemed to agree that affluent families should be expected to pay user fees, and they agreed that child care workers should be paid decent wages. Contributors made no comments about the provision of services by relatives and friends, but a couple of writers expressed interest in the provision of services by employers. There were no debates concerning a possible choice between making the services accessible to all children or only to children whose parents either were working or attending training or educational programs. A number of service providers were of the opinion that services should be provided by all three sectors, or by the private sector only with subsidies given to families too poor to pay for the full cost of services.

Several mothers wrote about their personal experiences when they had not been able to obtain the day care services that they needed, but they drew different conclusions from these experiences. Some, having managed on their own, objected to the use of their taxes to pay for the care of other women's children. Other mothers, however, wanted taxes to be used to ensure that working women and their children would not have to face the problems they had endured.

The day care issue remained unresolved and was not addressed very often in 1992. In 1993, there were indications that the debate could flare up again before or after a federal election campaign.

Another issue that had an impact on family and child welfare service involved school meal programs. The material dealing with this issue was written mostly by school administrators, board members, and parents. The material indicated that while some schools had set up good programs, school meals were considered to be an unfortunate necessity by most contributors. A couple of social welfare experts regarded them as being Band-Aid services, and a columnist condemned them because he believed that the real problem was the unwillingness of some poor people to budget properly and to cook decent meals for their children. A few mothers indicated that, while they were poor, they always had been able to feed their children properly without the help of school meals and that other women should be able to do the same. A couple of mothers were grateful for the help their children had received from a school meal program.

In general, those who strongly supported the initiatives taken by the government in the family and child welfare field liked them because they conformed to one or both of two agendas: an economic approach derived from neoconservative economic theories, and an attempt to return to traditional notions of the role of the family and particularly of the role of women. Proponents of the social services disliked the initiatives for precisely the same reasons.

Most contributors were interested in the development of a system of family and child welfare services that was quite different from the system that the government was setting up. They were not interested in political agendas and ideological squabbles but wanted parents to work with service providers and social welfare experts to plan and implement an efficient and effective system that would benefit all children and families. They were sensitive to the issue of cost but believed that investment in the welfare of the family deserved to be given a high priority. Many contributors were of the opinion that it was futile to design programs to help children at risk while ignoring the growing incidence of poverty in Canada and the lack of affordable day care services for parents who were trying to work rather than depend on public assistance. Many contributors suggested that the tax system should be revised, and a few contributors suggested that practices in the workplace should be modified to reflect changes in the structure of the family and in the roles of family members.

5.4.2 Income Support Programs
Data were collected on various types of income support provisions: Income Assistance, Unemployment Insurance, Food Banks, Old Age Security, and Housing Programs. The amount of material available on

Workers' Compensation and on the Canada Pension Plan was very limited.

What attracted attention to the first three of these programs in 1991 was the growing number of unemployed Canadians who had to use them to survive. These programs formed a system through which people in need travelled. People who were unemployable were eligible for public assistance. The unemployed were eligible normally to receive unemployment insurance benefits, but once these benefits were exhausted they too had to depend on public assistance. Many in both groups used the food banks at least occasionally. Funding for the three programs came from different sources, but even before 1991, they all faced a common problem: a persistent discrepancy between a soaring demand for help and insufficient resources to accommodate it.

All contributors shared a belief that an income assistance system of programs to help people who had no income and few assets was indispensable. They all indicated that fraudulent claims were not to be tolerated and that the Canadian system needed to be changed to meet the socioeconomic realities of the '90s. They agreed also that the programs for the unemployed should not provide handouts but should help them to re-enter the work force and become self-supporting as rapidly as possible. However, they did not agree about the underlying causes of the problems facing the system or about relevant solutions.

Comments about income security varied to some extent over time. In 1991, there were many more of the perennial complaints about workers who were unemployed because they were lazy, unwilling to take menial but respectable jobs, or reluctant to update their skills. But since concerns about "sturdy beggars" have been voiced through the whole history of social welfare in western countries, these comments hardly reflected a hardening in the views of the contributors toward the users of income support programs.

As the level of unemployment continued to remain quite high in 1992, this line of comments was supplanted by expressions of concern about the plight of the new poor, those workers who had always been steadily employed, who often had been skilled and experienced in their line of work but whose jobs were disappearing permanently at an alarming rate. Some of the comments reflected the ambivalent feelings of a number of contributors toward the situation. One could speculate that they felt sympathy for "people like us" but that being afraid that their own jobs could be the next ones to vanish, it was assuring to assume that the problems facing other workers had been caused by their inappropriate behaviour, and therefore could have been prevented had they behaved well. The belief that one could control one's destiny by engaging in the appropriate type of behaviour tended to be more attractive when contemplating the future than the belief that one was at the mercy of external forces over which one had little or no control. This tendency could be one factor accounting for the attractiveness of a number of conservative views on social welfare issues when the future looked so bleak to so many contributors. When contemplating the past, however, there could be emotional and practical advantages in believing that people who faced problems had been victims of external and destructive forces. By 1993, the debate between the lazy-and-incompetent-worker notion and the victim-of-inept-public-policy notion tended to reappear in some of the press content. They probably influenced by the stances taken by political opponents in the federal pre-election campaign.

From 1992 on, the contributors, reminded frequently that drastic cutbacks to the social programs were absolutely necessary to deal with the national debt and the deficits, offered suggestions to improve the income security system for adults under 65. One group of remedies was to conserve scarce resources by using them only to help those most in need and/or those most able to make effective use of them to get back into the labour force. A related suggestion was that this could be achieved by making eligibility requirements more stringent and by giving smaller cash benefits for shorter periods of time. The government was interested in similar ideas and acted accordingly.

Opponents of this point of view tended to believe that the benefits provided through unemployment insurance and public assistance were already too low and too difficult to obtain. They also objected to the assumptions that lay behind the suggestions, which seemed to ignore the nature of the drastic changes in the work situation. Retraining programs were sensible; however, since unemployment was not cyclical but the result of economic restructuring, many workers would never be able to re-enter the work force, at least not as full-time employees receiving adequate wages. New approaches were called for that involved an agenda that went well beyond a concern for traditional social service strategies. There were many debates about the role of the government and of the private sector in job creation. Most contributors favoured more intervention by the government, as well as more emphasis on the welfare of workers and less on the demands of employers in labour management issues involving big business. There was a consensus among all contributors about the importance of providing an adequate income to people who were unemployable because of severe disabilities, chronic illness, or advanced age.

The provision of a guaranteed annual income based on a means test and replacing all other income support programs was favoured by both neoconservative supporters and by some advocates of the poor. The first group wanted to use this approach because they believed it would be far less costly to taxpayers than the current one. The income to be guaranteed could be set at a minimal level, with the government retaining the initiative to further lower the means line any time it decided to cut down public expenditures. Advocates of the poor liked it because beneficiaries would not have to be subjected to any demeaning needs test, but would have the right to be eligible for benefits as soon as their income fell below a specified level. They also liked the idea that the program would have as a target the most needy Canadians. They seemed to assume that a shift to a selective program would automatically mean that the money saved would be used to give benefits that would be greater than those provided to the recipients by the various programs operating currently. This assumption did not seem to be shared by neoconservatives and it was not shared at all by opponents of guaranteed annual income programs.

These opponents, who usually were social welfare professionals and experts who had explored and assessed the value and drawbacks of different models of guaranteed annual income programs, had come to the conclusion that the approach was flawed. There were considerable administrative difficulties involved in the use of declaration of past income rather than use of evidence of present needs to establish eligibility, and emergency programs would therefore continued to be needed. Moreover, an approach that had been invented many years ago and supported ever since by conservative economists and politicians could be suspected of being one of the tools in the arsenal used to implement a neoconservative agenda.

By 1992, a growing number of contributors were in favour of a two-level approach to guide future directions of change in the field of income security. It included a short-term plan to improve the current system and do away with its more severe flaws – which were described fairly often by service users and providers – and a long-term process guided by a number of basic ideals. Most contributors were of the opinion that these ideals called for a charter of social rights and the development of a new social contract to replace the old social consensus. They believed that the cost of the income assistance system would go down when the employment situation improved.

The food banks were considered by all contributors to be a dismal consequence of the inadequacy of the current system of income support. A few people wrote that the banks had protected them from hunger but not from malnutrition, and that they had disliked the demeaning experience of having to use them. A couple of contributors believed that it was going to be very difficult to eliminate the food banks because they had become institutions, and because their demise would be resisted by their employees and by the growing number of users who did not have any alternative to turn to. A comment from one contributor, to the effect that people tended to abuse assistance less when it was given under the auspices of charity than when they believed that they had a statutory right to it, seemed to suggest another reason why the banks could continue to be supported.

An issue that elicited many comments was the support of single mothers and their children. Fears were expressed that providing these mothers with easy access to long-term assistance could not only encourage those who were very immature to keep infants who would have been better off placed for adoption, but would also ensure that many would remain untrained and therefore permanently unemployable. Another fear was that it would encourage fathers to shift the responsibility for supporting their children onto the taxpayers.

Most contributors, including several members of the helping professions, while agreeing that fathers should be expected to support their children, held the view that single mothers should receive support from public revenues when they needed help and that they never should be compelled to give their children up for adoption because of sheer financial necessity. The complexity of the issue was recognized by several writers, and the debates tended to link assistance for single mothers to other issues such as the provision of day care and the changing structure of the traditional family. The debates reflected concerns about the implications of the growing number of families headed by women and the lack of enforcement of child support orders. Most of the comments indicated that this concern was not so much about the morality of single parenthood than it was about concrete problems of economic and social costs affecting mothers, children, taxpayers, and society.

In 1991 and 1992, relatively little overt attention was paid to Old

Age Security Programs. Nevertheless, there were indications that concern about the income security of the elderly was very much alive. By 1992, several contributors were assuming or had sensed that the clawback approach that had ended the universality of old age pensions was only a first step in a process to turn a program of public insurance into a branch of the public assistance program for elderly Canadians who were very poor. Some politicians and commentators who were known to hold conservative views recommended that this step be taken. A small number of letter writers shared the same view. They indicated that this was either because they were wealthy and would not notice the disappearance of the old age pension, or because they were members of anti-poverty groups who favoured replacement of the pension with a guaranteed annual income program. Most contributors opposed the relinquishment of the insurance notion of old age security introduced in Canada many decades ago. Although most objected to the discriminatory aspect of the clawback, they did not object to the use of the normal tax system to recover all or part of the pension benefits from the income of wealthy seniors.

The debates about old age security indicated the emergence of a potential conflict of interest between low- and middle-income seniors. Concerns increasingly began to be expressed by contributors about the large group of seniors whose relatively modest investments were eroded by inflation and low interest rates, and whose pension and health care benefits now appeared to be in jeopardy as well. The major fear of these contributors was that a drop in their income, coupled with inflation in the cost of shelter, would result in the loss of their residence in a familiar neighbourhood. The trauma experienced by elderly people who had already been forced, in some cities, to relocate into cheaper accommodations and less desirable areas when urban renewal and shrinking incomes forced them out of their old homes was cited as a warning of what was in store for the considerable number of elderly people who were not poor but who were not rich either. A few contributors pointed out that unless there was a well-planned and gradual transition period from one system of old age security to another, Canadians who were near or over age 65 would not be able to make the necessary adjustments to their income strategies. They suggested that a new system should include the continuation of public sector programs, improvements to private pension plans, and a revision of the tax system. There were few if any comments about the Canada Pension Plan, most likely because it did not seem to have been placed on the first list of social programs to be restructured by the government.

The data available on the provision of affordable housing, while not very abundant, indicated that there was continuing support for the provision of social housing to the elderly and the disabled. But there were mixed feelings, or indifference, concerning the provision of social housing to other populations, as well as strong opposition to the location of social housing for low-income families and for the mentally handicapped in neighbourhoods other than those considered to be fairly undesirable. Home ownership in a "good" area continued to have a very important economic and social value for Canadians, and contributors who addressed this issue indicated quite clearly that they feared any potential threat to the social quality of their neighbourhood and to the value of their investment in a house. Their comments suggested that poverty and mental conditions continued to be associated with a financial or behaviourial inability to maintain dwellings in good condition, and with a propensity to engage in various forms of deviant or criminal behaviour.

5.4.3 Health Care

The bulk of the considerable amount of material available on health care dealt with two major components of the health care system: medicare and hospital insurance. The main issue of concern was the discrepancy between the soaring demand for services and the share of public revenues allocated to the system to meet this demand.

Two groups of contributors were not in favour of the continuation of a universal system of health care for different reasons. One group believed that patients who did not pay for the services they received soon tended to behave irresponsibly, to abuse the system, and to expect other taxpayers to cover the cost of superfluous services. The second group consisted of physicians who were engaged in fee-setting disputes with provincial governments and who were in favour of reintroducing a funding system based on private insurance and user fees. There was a general consensus among all contributors that the cost of health had become a problem in Canada, but the vast majority of these contributors wanted to keep the universal system, although they were prepared to support the introduction of some changes to the system in order to save it.

A large number of reasons were offered to explain the nature and the origin of the crisis, and the solutions proposed were equally abundant. The remedies fell into five categories, and between 1991 and 1993 many were implemented. The most popular category included measures to make better use of available funds through improvements in the planning, coordination, administration, monitoring, and evaluation of the services provided to the public. Also popular were suggestions to supplement public resources with other funding options: higher premiums, payroll deductions, user fees, and the use of lottery money. Each option, and particularly the last two, elicited many debates but no agreement about the choices considered to be most desirable.

A third category of remedies focused on the behaviour of users and providers, urging them to reduce the demands they placed on the system. A fourth category included suggestions about a variety of community care approaches to supplement or replace the costly care provided by hospital professionals. But in 1992 there were warnings that adequate community care was also quite expensive because it required the provision of an integrated network of professional and community services. A fifth and related category included suggestions to encourage, or even mandate, the replacement of hospital and institutional care with the labour of family members, usually women, and friends. Between 1991 and 1992, there were warnings from professionals and health care experts about overenthusiasm for the use of family labour when it was imposed on unwilling and overburdened family members to serve as a substitute for services that should be provided by the public sector. A number of articles appeared that described the damage to the physical and mental health of exhausted caregivers and established a link between this type of care and the inadequate or abusive care received by some elderly patients.

Between 1991 and 1992, any clashes of views between neoconservatives and proponents of the social services concerning health care were mild. Both camps tended to adopt a pragmatic stance and were simply trying to find ways to salvage the national health care system. In early 1993, however, there were strong indications that the federal government was about to remodel the system and to change its various programs from universal to selective ones. Provincial governments, faced every year with a decrease in their transfer payments, could be encouraged to turn to user fees, privatization, and other measures that would end the universality of health care services in

Canada. The process seemed to rest on the assumption that Canadians, terrified by the national debt crisis, would be ready to accept a return to residualism. When this press review ended, the proponents of the social services were raising strong objections to this potential scenario, but the final resolution of the debate would not take place until the federal election, due in the summer or fall of 1993.

5.5 The Extended System of Social Programs

The term "extended system of social programs" was used in this summary to refer to the system of programs, policies, and services added over the years to the basic social security net. Material available and collected included programs to help refugees and immigrants, human rights programs, foreign aid, and a few other programs.

5.5.1 Immigration

Contributors were interested not only in the services provided to refugees and immigrants following their arrival in Canada but also in the broader issue of immigration policies. In the case of family and child welfare and of income security, the government had taken the initiative to introduce changes. In the case of immigration, some of the demands for changes seemed to have originated with the general public, and concerns were related to sociocultural as well as economic costs and benefits. The debates pitted members of organizations and groups advocating on behalf of all refugees and immigrants in general, or on behalf of specific groups of newcomers, against other contributors. The advocates wanted the government to develop more flexible admission policies and more comprehensive and generous services to help newcomers settle comfortably in Canada. Their opponents wanted the government to modify the policies that were in place in 1991, which they believed to be too lax, as well as to modify admission processing procedures that were considered to be defective. Some of the opponents expressed concerns about the growing costs of post-settlement services. These concerns tended to focus particularly on costs affecting school taxes. Between 1991 and 1993, a strong current of caution against unquestioned support of the open approach to immigration and the generous provision of services to immigrants and refugees became more visible in the writings of an increasing number of contributors. The cautious views seemed to have gained ground for a variety of reasons, some spelled out and others only hinted at by the contributors. They included the following:

- the importance of extending the targeting approach to this field of social welfare in order to deal with the economic crisis and the national debt;
- the fear that Canada would be swamped by waves of people the country could not absorb, especially if the federal government chose to ignore the consequences of the fact that other western nations were tightening their immigration and refugees policies in response to a soaring growth in the number of genuine and bogus refugees across the world; and
- the belief that charity should begin at home when poverty was so high in many reserves and provinces.

A factor that played a significant role was the fact that whether or not the number of immigrants and refugees who had been engaged in criminal activities before or after they came to Canada was getting larger, the types of activities coming to the attention of the public appeared to many of the contributors to be quite violent, unusual, and frightening. They feared that it placed a strain on the resources of the police and the judicial system, and that it was proof of a growing invasion by members of international networks of criminals.

Contributors who gave indications that they belonged to a variety of ethnocultural groups believed that the theories about the high socioeconomic benefits and the negligible costs of wide-open immigration could no longer be accepted without some evaluation of the consequences of their implementation.

In general, the opinion of most contributors on the use of taxpayer money to fund post-immigration services was that it was useful and fair to fund and provide adequate services to help immigrants and refugees to settled in their new country. But from 1992 on, caution was urged by contributors – other than members of immigrant and refugee advocacy groups – about any tendency to continue to expand these services or to offer services which could prevent newcomers from integrating rapidly.

Lurking behind some of the negative comments were classic racist views about the origins of certain groups of immigrants and refugees. But other comments indicated the presence of more complex concerns. They seemed to consist of a blend of distrust of strangers, rejection of unwanted changes to the mainstream culture and to institutional arrangements that many Canadians, including some new Canadians, wanted to preserve, and fear that growing populations of newcomers of non-Judeo-Christian origin could choose, sooner or later, to introduce these changes if they became inclined to use their voting and lobbying influence collectively.

Some contributors who were very concerned about racism and xenophobia tended to have faith in the effectiveness of strong sanctions to suppress all unwanted views and attitudes. But a few contributors believed that suppression resulted in driving the problems underground, where they festered and became intractable. They placed more faith in the power of educational programs combined with the promotion of examples of sound patterns of intergroup relationships.

In general contributors appeared reluctant to deal openly and impartially with the issues of racism and ethnocentrism. Rather than promoting the use of calm, non-judgmental, and thorough explorations and discussions to try to resolve the difficulties positively and effectively, many showed a tendency to resort to a pattern of accusations and denials of racism coupled with emphasis on solutions that did not necessarily address the extreme complexity of a very serious and growing problem of intergroup hostility.

5.5.2 Human Rights Issues

The data available and collected under this heading dealt with policies, programs, and services to promote and to protect the rights of women, minority groups, disabled people, homosexuals, and victims of crime or past injustices. These data included writings pertaining to multiculturalism, sexual harassment, and victim compensation. Some of the material dovetailed with material collected on immigration.

Debates were related to the interpretations and consequences of the Canadian Charter of Rights and Freedom, and they touched on several issues:

- the inherent rights of aboriginal people;
- the distinct society status of Quebec;
- the cost and value of different notions of bilingualism and multiculturalism;
- the political, social, and cultural rights of minorities and of women;

- systemic racism
- freedom of speech and political correctness;
- intergroup relationships in a pluralistic society;
- the services and programs operating or needed to address most of these areas.

The debates were too numerous and complex to be presented in this brief summary. Suffice it to state, however, that they reflected a considerable degree of ambivalence, confusion, concerns, and uncertainty about two broad issues. The first was the issue of the relationship between the fair promotion of human rights for all Canadians, which all contributors supported in principle at least, and the promotion of human responsibilities, which was mentioned by an increasing number of contributors from 1992 on. The other was the issue of individual versus collective rights.

Most contributors supported policies and programs that promoted the basic equality rights of all individual Canadians and that protected them from discrimination and denial of access to the resources, amenities, and opportunities attached to Canadian citizenship. This majority was not in favour of programs promoted by advocates that were designed to give some individuals and collectives special privileges, opportunities, and powers for an indeterminate period. This interpretation of the notion of human rights seemed to them to perpetuate the acceptance of inequality and injustice in the distribution of resources and of power within the country. They were prepared to accept, however, the idea that some groups, particularly Aboriginals and women, should be given special opportunities for a limited period, to give them a chance to catch up in the race for equal opportunity. None of the contributors indicated that they were prepared to pay higher taxes to support human rights programs. They agreed for the most part with the view that human rights programs should be funded from public revenues, except in the case of compensation or punitive damages, which should be charged to individuals or organizations convicted of having perpetrated human rights violations, but they seemed to take it for granted that any additional funding needed to maintain or increase human rights services would come from the share of public funds allocated each year to all social welfare services.

The debates were extremely complex because often what was at stake was not a relatively simple issue of justice, tolerance, and fairness but a number of strong and complicated struggles pitting those who wanted to maintain elements of the socioeconomic power structure that happened to benefit them and those who objected to the way these elements treated them, and who therefore wanted them to be changed as soon as possible. The struggles transcended the standard boundaries between the neoconservative and the other ideological perspectives. They revealed or hinted at the existence of some unexpected and unstable alliances among Canadians who happened to contribute to the press under review. Because the debates dealt with controversial or taboo issues they were not always conducted in good faith, and a number of contributors were obviously using codes, probably because of fear of being accused of racism or sexism, or of contravening laws and measures against the promotion of hate. From 1992 on there was an increase in the types of comments that would seem to question the wisdom of analyzing human rights issues within a framework of simplistic notions about intergroup relationships and about the panacea that often are recommended to improve them.

5.5.3 Foreign Aid

The debates about foreign aid flared up only occasionally, and usually as the result of some international event or conference leading to statements from heads of foreign states, politicians, or advocates of foreign aid. The debates involved three different points of view:

- the unconditional approach, leading to the generous and long-term granting of foreign aid to developing nations, mostly to atone for colonial exploitation by western nations in the distant or recent past;
- the restricted approach, consisting of the granting of very limited aid, for limited periods of time, and only for compelling humanitarian or political reasons; and
- the conditional approach, whereby aid should be granted mostly to help developing nations help themselves and to help Canada achieve its own economic and diplomatic objectives. This approach also included such conditions as non-violation of human rights and restrictions on the use of any assistance for belligerent or corrupt purposes.

The number of debates was small, but conditional aid supporters carried out discussions about overpopulation and economic recovery in the developing nations, the validity or morality of making acceptance of family planning a condition of assistance, and the importance of providing more help to women in countries where their labour played a major role in sustaining the economy. One message recurring in the debates about foreign aid was the "charity begins at home" slogan already heard in the debates about immigration and refugee policies. The contributors wanted to see Canada maintain its reputation of generosity and fairness in its approach to foreign relations, but they believed that the country no longer could afford to be as generous as it wanted to be, and that it should not risk acquiring a reputation as a naive and soft "mark" within the international community.

Contributors tended to fluctuate in their views about humanitarian aid. Brief emotional appeals to the government to respond promptly to the plight of victims of civil war or of other massive calamities were followed by periods of indifference. Forceful and well-presented appeals, particularly when they described the sufferings undergone by children in countries or within populations that possessed a favourable image, elicited generous responses. The plight of members of countries and populations that had not been able to project as favourable an image were not highlighted, and there was little or no public support for the granting of assistance.

The provision of foreign aid by the voluntary sector appeared to be supported by all those who wrote about foreign aid, for one of two reasons. The first was that the assistance was voluntary, and did not involve compulsory contributions to fund programs that had relatively low priority; the other stemmed from the distrust of some contributors in the motives of the Canadian government in granting aid. They believed that these motives were political and economic rather than humanitarian.

5.5.4 Counselling Services

Support for the funding of counselling services from public revenues came mostly from professionals who provided them, from social welfare experts, and from users who believed that they had been denied services they were entitled to receive because of the lack of adequate funding from the government. When contributors supported the use of public funds for counselling, they usually wanted the money to be allocated to specific services that they considered to be crucial to the treatment, or to the prevention of problems detrimental to a particular group of sufferers. One possible reason for the rather low level of concrete priority, as opposed to priority in principle, given by contributors to counselling services could have been the competition from self-help and self-support groups. These were popular in 1991 and 1992, did not require the use of taxpayer money, and were considered by some contributors to be as effective as, or more effective than, services provided by professionals.

5.5.5 Other Programs, Issues, and Topics

The data on crime and delinquency reflected the presence of a general hardening of attitude towards criminals and young offenders. Commentators, community leaders, letter writers, and organizers of victim protection groups made strong recommendations for the use of tougher laws and for the introduction of a variety of law-and-order measures and policies. A growing number of contributors tended to place most or all responsibility for deviant behaviour on the offenders or on their parents. One exception, before the end of 1992, was when the offenders were Aboriginals. In these cases, contributors tended to mention the responsibility of white society in having destroyed aboriginal cultures and turned some Native Canadians into potential delinquents. By the end of 1992, there were a few signs of growing impatience with this view on the part of contributors who were members of the general public, especially when the offenses were severe or elicited a high level of fear and concern.

The two types of criminal activity that elicited a particularly high level of abhorrence were sexual or physical abuse of children. Little distinction seemed to be made between milder forms of abuse and abuse of children that was accompanied by extreme violence and cruelty, that occurred over a long period of time, or that affected very young children.

Contributors who were victims of crime, relatives of victims, or advocates of the rights of victims wanted a return to the death penalty, the introduction of more mandatory and lengthy sentences, the placement of severe restrictions on parole and probation, a revision of the Young Offenders Act, and an increase in the amount of authority given to the police. A few letter writers held views on the treatment of offenders that were based on retaliation and reflected a strong attraction for the use of cruel and brutal sanctions.

Opponents of the extremist supporters of law and order included a few academics, concerned about the decline of potential destruction and the growth of intransigence and cruelty; many lawyers, concerned about the preservation of a justice system that was reasonably humane and fair if principles that had taken centuries to develop were abandoned; and supporters of minority groups, afraid that the law-and-order trend could become an excuse to harass some Canadians. The debates about the treatment of various types of criminal offenses and of offenders indicated that there were many areas of confusion and inconsistency in the views of most contributors.

The data contained extensive debates about the revision of the income tax system, including different opinions about the fairness and wisdom of taxing more or less heavily one or another stratum of society, the handling of the national debt and yearly deficits, the pros and cons of a social charter and a social contract, and the use of public revenues to finance special and separate services for Native Canadians.

In 1993, a few contributors started to raise questions and to express some concerns about the possible size of the funding needed for Native self-governments and for the settlement of land claims. While these concerns tended to be dismissed by advocates as more ranting from racists, there were indications that they were not going away and that they could increase if it appeared that choices had to be made between these expenditures and social program expenditures.

In general the debates indicated that the views of contributors on the extended social services did not always correspond with the assumed divisions between neoconservative and other perspectives. Political expediency, as well as concerns for economic survival during a prolonged period of economic restructuring, created unexpected patterns of views. Contributors known to be neoconservatives did not raise objections, for instance, to the funding of services that promoted multiculturalism, a notion of culture that was considered to be favoured mostly by social service proponents. Most contributors were opposed to paying more taxes, and there was an increasing level of complaint about the impact of the cumulative nature of direct and indirect taxes. However, there were indications that some contributors would have been less opposed had they been more satisfied with the way the money was being used, or had they been kept better informed about the real patterns of funding allocations by the federal government.

There was no general consensus about the most appropriate allocations of public funds. But various interest groups, invoking the rights of taxpayers or other values, made it very clear that the causes or programs that they favoured deserved to receive generous allocations. It was difficult to envisage how the government would deal with the claims of groups powerful enough to influence an election and to call for reciprocal support afterwards.

5.6 Summary and Conclusions

The data available and collected from the press between 1991 and 1993 contained two levels of information. The first consisted of explicit comments and suggestions found in letters, editorials, articles, and press releases. The other included latent messages that provided insights into views and trends that had been present before 1991 but were becoming progressively more visible or widespread.

Between 1991 and 1993, the federal government carried out a substantial revision of the Canadian system of social welfare. Some programs were revised or terminated, openly through modifications to their goals and directions or indirectly through changes in funding allocations. Transfer payments to the provinces were subjected to a process of progressive reduction, benefits to individuals were clawed back or ceased to be granted, and several organizations lost all or part of their yearly grants. The provincial governments were left to cope somehow with the difficult and unpopular consequences of the cuts in federal contributions.

The pace of transformation accelerated between 1992 and 1993, and as the scope and the visibility of the changes increased, the debates in the press started to address different questions and issues. In early 1991, the questions most often raised were whether the social services were helping people effectively and whether the benefits they provided were too generous and leading to overdependency, or not generous enough and keeping users in a chronic state of need. These questions continued to be raised, but new issues appeared in the press in 1992.

The federal government and those contributors who supported its policies relentlessly imparted the message that, given the size of the national debt and the yearly budget deficits, Canada could no longer afford what was remaining of the social security net and the notion of welfare it reflected. A second message was that the Canadian public had reached the same conclusions and was, therefore, supporting the initiatives taken by the government. Several editors, commentators, and columnists disseminated these messages. But other views appeared in many of the articles, press releases, and letters, reflecting the extent to which contributors tended to agree or disagree with the analysis of the social welfare situation presented by the government.

In the debates conducted in the press there was a general consensus that something had to be done to reduce the size of the national debt and to eliminate the perennial deficits. But there was little agreement about the causes of the problem and about the types of measures to be taken in order to deal with it.

A minority of contributors favoured the elimination of all the so-called "frills" in the social security system, and perhaps in the extended network as well, and a return to a residual notion of social welfare. The restrictive measures they suggested included establishing more stringent conditions of eligibility, limiting the size and duration of benefits, targeting assistance to people in extreme need only or to recipients most likely to make appropriate use of the services, making users pay fees or higher premiums, and rationing health care services.

Most contributors were not in favour of a return to a residual notion of social welfare, and they began to question the view that social welfare expenditures were the main reason for the growth of the national debt and the persistence of yearly deficits. From this group of contributors came many suggestions about ways to increase national revenues and to improve the administration, delivery, and organization of the social and health care services to make them more efficient as well as more effective. Several contributors also suggested changes to behaviour patterns and customs of service users and providers that could lead to overuse or non-optimal use of services, particularly in the field of health care.

Contributors who feared that the government was going to continue to eliminate many of the social and health services, which had been once an integral part of the Canadian notion of social security, identified the programs they strongly wanted to keep. These programs were:

- Medicare
- Hospital Insurance and other health care services
- Old Age Security pensions
- Income Assistance for the unemployable
- Income assistance and job entry or re-entry programs for the unemployed
- Workers' Compensation
- services designed to help child victims of violence and neglect
- services to protect the public from criminals
- programs providing affordable housing to all Canadians

After 1991, there were, however, increasing expressions of mixed or even negative feelings toward certain programs in the extended welfare network. These were programs that were perceived to provide special benefits to selected categories of people for unlimited periods of time, and with broad or vague goals rather than specific objectives. The reasons given, or hinted at, were related partly to concerns about the feasibility or the wisdom of trying to maintain an ever-expanding network when the basic social security system was short of the resources it needed to fulfil its mandate effectively. But other factors were involved. One important one was the loss of faith in the validity of some of the theories that had influenced the growth of the extended system. An increasing number of contributors indicated that they were having second thoughts about the consequences of programs that had the potential to transform the social structure, not so much through the redistribution of incomes as through the redistribution of rights, privileges, status, and power. They feared that these programs were beginning to encourage the fragmentation of the Canadian society into a myriad of groups distrustful and resentful of each other. This line of thought was strongly opposed by individuals and organizations contending that a radical change in the social structure was absolutely necessary if the more disadvantaged members of society were to obtain their fair share of economic resources.

Some of the suggestions reflected a propensity to opt for rapid and simple, or even simplistic, solutions and to ignore the possibility of creating worse problems as a result. But there was an increase in the number of contributors interested in more thorough explorations of the social welfare issues. A number of themes emerged in the writings. These themes were not always particularly new or original, inasmuch as most had been explored previously by social welfare analysts. Their importance rested, however, in the indication of a rise in public understanding of the real nature of many of the social welfare issues at stake in the last decade of the century.

Several interesting themes emerged from the available press material. They included the following:

- The importance of improving the level of public participation in the revision of the whole system of social welfare in Canada, not only to make this system more relevant when it attempts to deal with those socioeconomic changes that could not be prevented or avoided but also to increase the sense of national unity and the sense of responsibility of each person for the welfare of the Canadian collective.

- The growing interest in the idea that the provision of social welfare could no longer be confined to the provision of more and bigger welfare programs and services. Many contributors, while rejecting the anti-social-service perspective, were nevertheless moving beyond the position of the more traditional social service proponents. They still wanted a system that protected individual Canadians equally from the most severe and unpredictable risks associated with life in a changing society, but they wanted to see more connections made between social welfare and the whole array of public policies. They no longer believed in an approach that had been developed around the assumption that an extensive system of services and programs could repair, or prevent, the problems caused by economic or other policies and arrangements. They believed instead in placing more emphasis upon assessing the role that taxation, fiscal, monetary, trade, employment, immigration, and foreign policies played in enhancing or detracting from social welfare.

  Several contributors were interested in the role of the government in condoning, supporting, or resisting the demands of transnational corporations and foreign governments that affected the well-being of Canadians. Depending on their angle of vision, contributors indicated that the government should be more forceful in supporting these demands, more forceful in resisting them, or more skilful in controlling them. A considerable number of contributors wanted the federal government to initiate a complete reform of the tax system.

- An increasing understanding that the social security system and the extended network reflected the culture of a particular society at a particular time in its history. The values that had been promoted strongly between 1945 and 1985 included a commitment to justice, tolerance, moderation, respect for the rights of the individual and the needs of the collective, as well as fairness in dealing with one another and in distributing socioeconomic benefits and responsibilities. In 1993, most contributors continued to support this value system but were afraid that it was threatened by the demands of the new economic reality that increasingly controlled most of the world's nations. Many contributors believed that in countries like Canada, decisions about the future pattern of social welfare provisions were slipping away from the hands of democratic governments and falling into the hands of powerful transnational corporations able to impose their special culture on millions of people.

One dimension of this theme, therefore, was the importance of deciding whether Canadians should try to resist, as strongly as possible, the slide into a survival of the fitness culture or to embrace it and learn to compete ruthlessly for access to economic amenities, including privileged access to restricted services. This theme was far from having been explored fully when this press review ended in the spring of 1993, but some of the writings revealed that the writers were attempting to reach a middle ground and to adapt to the new reality through a shift in their interpretation of the meaning of welfare. Instead of equating welfare with services that guaranteed security and protection from major life risks for everyone, they were equating it with access to the educational and life skills needed to succeed, or at least survive, in the competitive environment facing them in the next decade. Most of the contributors seemed to have made the shift, however, more from a sense of fear or resignation than from a genuine conversion to the survival of the fittest creed.

Other trends and factors were worth noting:

- The emergence of a mixture of simultaneous interest in tolerance and intolerance and in enlightenment and puritanism. Intolerant measures were recommended to promote support for a variety of causes, and while increasing acceptance of sexual and cultural freedoms for some Canadians was recommended, this was accompanied by a strong denial of greater freedom for others. Rather alarming to many contributors was the tendency to try to muzzle the free expression of ideas and opinions and to replace enlightening debates with legal sanctions.
- An interest in special causes that reflected new angles of visio appeared to be growing within some segments of the public. Members of these segments tended as a result to replace support for traditional political and economic perspectives, such as conservatism or socialism, with support for goals such as the preservation of the environment or of the culture of a minority group. But there was evidence also of fluctuations in the popularity of new views, con-

cepts, or beliefs. The concept of victimization, for instance, was quite popular in 1991 but appeared to be hit subsequently by a mild backlash when some contributors started to believe that it was overused and in danger of becoming a political strategy to gain hasty and uncritical public endorsement for cases that required more intensive scrutiny.

- The data tended to reconfirm the influential role of images in the debates between proponents and opponents of the social services. In general, the statistics, studies, and reports from experts cited by the dedicated supporters of a perspective to bolster their arguments were ignored by their equally dedicated opponents, or simply reinterpreted to conform to the angle of vision that happened to be used as a point of reference. Nevertheless, the persistence and forcefulness of the images used by the parties appeared to have an impact upon the general public. The side that could present the stronger and more colourful images or could display the greater velocity of tongue could sway the opinions of many members of the public. Pollsters, image-maker specialists, editors, and syndicated columnists seemed to become increasingly influential between 1991 and 1993, although the less partisan newspapers and periodicals were making reasonable attempts to equitably provide a range of opposing views and arguments on important social welfare issues.

Some issues were addressed only superficially, while others were not addressed at all.

- In the field of health care, for instance, the potential impact on universality of an increase in the number of private hospitals, clinics, and other facilities that would create several tiers of services was mentioned, but not the reduction in public revenues that would occur when users of the private system began to claim tax exemptions.
- Also not explored was the potential impact on the equitable distribution of funding to services used by the general public of the popular notion that members of selected groups should have the right to direct the use of their tax dollars toward services of their choice.
- The implications of the disappearance of universality for the future of the middle income stratum of the population were addressed before 1993 only, and rather slightly, in relation to Old Age Security.

Yet the impact of this disappearance on the lives of a huge number of Canadians of average means who have been depending on access to various services to remain above the poverty line could be devastating. In general, there was a tendency on the part of experts and advocates to polarize. Small business and ordinary, average-income Canadians were less well represented or tended to be ignored. By 1993, however, there was an increase in the number of contributors who could be identified as belonging to these two groups. They were showing signs of balking at the possibility of being expected to pay more taxes and receive a diminishing share of social and health benefits and services.

- While there was much interest in public participation, not many useful suggestions were offered to deal with the many concrete difficulties of applying the principle of participation to the actual revision and re- evaluation of social welfare provisions. A key issue is going to be the need to formulate relevant principles and criteria to guide the equitable allocation of social benefits and responsibilities, in the event that the political party forming the next federal government in the fall of 1993 decides to further decrease social program expenditures. Whether the process of equitable distribution would be achieved through reasonable debates and compromises or through brutal struggles among parties and vested interest groups, hidden under a flood of sophisticated rhetoric, had not been explored adequately by the time the review ended in 1993.

- The views of contributors about the role of the government showed several contradictions. A fair number of writers favoured maximum feasible decentralization, the transfer of control over the development of the Canadian society from the government to the people at the level of local communities, and the rights of people to control their own destiny. At the same time, however, there appeared to be a strong faith in the validity of using centralized forms of government intervention to compel people to modify their behaviour and attitudes and to transform the economic system, and society itself. A number of plausible explanations could account for the contradictions, but these were not explored in the press under review. There were also interesting contradictions between negative attitudes toward groups such as single mothers on welfare or immigrants and compassionate views and activities directed at individuals belonging to these groups when their plight was reported by the media.

Contributors, including so-called ordinary Canadians, seemed to be relatively unaware of the impact of those insidious and cumulative types of inflationary pressures that affect lower-income people more than affluent ones. Small but relentless rent increases and increases in the cost of shoe repair, dry cleaning, and other such services must have caused more hardship to the working poor, to recipients of income assistance, and to pensioners than was mentioned in the press between 1991 and 1993. The impact upon the economy of widespread shopping across the border and of the underground economy were discussed but not explored to deal more systematically with the influence of personal and collective spending patterns upon job creation.

The content of the press under review conveyed a rather grim impression of a society faced with acute turbulence and with changes that were not seen as contributing to any enhancement in the quality of life for most Canadians. It was quite evident that the vast majority of contributors wanted very much to keep the network of basic social security programs, as well as some of the programs in the extended system. This was in spite of concerns that the social services had not been able to fulfil all the expectations held of them in the past, and in spite of complaints about the delivery, quality, validity, and effectiveness of some services.

It was clear that most of the contributors greatly feared an acceleration in a process of erosion that would lead inevitably to the annihilation of the whole system of social security in Canada in the near future. Some felt rather helpless to halt this process because they did not have any effective remedies to seek protection from the economic and political arrangements prevailing in the country and in the world. Others were nevertheless determined to find solutions to the problems Canada was struggling with on the eve of the next millennium.

One of the most positive findings to emerge from the press review was the strength of the conviction, displayed by a large majority of contributors, that the values reflected in the Canadian welfare system should be preserved.

6

Neoconservative versus Proponents' Views of Social Programs

6.1 Proponents and Neoconservative Critics

Canadian neoconservatives have energetically promoted a fully developed anti-welfare-state ideology. An important feature of this ideology is that it is imported from abroad, in prepackaged form, as part of a worldwide campaign, which I shall describe below in more detail. It is rather like a TV dinner, the recipes for which have been written elsewhere than in Canada. To analyze it, we need to examine the work of the chefs, who were mainly U.S. neoconservative theologians.

Proponents of broad-scale social programs in Canada, on the other hand, are a more indigenous and much more varied group, who defend the social services from a number of different perspectives. In 1992 perhaps the most important members of this group were those, like the Council of Canadians, who linked the problem of threats to the social safety net in Canada to the issues of Canadian autonomy and unity. This linkage has been powerfully affirmed in the recently published book by Radwanski and Luttrell:

> All the things that we took for granted about Canada have been disappearing before our eyes. In a nation where some 435,000 manufacturing jobs have disappeared in just two years, prosperity seems an irretrievable dream. Where until so recently we prided ourselves on being a caring society, we see the safety net unravelling at every seam. Unemployment insurance has been cut back, funding for welfare has been slashed, we see the homeless in our streets. Food banks – the soup lines of the 1990s – are proliferating. And now even medicare is threatened. Taxes keep rising, and we are getting less and less for our money.
>
> National institutions that were symbolic of our identity are being

abolished at every turn. Our railways, our air transportation network, the CBC, the Canada Council, Petro-Canada and other key elements of the Canadian foundation that were built up over decades have all come under relentless attack.[1]

Other proponents of the Canadian social services include corporatists such as Mishra, as well as traditional conservatives of the Red Tory variety who are seeking ways to make the welfare state work under changing economic conditions; international labour groups, who are increasingly borrowing ideas from the human capital theorists and applying them in an international context; proponents of a Canadian social charter; and communitarians and Greens, for whom social services are a part of larger schemes of revamping our values and social organization.[2] Thus proponents have no single social services ideology. In this chapter, therefore, I shall refer to them not by such terms as "liberals" or "social democrats" but simply as proponents or defenders of broad-scale social programs.

6.2 Neoconservative Standpoint

6.2.1 Credo
Steinfels began his important book on the neoconservatives, published in 1979,[3] with the observation that neoconservatism may be identified as "a distinct and powerful outlook that has recently emerged in the United States." Neoconservatives themselves frequently cited the following definition: "A neoconservative is a liberal who has been mugged by reality."

This definition can be decoded to reveal a good part of the neoconservative credo:

- liberals' naive belief in the ability of governments and social planners to cope effectively with social problems, such as the intractable problem of the ghetto "underclasses"; the public's excessive expectations of government created by the liberal romanticism;
- the resulting danger of overloading government with responsibilities for which it is unsuited and at which it is bound to fail;
- worse, the decline of respect for the authoritative institutions of society that would follow from such failures, for which there is already evidence;

- worse still, the decline in individuals' sense of responsibility for their own problems, their greater willingness to say "the system is to blame";
- conclusion: to restore its powers to govern, government must hold individuals and families more accountable for their problems.

6.2.2 Theory of "Popular Wisdom"

The neoconservative theory of welfare contains some specific propositions concerning the "popular wisdom" about the welfare state that we may expect to find in a survey of public opinion. Murray formulates these propositions as follows:[4]

- hostility towards welfare (it makes people lazy);
- hostility towards lenient judges;
- disapproval of "favouritism" in the form of too many written-in rights for disadvantaged minorities of all kinds;
- view that the government is meddling far too much in things that are none of its business;
- conviction that people respond to incentives: carrots and sticks work;
- people are not inherently hardworking or moral: in the absence of countervailing influences, people will avoid work and be amoral;
- people must be held responsible for their actions; whether they are responsible in some ultimate sense cannot be the issue if society is to function;
- by ignoring these premises, the enlarged welfare state instituted in the mid-1960s has created much of the mess we are in.

6.3 Neoconservative Campaigns

6.3.1 The Campaign against the "New Class"

As the foregoing concerns suggest, the neoconservatives have distrusted intellectuals (especially in the earlier days of their movement), an attitude nicely reflected in a remark by William F. Buckley: it would be better to be governed by the first five thousand names in the Boston telephone directory than by the faculty of Harvard.[5] Daniel Patrick Moynihan, a major contributor to the neoconservative canon, put it differently but with much the same point: "Liberals will simply have to restrain their enthusiasm for civilizing others."[6]

These quotations illustrate what many neoconservatives have from

the beginning seen as perhaps their most important mission: the res-
cue of the polity from the undue influence of a group they label the
"new class." They have perceived this new class as an entrenched intellectual elite, a cadre of social researchers and policy technocrats out
of academia, who acquired in the Kennedy administration of the early
1960s a dangerous influence over the public policy agenda and the
politicians. Part of the new class thesis is that whole new categories of
social problems that otherwise would never have become part of the
policy agenda were defined into existence by the theories of these academics, who imposed their own theories on their data.[7]

6.3.2 The Neoconservative "Counter-intelligentsia"

Fischer provides an account of the emergence of conservative policy
analysis during the 1970s,[8] showing that this was a major change
from the traditional anti-intellectual stance of conservatives that identified all policy analysts as liberals, witting or unwitting tools of
"creeping socialism." The goal of the analysis was to *"sever the connection between liberal reform and policy expertise."* Conservatives were to
be urged to drop their traditional animosity towards the academy and
instead find and create allies within it. They must be made to realize
that the knowledge society is here to stay, and that to get control over
it or at least reduce its potential for harm, they must create a "conservative counter-intelligentsia."[9] This must be supported by the business community: *"Funds generated by business [including money from
business foundations – my condensation] must rush by the multimillions to
scholars ... who understand the relationship between political and economic
liberty ... [must support] books and more books."*[10] Most important, business must end "the mindless subsidizing of colleges and universities
whose departments of economics, government, politics, and history
are hostile to capitalism."[11]

A similar analysis had been provided by Irving Kristol, an originator
of the new class thesis. Kristol, who was originally a Marxist, developed a curiously Marxist style of analysis. The intellectual policy elite,
he pointed out, having become a "permanent brain trust" were in the
process of seizing and consolidating their political position. The conservatives must find ways to appeal to significant numbers of intellectuals. The principal mission of the neoconservative movement must
be to provide the policy elites with an ideology that makes ample
room for the private sector as prime mover in the economy.[12]

Objection to redistributive aims: Neoconservatives take particular aim at social programs that redistribute resources from higher- to lower-income groups. This point of view is summarized in Murray's *"law of unintended rewards":* any social transfer increases the net value of being in the condition that prompted the transfer.[13] This "law" operates to increase the number of persons with the condition in question. As a result, the original problem (e.g., poverty) worsens. Therefore, redistributive programs should be opposed. Instead, there should be small-scale privately run or at least local programs.

6.4 Proponents' Defense of Social Programs
Canadian defenders of social programs hold that:

- Social programs are an essential safety net that Canadians have painstakingly woven over a period of many decades.[14]
- Economics must sometimes at least come second to human solidarity; [the] responsibility of the fortunate for the unfortunate cannot be left to the discretion of the fortunate but must be embodied in our collective institutions.[15]
- Far being harmful to the economy, the social services are sensible economics. Those who cut back such programs for economic reasons are undermining the "very capacity for economic competitiveness they claim to want so badly."[16]
- In the new and emerging world economy, Canada, with its greatly increased services sector will succeed only to the extent that it is able to invest in skills, knowledge, and performance of its workforce. We cannot afford to waste human potential.[17]
- It is a serious error to regard social programs as a tax on the rich to help the poor. In major part they are a "redistribution between people in different circumstances within the middle income groups."[18]
- Most important is the symbolic meaning of the social programs: "because everyone has some exposure to social programs, we have an early warning system to alert us to governments that seek to erode our most basic and fundamental Canadian values ... it is only by ensuring that the great majority of Canadians – the middle class – will have the awareness and the motivation to make common cause with [the poor], that we can remain the kind of society Canadians wish us to be."[19]

6.5 Comparisons: Neoconservative versus Proponents' Views
Five basic elements of the neoconservative ideology of the social ser-

vices can be used as a test of neoconservative leanings in the Canadian public: general opposition to broad-scale social programs; opposition to public sector responsibility for such programs; preference for the private sector; particular objection to social policies that have redistributive aims, and to affirmative action programs; demand that benefits be conditioned on recipients' meritorious behaviour. I present data on each of these points.

6.5.1 Opposition to Broad-Scale Social Programs

"Broad-scale" refers to policies and programs aimed at entire populations. Because of their scope and the need for uniformity of standards in different areas of the country, such programs generally require a heavy involvement of the national government. Neoconservatives see such programs as inevitably leading to metastasizing bureaucracies, government deficits, weakening of the economy, granting of benefits to large numbers of persons not entitled to them, and adding to the general disillusionment with the effectiveness of government.[20] In Canada the argument by neoconservatives against public sector commitment to broad-scale social programs has had the same form, but varying content, since 1970. The form of the argument is as follows:

> We are faced with an unprecedented economic crisis that confronts us with a grim choice of alternatives: either we deal with this economic crisis by cutting government spending (i.e., cutting back on social programs) or face consequences that are much worse. Though we regard social programs as a sacred trust, there is no present alternative but to scale them back.

Though this argument has been unvarying since about 1970, the economic ogre confronting Canada that serves as a part of the argument has changed every few years. In the 1970s it was inflation, then stagflation, then a fiscal crisis. By the 1980s it had become a crisis of high interest rates, followed by a crisis of low economic growth and unemployment, then a record deficit, and currently a crisis of productivity and competitiveness on the world market.

Proponents, in contrast, emphasize the need for universality of coverage and for equality of access to services over large populations. Problems of bureaucracy and service delivery are admitted, but are seen as less harmful and as more tractable than in the neoconservative view. Since such programs are investments in "human" capital, they need not entail the disastrous economic consequences predicted by the neoconservatives.[21] If government becomes part of the problem rather than of the solution, this is not, in the proponents' view, because there is any inherent reason why government is unable to deal effectively with social problems, as the neoconservatives claim (an exception for the neoconservatives is moral problems, as illustrated below). Rather, it is because government has been made captive by powerful corporate interests, both national and multinational.[22] The remedy for this is not to dismantle social programs but to find ways to make government more accountable and efficient. Consequently, proponents take a much more positive view of both the social and economic outcomes of public sector interventions.[23]

6.5.2 Against Programs with Redistributive Aims: The Argument from Precept

As I have noted, neoconservatives have raised particularly strong objections to social programs with redistributive aims. Their objections to such programs are a variation on their theme that "people must be held responsible for their actions" and that government's failure to maintain this principle is responsible for "much of the mess we are in."[24]

One side to this neoconservative argument is the George Gilder panegyric to aggressive males: "entrepreneurs, business men, risk takers and the thrifty poor."[25] According to Gilder's version of the neoconservative credo, in which the twin enemies of economic progress are the welfare state and feminism,[26] impoverished aggressive males are the true source of the nation's wealth. The spur of their poverty motivates these males to take the risks that are a necessary part of moving up the socioeconomic scale in our society: becoming wealthy and creating wealth. Programs that remove this spur of poverty condemn these otherwise productive members of society to a life of dependency and moral decay. On a broader scale, social programs that redistribute wealth make society poorer in the end.

Other neoconservative writers, without necessarily subscribing to Gilder's anti-feminism, agree with Gilder that a principal cause of decline in the industrial economies of the capitalist world is government activity of any kind, of which social programs are an example, that impedes the "born leaders" of society. Here we meet Schumpeter's elite[27] on whom the survival, not just the progress of an industrial order, is supposed to depend.

Probably the most popular argument among neoconservatives against redistributive programs are elaborations of the simple precept, considered by neoconservatives to be a part of popular wisdom, that welfare makes people lazy. There are two versions of this, one found in more academic writings and the other promulgated by the religious right. The first, which we find clearly expressed in Charles Murray's writings, is a version of rational choice theory, a currently popular theory of crime.[28]

This theory is applied to welfare in Murray's parable of the case of Harold and Phyllis, a (hypothetical) young American couple "unremarkable except for the bare fact of being poor ... [neither] ... particularly industrious or indolent, intelligent or dull."[29] They are high school graduates with no special vocational skills and no desire to go to college. They went together in high school and Phyllis is pregnant. Thus they have a series of decisions to make: whether or not to get married, to live together without getting married, or to live separately; whether to keep the baby or give it up for adoption. If Phyllis decides to keep the baby, she will have to decide whether to find work or go on Aid to Families with Dependent Children (AFDC), a form of welfare. Harold has to decide whether to find a job or try to get Phyllis to help support him. The only job Harold can get is at rock- bottom minimum wage rates, working in a laundry, on his feet all day, in an unpleasantly hot environment.

In a series of calculations complete with loss tables, Murray shows that the benefits and losses of each of these decisions are heavily affected by the liberality of the rules of the welfare programs available to the couple. He contrasts 1960 (restrictive) welfare rules with 1970 (liberal, Great Society reform) welfare rules to show these effects. Some examples:

- The liberalization of benefits introduced in the 1960s made welfare more remunerative for Phyllis than working.
- Before the 1960s, the AFDC program had a "no man in the house rule" that applied to single mothers. The striking down of this rule by the courts in 1964, coupled with the liberalization of benefits, meant that Harold could move into the household without having to work regularly.
- For Harold, after the liberalization of benefits, getting married became, from an economic point of view, "a dumb decision."[30] He could "get married and work forty hours a week in a hot tiresome

job, or he could live with Phyllis and their baby without getting married, not work, and have more disposable income."

Thus, Murray contends, what liberals would consider to be Great Society welfare policies make it rational for the recipients to make irresponsible decisions, at least in the short run, the only practical time frame in which to make such decisions for persons whose options are extremely limited. Murray further contends that the same general logic would apply both to severely disadvantaged recipients, such as ghetto residents, and couples like Harold and Phyllis, children of the working class (p. 160):

> There is no "breakdown of the work ethic" in this account of rational choice amongst alternatives. There is no shiftless irresponsibility. It makes no difference whether Harold is white or black. There is no need to invoke the spectres of cultural pathologies or inferior upbringing. The choices may be seen much more simply, much more naturally, as people responding to the reality of the world around them ...

Murray's straightforward application of precepts from neoclassical economics, which we see in this parable of Harold and Phyllis, is echoed in the work on poverty in Canada published by the Fraser Institute.[31]

The Religious Right, not generally regarded as a part of the neoconservative movement but energetically wooed by neoconservative politicians, takes a different view of the moral aspects of going on welfare. Its concern about the moral aspect of going on welfare is part of its anxiety about the breakdown of the traditional family and of sexual morality. It regards welfare as government support to persons who wish to flout both traditional sexual mores and the work ethic. Mothers on welfare must therefore *"repent of complacency and instill in themselves, by seeking God's help and neighbours', a desire to achieve. To rise from public assistance to self assistance."*[32]

Though we see a number of differences among elite theorists of the Schumpeterian or Gilder variety, rational choice theorists like Murray and Sarlo, and moralists of the religious right, all arrive at the same general policy conclusion regarding redistributive programs: *they are public policy blunders that worsen the conditions they are intended to remedy and pose a general threat to the economy and social welfare.* Therefore they should be severely restricted or, as Murray and others suggest about welfare, phased out. The disastrous consequences of such policies as seen by the neoconservatives are exemplified in Murray's account (above) of the outcomes of the Great Society programs.

6.5.3 For Targeting: The Argument from Efficiency

A number of American states are literally applying Murray's prescriptions for setting time limits on or for the phasing out of welfare.[33] In many states, and in Canada, such drastic measures are politically risky, as illustrated by the Conservative government's hasty retreat from its initial ventures into "deindexing" Old Age Security.[34]

An alternative theme of the neoconservative attack on social programs has been that these programs should be directed only at those who need them. Though this position is inconsistent with neoconservative opposition to redistributive programs, it is much easier to sell. The Conservative party of Canada sold it very successfully in the 1988 Canadian general election, with the slogan that "Conrad Black, multimillionaire, should not be eligible for Family Allowances."[35] This message is all the more saleable if it is accompanied by constant hammering on economic themes:

- Social programs are a principal cause of record national debt and annual fiscal deficits.[36]
- Canada has one of the world's "most overly governed and foolishly generous welfare states."[37]
- In the new global economy, Canada must become "more like its competitors," i.e., spend less on social programs, in order to be playing on equal terms with these competitors.
- The logical way to maximize the value of the social welfare dollar is to see to it that it is spent on those who need it most.
- We should certainly not be wasting precious welfare dollars on the Conrad Blacks (multimillionaires) of this world, who can well take care of themselves.
- By the same logic, we should be careful to so design and manage social programs that they reach those who need them most.

6.5.4 Demand that Benefits Be Conditioned on the Meritorious Behaviour of Recipients

Murray reasons that since social programs reward and reinforce the problem behaviours that they are designed to treat, thus making the problems worse, the obvious solution is to do away with such programs. Others in the neoconservative movement draw a different conclusion: make the benefits of social programs conditional on good behaviour. This view is set forth in detail in Mead's book on entitlement.[38] What's wrong with welfare, according to Mead, is that nothing is demanded of the recipients in return for the benefits. Entitlement, he maintains should be based not merely on need, but on merit, assessed at the beginning of service and on an ongoing basis thereafter.

There are two parts to this argument. First there is the contention that merit considerations ought to enter into decisions about entitlement. The second is the more administrative problem of deciding how to apply such a rule: whether for instance to deal with "non-meritorious" applicants simply by denying their applications or by stipulating conditions that they must satisfy in order to continue to collect benefits.

In this study we opted to explore the first part of this argument by asking: *to what extent do the respondents take personal merit of the recipients into account in deciding whether they favour or oppose a given example of social service benefits?* To obtain evidence on this question, we made use of a factorial experiment design, which I have described in detail in three earlier papers.[39] The results are presented in Chapter 8.

6.6 Note on Data Analysis

In Chapter 8, I use the major differences between neoconservatives and proponents, which I have presented in section 6.5, as a framework for analyzing both the survey and the focus group data. From this analysis one can see where the public stands on the key issues that divide proponents from neoconservatives.

7

Beverley Scott

Against Social Programs: The Campaigns of the Fraser Institute

7.1 The Fraser Institute: Advocating Against Public Programs

The purpose of this chapter is to present in detail an example of neoconservative campaigns against social programs in Canada. I describe how the goal of the Fraser Institute influences its research on public programs, and how its publications consistently present a specific range of facts that are chosen in accordance with the Institute's ideological free market orientation. I describe, largely in the Fraser Institute's own words, some of the assumptions and social implications of its free market philosophy.

In Chapters 7 and 8, the neoconservative outlook on social policies and programs is compared with the public's point of view. This enables us to judge the extent to which the public still holds to some of the basic objectives of the classic welfare state.

The approach taken in this chapter is to present some basic facts about the Fraser Institute as an organization and then to set forth the themes and tactics of its advocacy campaigns.

7.2 Origins of the Fraser Institute

The Fraser Institute was founded in British Columbia in 1974, two years after the New Democratic Party took office in the province. The Institute was not set up in specific reaction to the New Democratic Party, but it was established to counter government interventionist economic policies, as 1974 was a year in an era of large government spending programs and increasing deficits. T. Patrick Boyle, then vice president and comptroller of the giant MacMillan Bloedel forest products company, had been alarmed to note both in Canada and abroad that governments over the past several years had been entrenching a pattern of inflationary spending and aggressive economic intervention that was, in his opinion, reducing the private sector's capacity to invest. Mr. Boyle, who became instrumental in establishing the Fraser Institute, saw the need for an institute to create a climate more conducive to non-interventionist policies, particularly when governments were funding institutes favouring government intervention. The newly elected New Democratic Party used taxpayers' money to fund the British Columbia Institute for Public Policy. As regards the federal government, Mr. Boyle said: "I realized that as prime minister, Trudeau was creating intellectual sources and organizations to sprinkle holy water on his policies. There was nothing being done by the good guys to counter that influence ... I reached the point of being utterly fed up."[1]

7.3 Philosophy and Objectives of the Fraser Institute

According to the Fraser Institute's public statement of its objectives, the Institute assumes that the competitive market system is usually best able to provide for the well-being of Canadians, but it does not rule out the possibility that government programs may sometimes be superior to purely market forces. In its own words:

> The Fraser Institute is an independent Canadian economic and social research and educational organization. It has as its objective the redirection of public attention to the role of competitive markets in providing for the well-being of Canadians. Where markets work, the Institute's interest lies in trying to discover prospects for improvement. Where markets do not work, its interest lies in finding the reasons. Where competitive markets have been replaced by government control, the interest of the Institute lies in documenting objectively the nature of the improvement or deterioration resulting from government intervention.[2]

However, the Fraser Institute's studies never interpret their research findings as indicating a need for greater government involvement. The Institute's *Lexicon of Economic Thought* puts its this way:

> Government Programmes. Why aren't we more positive? Instead of simply bellyaching about government programmes and their applications, why don't we provide some concrete, positive proposals for government programmes which would work? Quite candidly, that is a tough question. We do spend a great deal of time pointing out the errors in government actions and not much making proposals with

which to replace those criticized. Unfortunately, that is the nature of the position to which economic analysis pushes us.[3]

A more honest answer would have been that the Institute is opposed to the existing levels of funding of the programs it criticizes. Dr. Walker, the Institute's director, believes that the role of the state is to act as an umpire to the free market system. It must not, in Dr. Walker's view, be an active player.[4]

The objectives of the Institute are more clearly stated in documents that are not intended for the public and are written for prospective financial supporters. For example, the handout included in the Institute's Application for Membership folder is as direct as can be: "Why Support the Fraser Institute? ... The Fraser Institute argues for free markets in a way which is not possible for those in business who are perceived as having a vested interest. We give alternative solutions to offset growing government intervention in the economy, which has become all-too-common."[5]

A more ideological summary of the organization's purpose is given in its booklet *The Fraser Institute Endowment Fund,* which states:

In the period since the last World War, scholars in economics, sociology, and politics have tended to be particularly influenced by the work of Marx and Keynes. As a result, these scholars and their interpreters in the media have produced an enormous intellectual outpouring in favour of statism.

Political expediency, ideological motivation, or an inability to see the end consequences of this tendency, have led elected officials to follow the course charted by this intellectual consensus. The electorate, for its part, faced with political rhetoric and attracted by promises of ever-increasing affluence, is seldom made aware of the adverse effects that spreading government controls have on individual freedoms and the standard of living.

Since ideas do have such consequences, the Fraser Institute was created to redirect the public's attention to the use of competitive markets as the best means of organizing people, capital, and natural resources. By means of its research, its ensuing publications and their widespread dissemination, the Fraser Institute seeks to demonstrate how, under such a system, the best way will be found to ensure the freedom, and material well-being of all Canadians both now and in the future.

How will Canadians choose which way of life? So much will

depend on the ideas with which they are confronted. In this battle of ideas, the organized involvement of informed and concerned individuals can greatly affect Canadians in their choice between the two ways of life.[6]

7.4 Funding and Organization of the Fraser Institute

The Fraser Institute is a national, federally incorporated non-profit organization. In Canada it is a registered charity for the purposes of income tax, and in the United States it has an equivalent status. It is headquartered in Vancouver, British Columbia, and has an office in Toronto, Ontario. It also has a Seattle, Washington, address. The Institute is directed by a Board of Trustees who are elected annually by the membership.

There is considerable overlap between the trustees of 1992 and the trustees of 1982 and 1983. In 1983 the Solidarity Coalition was alarmed at the influence the Fraser Institute was having on the government of British Columbia. It undertook to increase its knowledge of the Institute and concluded:

> Over the years 1982 and 1983 there were 53 different directors and permanent members holding a total of 237 directorships ... the primary affiliation of the 1982 trustees and the assets and sales of the companies concerned ... shows 22 corporations with total 1982 assets of $248,740,500,000 and total sales of $76,475,200,000. Clearly the Fraser Institute's trustees do not represent the average Canadian company of citizen but rather, the very large corporation.[7]

Ben Swankey, who was the director of the Centre for Socialist Education in Vancouver in the early eighties, also did some fact finding on the Fraser Institute. He came to conclusions similar to those of the Solidarity Coalition:

> The Institute is in reality funded and controlled by big corporations, many of them foreign-owned; and its policies and activities are designed to promote the interests of the corporations who fund it. It is in fact a political propaganda organization of big business. Unless the direction B.C. has taken under the Bennett government on the advice of the Fraser Institute is reversed, then human rights, trade union rights and social services as we know them today will soon become unrecognizable.[8]

7.5 International Connections
As one would expect, the Fraser Institute has ties with similar institutions around the world. These ties are seen in the notations of visitors to the Institute mentioned in *Fraser Forum*, in the affiliations of the researchers authoring its books and appearing at conferences and as luncheon speakers. These natural links are formalized and strengthened through the Mont Pelegrin Society. The Society was founded in Switzerland in 1947 to promote the "social free market economy." This economic society denies that capitalist economies tend to develop large monopolies that are not beneficial to society as a whole. The members maintain that although corporations increase in size, there can still be effective competition. They believe that the postwar extension of government economic intervention has caused poor allocation of resources.[9] In 1983 the Fraser Institute hosted a regional Mont Pelegrin Society conference, and in 1992 the Institute was host for the Society's annual general meeting.

7.6 Publications
The publications of the Fraser Institute all promote a free market economy. The Institute's 1991-92 book catalogue lists 12 current titles and 75 titles in its back list. The 12 current titles and abbreviated annotations are:

- *Government Spending Facts.* "One of the most pressing economic issues of the 1990s is the concern about out-of-control spending by our governments."
- *Landlords as Scapegoat.* "... shows that in any confrontation between landlord and tenant, especially in areas where rent control is still in force, it is the landlord, not the tenant, who is likely to be vanquished."
- *Economic Freedom: Toward a Theory of Measurement.* "Participants argue against value-laden rating systems which indicate that democracy is the best way to advance economic freedom, and that political and civil freedom are bases for establishing economic freedom – beliefs that defy the real world examples of Sweden, Hong Kong, Singapore and South Korea. This book attempts to measure economic freedom in all nations."
- *Continental Accord.* North American economic integration: "International competition is a fact of life facing all sovereign countries. If Canadians wish to compete in the global marketplace then they

must begin to explain more closely the implications of a North American trilateral trade agreement."

- *Election Finance Regulation in Canada: A Critical Review.* "Competition in Canadian elections is in danger and election finance laws may be to blame. Campaign spending limits, government subsidies to politicians, and the regulation of contributions may all work against the public interest by entrenching incumbent candidates. This surprising claim contradicts the popular view that money in elections is a corrupting evil. By drawing on recent research, this book provides a thoughtful explanation of the role of money in elections and challenges simplistic arguments for government intervention."
- *The Economic Consequences of Quebec Sovereignty.* "Quebec sovereignty is a threat to that [Canadian] prosperity."
- *Breaking the Shackles: Deregulating Canadian Industry.* "Each author provides an evaluation of the current state of affairs in these various field and contrasts those developments with the U.S. experience."
- *Tax Facts #7: The Canadian Consumer Tax Index and You.* "See how your province is doing in this detailed province-by-province analysis of the total direct and hidden tax bill."
- *The Mail Monopoly: Analyzing Canadian Postal Service.* "This in-depth analysis explains why service is not likely to improve until the crown corporation is privatized and subject to competition."
- *Religion, Wealth, and Poverty.* "Father Schall, a Jesuit priest who is a member of the Political Science Faculty of Washington's Georgetown University, views 'social justice' as an attempt to wrest control of the economy from the citizen and thereby strengthen the state. He lauds the profit motive as a great boon to the poor, and criticizes government welfare programs as dependence creators. In his view, the poor are poor not because the rich are rich but in spite of the fact. He sees an important role for religion as a wealth-creating institution, but strenuously opposes the church's persistent opposition to democratic capitalism, the last hope for the poor."
- *Petro Markets: Probing the Economics of Continental Energy.* "How sensitive is energy demand to energy prices and to economic growth? ... Should oil self-sufficiency be a national objective?"
- *Economics and the Environment: A Reconciliation.* "Is the market system inherently wasteful? Is free enterprise necessarily incompatible with conservation? Does the business ethic lead to pollution of the environment? Will population growth outstrip our ability to pro-

duce foodstuffs? There are many so-called environmentalists who would answer these questions in the affirmative and call for greater government intervention in the economy as a solution. Contributors to this volume examine the ability of the marketplace to deal with the problems of the environment. This book is an eye-opener. First prize winner of the Atlas Foundation's Sir Anthony Fisher International Memorial Award for 1991."

7.7 Themes of the Fraser Institute's Publications

7.7.1 One Value versus Several Values
In the free market system, the value is determined by price. For example, Walter Block, when senior economist for the Fraser Institute, argued that there should be no government restrictions on land use. The fact that some land near Vancouver is being preserved for agricultural use when it could command a high price in the housing market shows that people value the land most for housing and are actually crying out, through the price mechanism, for more land for housing.[10] Or, as Michael Walker said in the "Consumer Sovereignty" entry in the *Lexicon of Economic Thought*:

> Value is not an objective reality. Value exists because people place a value on something. They do so by freely giving up some of their voting power (some of their money) to acquire the object of interest. A freely made decision to exchange creates wealth and therefore has value.[11]

7.7.2 Economic Freedom versus Democracy
The Fraser Institute wants the role of government narrowed in the name of economic freedom. Instead of focusing on the role of government directly, it focuses on the need to limit government spending. It is not against deficit financing, which it accurately points out provides a measure of stability against the ups and downs of business cycles.

Dr. Walker appeared before the House of Commons Standing Committee on Finance regarding the proposed Spending Control Act on 17 September 1991, and said:

> The Fraser Institute, through its National Tax Limitation Committee, has been investigating ways in which the self-destructive economic forces unleashed by democratic political choice might be restrained.

We see this search as an economic parallel to the attempt, via the Charter of Rights in our Constitution, to restrain the choices that may be made by legislators with regard to those fundamental rights. The imposition of a limitation on the sovereignty of Parliament in the form of a constitutional restraint prohibiting the legislative infringement of certain rights is an acknowledgement of the same kind of tyranny of the majority that in effect haunts us with regard to government expenditure. Our research has led us to the view that the problem ultimately will not be solved until the Constitution contains a limitation on the ability of Parliament to legislate with regard to the extraction of a person's income in the same way that it is bound not to legislate with regard to the removal of a person's liberty, their right to speak out on the issues that concern them and, hopefully with the current constitutional revisions, the right of citizens to own and enjoy the use of property.[12]

As the above quote shows, the belief to limit government spending in order to provide economic freedom is mixed with a distrust of the democratic process. This mistrust runs through many of the Fraser Institute's publications:

Elected representatives, labour leaders, government officials and the media often do not bring careful, long-range perspective to their undertakings. Rather, their goals are often short term and expedient in nature. Elected representatives are, in this connection, anxious to either stay in or return to power. Buffeted as they are by the adversary climate of their legislative assemblies, and their need to win the next election, they often feel compelled to adopt a populist mode of behaviour even against their better judgement. Generally speaking, an unvarying adherence to economically sound principles is not perceived as politically feasible conduct ... [13]

Or, as Milton Friedman, who is highly regarded by the Institute, and a world-renowned economist, was quoted in the *Fraser Forum* as saying:

One of the things that troubles me very much is that I believe a relatively free economy is a necessary condition for a democratic society. But I also believe there is evidence that a democratic society, once established, destroys a free economy. So rolling back the welfare state is exceedingly difficult, there's no question about that.[14]

Why does a democratic society destroy a free economy? Could it be that the population does not equate a free economy as being the same thing as justice? It is not enough that the Fraser Institute calls for economic freedom for those with wealth. The possibility that society as a whole might have suffered in order for individuals to have created their wealth is not admitted. The possibility that even those with wealth might be better served through government services than through private services is not admitted. The Fraser Institute's research, in its book *Economic Freedom,* is anchored in the philosophy of John Locke, Milton Friedman, and Murray Rothbard. It has not hired or referred to the work of any political scientists, sociologists, constitutional lawyers, and human rights experts. It knows that it does not have public support, yet it continues to advocate for a spending limit. Two of its staff economists, Isabella Horry and Filip Palda, in the January 1992 *Fraser Forum,* wrote:

Of course, the major part of government spending is not for tangible projects such as roads or buildings, but for redistribution of money among interest groups. The benefits of this redistribution are difficult to assess but the high cost of taxation described above gives some weight to the argument for a spending limit.

The political climate in Canada may be ready for a balanced budget amendment, but not for a legislated limit on government spending. A balanced budget requirement would keep spending down. However, it is not a perfect instrument because government has some ability to fund extra spending with taxes, even though taxes are politically dangerous. A spending limit would be a more direct and effective method of controlling the growth of government but may not be acceptable because, in Canada, even if we feel that governments spend too much, it is often considered unfair to suggest that support for any particular project should end ...

At the same time they believe that, overall, government spends too much and may express this in the roundabout cry for a lower national debt. However, as Gorbachev discovered in his reform of the Soviet economy, roundabout paths are longer, costlier, and riskier.[15]

The public interest is dismissed as "interest groups." Nevertheless, according to the Fraser Institute, the public supports government spending because for some unexplained reason, the public considers it "unfair" to cut the programs. Perhaps, instead, the public simply wonders how a low spending limit would get rid of the deficit. The "problem" with democracy may be a value system that does not value economic freedom for those with wealth.

7.7.3 Charity versus Broad-Scale Public Programs

The Fraser Institute advocates charity over broad-scale public programs. In the February 1988 issue of the *Fraser Forum*, Michael Walker made the reason for the Institute's preference clear:

> One of the most cherished notions about Canada is that we care for each other. This is reflected in the extent of social welfare programmes and the relatively large amount of public charity. By comparison, many Canadians believe our American neighbours are more independently minded and are less likely to have concern for their neighbours. Certainly in the currently raging debate about free trade, this characteristic about our two societies has often been mentioned. The facts of the matter are somewhat different than the perception, however.
>
> First of all, it may be true that we spend more money through the government sector to support social services and other people-oriented programs. However, this is not a voluntary activity for Canadians since the payment of the taxes which support the programmes is not voluntary. When we look at those areas of voluntary support for community and service activities, the average American looks much better than the average Canadian. For example, the average American donates to charitable activities twice as much, in proportion to his or her income, than the average Canadian. This according to the Canadian Centre for Philanthropy.
>
> Meanwhile a study in the United States, comparing the community involvement activities of Canadians and Americans has determined that Canadians are less inclined to volunteer than their American counterparts. Now, from this comparison we should not infer that Canadians are less caring than Americans, to invert the popular myth. What we should learn is that perhaps those comparisons between Americans and Canadians don't tell us anything about how charitable or community-minded we are. What they may tell us is that Americans and Canadians have a different propensity to have governments do things. Maybe the same level of charity is accomplished in both countries but in Canada more of it is done by government.[16]

7.7.4 Economic Freedom versus Necessities

In 1992, the Fraser Institute published the book *Poverty in Canada*, by Christopher Sarlo. He concludes that poverty is greatly exaggerated because of the way it is defined.

> Specifically, I define poverty as the inability to acquire all basic necessities of life where those basic needs are any items without which long term physical well being would be jeopardized. The list of necessities, which includes food, shelter, clothing, health care, personal hygiene and a variety of household requirements, would stay fixed to permit legitimate comparisons over time. However, the quality of each item on the list would reflect the minimum adequate standard in the community in which one is a member. This aspect is the relative component.[17]
>
> There are a number of good reasons for preserving the "basic needs" approach to poverty – the most important of which is that it is the most "useful" way of distinguishing between the poor and the nonpoor. And this brings me to the fundamental reason why I strongly favour the absolute or basic necessities approach ... Impoverishment will occur at different living standards for different people ... It seems to me that the most useful cut-off is at the level of basic physical necessities of life.[18]

The book states that single employable individuals receive less assistance than is necessary to provide for the basic physical necessities. Therefore, why does the Fraser Institute not advocate a raise in social assistance rates for single employable persons on the basis of its own research? The Fraser Institute instead promotes a climate that supports the prejudice against employable people. Michael Walker spoke out against the Supreme Court of British Columbia's decision in 1987, when the court ruled that the government could no longer discriminate against able-bodied welfare recipients on the basis of age. He said:

> The reason for making the change is to attempt in the crudest fashion possible to distinguish between the irresponsible and the unfortunate in making payments to welfare recipients. The former, broadly speaking, are those who collect welfare because they have made risky choices with regard to their lifestyle or have decided, in one way or another to opt out ... Generally speaking, the probability is high that

if someone is under twenty-six years of age, is able bodied and is collecting welfare they are in the irresponsible group.[19]

The Fraser Institute, when arguing for the right of individuals to spend their money as they choose, is very vocal in its opposition to the government's right to tax calling it the "tyranny of the majority." However, the "tyranny of the majority" in the form of low social assistance payments that fail to provide individuals with the basic necessities because of the "crude" assumption of irresponsibility is not raised as an issue. In fact, the assumption is promoted by the Institute.

The Fraser Institute wants property rights and "economic freedom" entrenched in the constitution. The Fraser Institute does not want any social rights that would provide for the basic necessities of Canadians entrenched in the constitution.[20]

7.7.5 Medical Care

The Fraser Institute's position on medical care is much like its position on poverty. Only a very low level of care needs to be available to everyone. Michael Walker put it this way:

> There is, however, a bright light on the horizon, which could over a period of time, transform the whole discussion about medical insurance in the United States. Many states are now enacting legislation (17 such laws have already been passed) waiving some or all of the [private insurance] coverage mandates such as drug and alcohol treatment, mental health benefits and some aspects of preventative care. The result has already been the emergence of new plans like that in the state of Kansas, that costs $900 a year, and has a $5,000 deductible, but which covers the family for expenses above that level for catastrophic illness, like a cancer treatment or for the care of injuries received in an automobile accident or other such misfortune.[21]

On the question of health service providers, the Fraser Institute published a book in 1985 entitled *Canadian Medicine: A Study in Restricted Entry*, which argues for competitive certification rather than compulsory monopoly licensing.

7.7.6 Unmet Needs and Responsibility

The Fraser Institute sees injustice as stemming basically from genetics, not society, and it points out that those who are better off cannot be held responsible for the innate disabilities of others. Quite the contrary, they are the ones who can aid those with disabilities. Or in Michael Walker's words:

> In some cases ... poverty is simply a reflection of the fact that the sufferers were dealt an unlucky intellectual or physical allocation from the roulette wheel of genetic inheritance. Others suffer physical handicaps due to no fault of their own. These unfortunates are the normal objects of private charity and should be the target of public charity. Obviously, their position in life is not due to the success of failure of others who have been more fortunate. However, they are dependent on the success of the more fortunate for their maintenance for it is only the successful who generate income which supports those who are unable to support themselves.[22]

However, the writings of the Fraser Institute do not research the possibility that the economic system is contributing to the psychological desperation of individuals that is directly related to their irresponsible behaviour. The consequence is that the Fraser Institute's publications consistently assign primary responsibility to the individual and conclude that few deserve society's assistance. The mentally ill are rarely mentioned, psychological abuse is not mentioned, and childhood abuse that has left individuals traumatized at a very deep level is not mentioned.

The existing public programs provide income and health services with few conditions attached to those receiving the benefits. If a person meets the basic criteria for assistance, then he or she is entitled to that assistance. The person has a right to it. The Fraser Institute does not believe that the answer is to continue social programs that entitle those in need to assistance:

> Rights. Notice how different are these new positive rights from the negative rights of classical origin. In this view, the obligation of other people is not merely to refrain from invading person and property. Not at all. Here, the demand is that other people provide the food, clothing, and shelter that is their right. But this, it should be obvious, is merely a disguised way of demanding the products that other people have earned, produced, and created. It is an attempt to smuggle

compulsory income distribution into the language – under the guise of human rights.[23]

While the Fraser Institute believes that members of society should not make many demands upon other members, it does still find some deserving of assistance. Those that are deserving can be best assisted through a guaranteed annual income, in the form of a negative income tax.[24] Groups with differing ideas about the role of the state support the concept of a guaranteed annual income. Where the groups differ is in the level of support to be provided and the criteria for eligibility: these are not minor differences.

7.7.7 Unemployment

On the topic of unemployment, Michael Walker has said:

> While there continue to be unemployment problems that cause real distress to individuals, this is much less true than was the case in the past. The regular and incessant unemployment experienced by many Canadians these days ought to be the occasion for public questioning of the functioning of the social welfare apparatus which induces this unemployment. And governments ought to be much less anxious to use the unemployment rate produced by this kind of social policy as an indicator of the functioning of the economy and extent of economic and social distress caused by an economic slowdown. While we must continue to have sympathy for individuals who face harsh conditions because they have been let go from their employment, we must realize that for the vast majority of those who are measured by the monthly unemployment numbers, idleness is neither a sign of distress nor involuntary. It is, rather, a symptom of job search and a result of the fact that our employment insurance program encourages people to be choosy.[25]

7.8 Lobbying Tactics

The Fraser Institute uses a wide variety of tactics to influence public opinion. Its methods are imaginative, sophisticated, and highly successful, right down to the smallest detail. For example, instead of just the mundane button with a slogan, the Institute also has ties and scarves, featuring Adam Smith, one of the founders of the free market system, who minimized the individual differences in innate ability.

Its books are written by well-qualified economists and the publications, along with other media information, are widely distributed through a multifaceted marketing plan. As early as 1983, the Institute was able to say that nearly a quarter of a million copies of its publications had been sold and that some of the publications qualified as bestsellers by Canadian commercial standards. By 1983 it was receiving over 15,000 column inches annually in over 250 newspapers and journals,[26] and on 10 October 1986, Michael Walker taped the thousandth edition of "Perspective." The Fraser Institute made a "focused" marketing effort in 1992 and doubled the number of its standing orders. Its expected revenue from sales of publications for 1992 is nearly $100,000. Currently, its editorials appear in more than 50 journals and it runs an editorial program: "This program gives us the opportunity to explain the merits of the free market system, issue by issue, and add to the effectiveness of the Institute's programs."[27]

The Institute's influence is reaching well beyond the Canadian borders. For example, it reported an increase for information on health care because of the 1992 U.S. election. In each issue of the *Fraser Forum*, visitors to the Institute are listed. The latest monthly issue, February 1993, lists the visitors as:

- From the Japan Centre for International Finance, Tokyo: Mr. Hiroshi Tsukada, Chief Economist, Director, Latin America and Canada Department, and Mr. Masashi Otsuka, Economist, Latin America and Canada Department
- Mr. Alan Gardner, Planning Facilitator from IBM
- Mr. Bruce Chapman, President, Discovery Institute of Seattle
- Mr. Michael Planque, Financial Attaché to the French Embassy in Washington, D.C.
- From the State Council and Trade Office of the People's Republic of China, a delegation headed by its vice-premier and chairperson, Zhu Rongji

7.8.1 The Report Card Tactic

In addition to the traditional articles and news broadcasts analyzing and criticizing government policies, the Institute issues a government report card. This report card often awakens enough interest to be featured in publications other than the Institute's, such as major daily newspapers. Most of the report cards have been on the federal government, but the Institute has also reported on the Ontario government. Following are samples from the rating of the Mulroney government for 1989:

Foreign Investment: "A" FIRA gone, FTA investment provisions good, protection of intellectual property and patents. Potential problem with mergers policy and the Competition Tribunal needs immediate attention.

Unemployment Insurance Reform: "D" Premium financing a good start. Tightening requirements right direction. Too timid. Suggest reading of Forget Commission Report, also Fraser Institute, Canadian Tax Foundation Report, et cetera.

Reform of Universal Social Programmes: "D" Repayment of Family Allowance and Old Age Pension by higher incomes eliminates effective universality. Good move. Need to appoint ethics committee to review who should get payments from welfare system like medical ethics committees review who should get high priced surgery. Must separate the irresponsible from the unfortunate.

Job Creation: "C" Structural unemployment caused by legislation prevents Canada matching U.S. jobless rate. If Canada had same unemployment rate as the U.S., 298,000 more Canadians would have a job.

Privatization: "A" Air Canada, Petro-Canada et cetera. Well done!

Attitudes of Government: "F" GST reveals intent to allow government to grow. Willingness to accept lowest poll standing in history over a tax measure designed to fight the deficit by unwillingness to tolerate any political discomfort to eliminate major sources of overspending reveals bias toward government growth.[28]

The Ontario government's report card for mid-year 1991 said, in part:

Microeconomic Policy: "F" Punishes success, rewards failure and eliminates choice. During the campaign and after the election Premier Rae and his colleagues repeatedly asserted that they had learned the same lessons as their Social Democratic and Socialist colleagues in, for example, New Zealand, Australia, Spain, France and even Sweden. They have not done so. It is recommended that they study their socialist colleagues more closely and read the recommended [Fraser Institute] readings at the end of this report card.

Macroeconomic Policy: "F" Main focus here is the budget, with a huge deficit that is economically damaging. Also to be considered are the government's clinging to job creation, and its devious explanations of the size of its budget and its deficit.

Structural Policy: "F" This is the worst area by far. Between high taxes, expanded privileges for unions, and policies designed to make starting companies unattractive and operating them difficult, the government is doing enormous damage. Add to that its desire to reassign half the workers of Ontario to different jobs (see Employment Equity below) and the only possible consolation is that many of its preferred policies are not yet being carried out.

Employment Equity: "F" A serious contender for the worst idea in the history of economics. Employment quotas imply reverse discrimination and if followed to the extent desired would result in widespread disruption in labour markets. Under certain circumstances, if only one employer hired more than its "share" of a targeted group, no other employer could meet the legal requirement. Can become a serious impediment to structural change as well if unions given important role in policy.

Pay Equity: "D" Continuing and strengthening equal pay for work of equal value legislation earns government a D. Saved from an F by the previous government which inaugurated this policy which is the other contender for the worst idea in the history of economics.[29]

7.8.2 Judging the Media
The Fraser Institute is aware of the power the media has to influence public policy making, and it therefore set up an important sounding division within the Institute – the National Media Archive – to scrutinize the media: "The Archive aims to provide, and encourage other researchers to produce, a flow of research on the fidelity of the public information function performed by national media."[30]

The Archive has the transcripts of news and public affairs programming of both the Canadian Broadcasting Corporation and the CTV

Television Network. Its findings of media coverage are published in *On Balance: Media Treatment of Public Policy Issues,* a newsletter it publishes 10 times a year. A typical example of an *On Balance* news story is the following:

DECREASES IN UNEMPLOYMENT NOT NEWSWORTHY: Every month Statistics Canada provides the country's unemployment rate. From the third quarter in 1988 to the second quarter in 1992, they reported increases in the unemployment rate 25 times. The rate decreased 16 times, and showed no change in 4 of the months reported. To determine whether Canadian television news accurately reflected the change in the rate, we compared the amount of attention television gave to the unemployment rate with that of Statistics Canada's monthly reporting ... Both networks overemphasized increases in the rate and de-emphasized the instances when the unemployment rate went down. Almost three-quarters of the attention to unemployment occurred when the rate increased, despite the fact that in reality the rate was increasing only slightly over half the time. In contrast, while the rate decreased over one-third of the time, attention to the decrease accounted for only 14 percent of CBC and 21 percent of CTV attention to unemployment.[31]

The staff of *On Balance* claim that their analysis of the news is "completely objective" since they use content analysis, that is, the news content is systematically examined according to specified categories. But the very construction of the categories involves a lot of decision making on the part of the category selector. A recent detailed study of *On Balance* (OB) found it to be lacking in objectivity:

In addition to methodological and conceptual difficulties, OB often undercuts its stated goal of scientific objectivity by an editorial mode of reporting results. One disturbing tendency is the use of graphs suggesting that the reporting of particular, named journalists is overwhelmingly imbalanced on a particular issue – sometimes on the basis of only one or two news stories ... (OB October 1988, p. 4).

The use of headlines and quotations in sidebars in OB, while it can be a legitimate reporting device and an aid to readers, often presents a clear point of view. Moreover, the reader of OB is sometimes confronted with gaps between evidence and conclusions, gaps which are seemingly bridged by interpretations which more often than not are consistent with the ideological stance of the Fraser Institute ... The rhetoric of OB reports largely work by a process of implication ... Columnist Andrew Coyne was surely not far from the mark in his interpretation of the On Balance research agenda: "Ostensibly, it's just disinterested empirical observation, like birdwatching, but the intention is clear: to gather proof of the leftist conspiracy conservatives are convinced is running the media" (*Financial Post*, August 9, 1989, p. 11). Such a view of the media can be sustained only by ignoring a great deal of reputable research which suggests that mainstream media tend to amplify official definitions of reality and to marginalize and delegitimize fundamental opposition.[32]

The Fraser Institute uses *On Balance* to draw attention to the issues it wishes the media to place greater emphasis on, and through its analysis, indicates how it would like issues treated in the media. It contends that the answer to the media bias that results in more attention being focused on negative economic news than on positive economic news is to privatize the CBC and deregulate the media. The media is not seen as responsive to public demands for the type of news stories it wishes to receive, and increased competition is seen as the best way to correct this problem.[33]

It is rather ironic that the Fraser Institute is so concerned with the objectivity of the media, when its own publications give only information congruent with a free market philosophy. Since the Fraser Institute was consulted extensively in 1983, as the new British Columbia government brought in a restraint program, the publications of the Institute are viewed as having, or potentially having, significant influence. And it was therefore pointed out as "disturbing" and "serious" in articles appearing in 1984 that the Thompson and Southam newspaper chains, Maclean-Hunter, BCTV, Moffat Communications, and Premier Cablevision all contribute funds to the Fraser Institute.[34]

7.8.3 Prizes

Prizes are another way that attention is brought to the ideas espoused by the Fraser Institute. In 1991, 773 contestants entered the annual Fraser Institute Economy in Government Competition. More than $70,000 in prizes were awarded to the best proposals to restructure activities of the federal, provincial, and territorial governments in ways that reduce the cost of government per unit of service delivered. In

1992 there was an Awards Dinner in Ottawa with the federal Minister
of State for Finance, who presented the prizes. The first prize went to
the proposal to reduce costs associated with the mint, the second
prize went to a proposal to alter the civil service by reversing the
Glassco Commission's recommendations, and the third prize to proposals to reduce waste and extravagance in the foreign service.[35]

The prize technique is used by other groups who foster a free market economy. Thus, the Fraser Institute wins prizes, with attendant
publicity for its activities. For example, the National Citizens'
Coalition annually gives the Colin M. Brown Freedom Medal to hon-
our an individual who has made "outstanding contributions to the
advancement and defence of Canada's basic political and economic
freedoms." Past winners have been Barbara Amiel, Senator Stan
Waters, and Thomas Bata who is married to Sonja Bata, a Fraser
Institute trustee. On 8 September 1992, the *Vancouver Sun* informed its
readers that Michael Walker was the 1992 winner "for his efforts to
give Canadians a better understanding of the free market system, government spending and taxation."[36] The medal comes with $10,000.

Book prizes have also been won by the Fraser Institute. The prizes
are helpful in book promotion. They are given by groups whose purposes are similar to the Institute's. For example, the Institute's 1991
annual report notes:

> The Atlas Economic Research Foundation awarded first prize (U.S.
> $10,000) in the 1991 Sir Anthony Fisher International Memorial
> Awards to the Fraser Institute for *Economics and the Environment: A
> Reconciliation,* edited by Walter Block. The winning entries were those
> which the judges felt made the greatest contribution to the under-
> standing of the free market economy over the past two years.[37]

7.9 Conclusions

The Fraser Institute exists to demonstrate through its research the su-
periority of a free market economy over a government-regulated economy. It claims to be a social as well as an economic research organization, yet it conducts only economic research. It muddies the waters
between values and economics and between the particular findings
from a limited brand of economic research and the much wider truth.

The Fraser Institute points out the weaknesses of government regulation and suggests that the solution is much less government regulation. Free markets are said to be best for both those with capital and

those without capital. Only in a few limited cases is society to act as a collective. The reason collective action is typically viewed as negative is that it restricts the financial freedom of individuals. The capitalist system is not admitted to be biased in any serious way. Thus, its research in areas related to public programs consistently assume that individuals are responsible for their own well being and have extremely little claim to the assistance of others. The general conclusions the Fraser Institute will draw from its research into any public program are quite predictable.

The Fraser Institute has succinctly summarized its views on social programs. In answer to the question "what social services should the public sector provide?" Walter Block, then senior economist for the Institute, said:

Little or none. The classical liberal tradition, the tradition of Adam Smith, John Stuart Mill, and David Hume was that government was mainly for defence, judiciary. And when it tries to act in the public good it actually worsens the situation of the people that it is acting in behalf of. The Fraser Institute would certainly advocate the government as a safety net of last resort but not one of first resort as is all too popular in this province and this country.[38]

Part IV:
The Public's Views of Social Programs

8

Public Support for Comprehensive Social Programs in Canada

8.1 Support for or Opposition to Broad-Scale Social Programs

An indication of the degree of the public's adoption of the neoconservative arguments concerning social programs is the general trend in support of or opposition to such programs across a sample of programs that have varied objectives but have in common that they are broad-scale (aimed at large populations of beneficiaries) and involve the public sector as major sponsor. Table 8.1 summarizes the results for a set of nine items in which a rating was obtained of support of or opposition to broad-scale social programs.

For eight of the nine programs, there are strong majorities supporting the program and only small minorities expressing any degree of opposition to the program. The general pattern of these findings is consistent with the proponents' position we have outlined in Chapter 6 and inconsistent with the neoconservative position.

The only program that fails to achieve a firm majority support in our sample is a program of tax exemptions for investment opportunities. The results for this item contrast with the results for the similar items of tax exemptions for small business and RRSPs, both of which are clearly supported. This difference, however, also appears to be consistent with a proponents' view, in that the several tax exemption programs receiving support are benefits for middle- or lower-income taxpayers, whereas tax deductions for investment are more likely to be seen as aid for the more prosperous taxpayer and for large corporations. This pattern of findings amounts to support for using the tax system for income redistributive purposes, a view that is favoured by proponents and opposed by conservatives.

A second body of data on support for and opposition to broad-scale

Table 8.1

Percentages of Responses Supporting or Opposing Nine Social Programs with Varied Objectives

Social Programs	N	Strongly Support	Support	Mixed: Support & Oppose	Oppose	Strongly Oppose
Alcohol and Drug Rehab. Services	124	42.7	35.5	13.7	4.8	3.2
Child Tax Deduction: Low Income Families	123	54.5	31.7	8.9	3.3	1.6
Job Retraining: Injured Workers	123	67.5	29.3	0.8	1.6	0.8
Services to Help Immigrants	124	37.1	27.4	20.2	8.1	7.3
Income Assistance (Welfare)	123	39.8	28.5	26.0	4.1	1.6
Tax Credits for Investments	121	13.2	18.2	28.9	15.7	24.0
Home Nursing Services	121	62.8	28.9	5.0	1.7	0.8
Family Allowances	123	35.0	18.7	31.7	10.6	4.1
Tax Deductions for RRSP	124	60.5	25.8	9.7	1.6	2.4

social programs is available from our vignette database. As explained in Chapter 1, the design of the vignettes study was a factorial experiment in which the judgments of support were made in response to vignettes incorporating 11 variables, one of which was the type of social program.[1] A sample vignette and the seven-point bipolar rating of support/opposition, as well as preferences for funding are also presented in Chapter 1. The seven-point scale is used primarily for the regression analysis.[2] In this chapter, the seven are reduced to five.

We designed the vignettes database primarily to examine the effects on support of these 11 variables in conjunction with respondent variables (e.g., gender, age, income). Twenty-three social programs were included. For the present analysis we use 22 of these.

We may use this database to look at overall support for or opposition to each social program by averaging over the other 10 variables. This provides us with a measure of support for or opposition to each social program when the effects of the other variables have been randomized over all values. Table 8.2 shows a percentage distribution of the judgments made on each social program, in response to the following question:

Based on the information provided in the vignette, please tell me which answer expresses your opinion.

How strongly are you in favour of or opposed to this program/ service?

1	2	3	4	5	6	7
Strongly			Mixed:			Strongly
Oppose			Favour and Oppose			Favour

These ratings may be grouped as follows:

1   Majority support of two-thirds or better is shown for the two workers' compensation programs, family counselling programs, welfare programs with job retraining, unemployment insurance, universal retirement pensions, contributory retirement pensions, pharmacare, group homes for behaviourally handicapped adults, English as a second language classes, supplementary university preparation for Native students, legal aid for a woman's equal pay suit.

2   Majority support of between one-half and two-thirds is shown for

Table 8.2

Percentages of Responses Opposed to or in Favour of 22 Social Programs with Varied Objectives (Vignettes Database: N = 1700)

Social Programs	N	Strongly Favour	Favour	Mixed: Favour & Oppose	Oppose	Strongly Oppose
Workers' Compensation Pension	37	35.1	45.9	13.5	5.4	0.0
Workers' Compensation Physiotherapy	32	50.0	40.6	3.1	0.0	6.3
Counselling for Individuals	176	28.4	35.5	12.5	8.5	15.3
Family Counselling	46	34.8	30.5	10.9	15.2	8.7
Tax Exemptions for RRSP	79	30.4	26.6	19.0	11.4	12.7
Welfare with Job Retraining	48	27.1	43.8	12.5	10.4	6.3
Government Scholarships	98	27.6	31.6	21.4	9.2	10.2
Unemployment Insurance	97	40.2	42.3	12.4	2.1	3.1
Subsidized Rent	88	22.7	27.3	21.6	9.1	19.3
Tax Shelters for Investment	68	5.9	7.4	20.6	14.7	51.5
Universal Retirement Pensions	75	41.3	30.7	18.7	4.0	5.3
Income Assistance (Welfare)	96	19.8	31.3	17.7	13.5	17.7
Tax Writeoffs for Small Business Expenses	69	17.4	34.7	26.2	11.6	10.1

Pharmacare	80	43.8	33.8	13.8	5.0	3.8
Contributory Survivor's Pension	77	46.8	39.0	9.1	2.6	2.6
Group Home for Handicapped Adults	58	24.1	51.8	13.8	3.4	6.9
Voice Box to Replace Cancerous Larynx	66	31.8	33.4	21.2	7.5	6.1
ESL Classes	90	34.4	33.3	16.7	2.2	13.3
Homemaker to Assist with Child Care	82	19.5	32.9	19.5	13.4	14.6
School Lunch Program (no means test)	72	36.1	18.0	23.6	4.2	18.1
Aid for Plaintiff in Sexual Abuse Case vs. Church	23	34.8	21.7	21.7	4.3	17.4
Supplementary College Preparation: Native Students	35	37.1	31.5	8.6	11.4	11.4
Aid for Discrimination Suits: Metis vs. Government	36	13.9	41.6	19.4	13.9	11.1
Ombudsman's Suit vs. Employer re Equal Pay for Females	43	46.5	28.0	7.0	4.6	14.0

counselling for individual problems, government scholarships for college students, tax writeoffs for small businesses, welfare without job training, and school lunch programs.

3   Majority opposition greater than two-thirds is shown to tax deductions to provide investment incentives. No other programs are opposed by a majority of respondents.

The general pattern of these findings is similar to that of the first batch of data on support displayed in Table 8.1. The results are quite consistent with proponents' views of social programs and inconsistent with the neoconservative views we have summarized in the preceding chapter.

Both programs that are targeted towards low-income groups and programs with no particular income targeting are strongly supported. This pattern is reminiscent of Kent's observation, published in 1960,[3] that comprehensive social security is mainly a redistribution of income within middle-income groups.

Willingness to Pay More Taxes. A more stringent test of support for social programs is willingness to pay increased taxes to maintain them. To get at this, we asked the respondents for the following rating on each of the vignettes:

If funding the service should call for an increase in tax rates, how strongly would you favour or oppose this increase?

The rating scale employed here was the same one employed for the question on support:

Based on the information provided in the vignette, please tell me which answer expresses your opinion. How strongly would you favour or oppose this increase?

1	2	3	4	5	6	7
Strongly Oppose			Mixed: Favour and Oppose			Strongly Favour

The results are shown in Table 8.3.

In summary, for the following programs *a majority of respondents are in favour of increasing taxes should funding the program call for such in-*

Table 8.3

Percentages of Responses Opposed to or in Favour of Increased Taxes, If Needed, to Maintain 22 Social Programs with Varied Objectives
(Vignettes Database: N = 1700)

Social Programs	N	Strongly Favour	Favour	Mixed: Favour & Oppose	Oppose	Strongly Oppose
Worker's Compensation Pension	37	16.2	21.6	27.0	8.1	27.0
Worker's Compensation Physiotherapy	31	16.1	25.8	25.8	13.0	19.4
Counselling for Individuals	174	6.3	25.9	25.3	16.1	26.4
Family Counselling	45	20.0	31.1	13.3	16.6	17.8
Tax Exemptions for RRSP	77	9.0	9.0	24.7	16.9	40.3
Welfare with Job Retraining	47	6.4	40.4	25.5	8.5	19.1
Government Scholarships	98	11.2	21.4	29.6	16.4	21.4
Unemployment Insurance	98	10.2	34.7	26.5	8.1	20.4
Subsidized Rent	87	10.3	18.3	28.7	13.7	28.7
Tax Shelters for Investment	65	1.5	4.6	16.9	10.8	66.2
Universal Retirement Pensions	75	22.7	38.7	18.7	9.3	10.7
Income Assistance (Welfare)	91	11.0	20.9	31.9	13.2	23.1
Tax Writeoffs for Small Business Expenses	62	3.2	17.7	27.4	22.6	29.0

(continued on next page)

Table 8.3 (continued)

Percentages of Responses Opposed to or in Favour of Increased Taxes, If Needed, to Maintain 22 Social Programs with Varied Objectives
(Vignettes Database: N = 1700)

Social Programs	N	Strongly Favour	Favour	Mixed: Favour & Oppose	Oppose	Strongly Oppose
Pharmacare	79	17.7	34.2	25.3	10.1	12.7
Contributory Survivor's Pension	77	10.4	41.6	16.9	10.4	20.8
Group Home for Handicapped Adults	58	10.3	25.9	37.9	10.4	15.5
Voice Box to Replace Cancerous Larynx	64	18.8	20.3	28.1	14.1	18.8
ESL Classes	89	13.5	28.1	23.6	13.5	21.3
Homemaker to Assist with Child Care	81	7.4	28.4	19.8	11.1	33.3
School Lunch Program (no means test)	70	15.7	38.6	17.1	10.0	18.6
Aid for Plaintiff in Sexual Abuse Case vs. Church	21	28.6	23.8	14.3	9.5	23.8
Supplementary College Preparation: Native Students	35	8.6	45.7	20.0	14.3	11.4
Aid for Discrimination Suits: Metis vs. Government	36	11.1	16.7	33.3	16.6	22.2
Ombudsman's Suit vs. Employer re Equal Pay for Females	41	14.6	39.1	12.2	9.7	24.4

creases: family counselling; unemployment insurance; universal retirement pensions; contributory pensions; pharmacare; school lunch programs; supplementary schooling to help Native students prepare for university; financial assistance for suits against a church for sexual abuse of students; financial assistance for suits against an employer on behalf of equal pay for female employees.

Pluralities are in favour of increasing taxes, should these be necessary to fund the following programs: ESL classes; workers' compensation pensions; physiotherapy for workers' compensation cases; welfare programs with job training provisions; welfare programs with no mention of job training provisions; provision of a voice box in the case of a smoker who developed cancer of the larynx.

Majorities are opposed to increasing taxes to maintain the following programs: tax exemptions as investment incentives; tax writeoffs for small business.

Pluralities are opposed to increasing taxes, should these prove necessary to fund the following programs: counselling for individual problems (e.g., drug and alcohol addiction); government college scholarships; home child care (homemaker) services; aid to a discrimination suit against the government on behalf of Métis.

As expected, the percentages favouring increased taxes to maintain social programs are not as large as those favouring the programs. Nevertheless, the results seem consistent with the former set of findings and with the data on responsibility for funding. A most striking finding is the percentage of respondents who are willing to pay increased taxes to support government intervention to remedy injustices or institutional discrimination (Native students, female employees). This hardly bespeaks a narrow, small-safety-net conception of the social services. It again looks more like the comprehensive social security vision of Kent et al.[4]

The two programs to which there is majority opposition are tax incentives for business activity and for investments (see above). These seem to have in common that they are aid to "those who have." One sees this same theme in the programs for which tax increases are opposed by a plurality of respondents. There is evidence of a concern to ensure that benefits go to those who need them, but this also looks like pragmatism – making the best use of limited resources – rather than any principled view that the only programs we should have are those aimed at the poor and severely disadvantaged.

8.2 Support for or Opposition to Public Sector Responsibility for Social Programs

Neoconservatives, we noted in the preceding chapter, are opposed to or reluctantly acquiesce in policies that place responsibility for funding social programs in the public sector. Their motto is, "when you give it to the government, you make a racket out of it." We have examined how far the public has moved, if at all, towards this neoconservative view by a series of items concerning preferred means of funding social programs. Table 8.4 shows the results of a question that asked respondents to check one or more of the following methods of funding: taxes, user fees, lotteries, and charitable donations. Any of these options could be checked – they were not treated as mutually exclusive. Respondents who were not in favour of a given program checked none of them. To explore the public's preferences for public versus alternative means of funding, we compare in Table 8.4 the percentages of respondents who checked taxes, user fees, lotteries, and charities for six social programs. Tax exemptions are not included in this list, as a number of our respondents had difficulty with the idea that such incentives have to be "funded." In Table 8.5, I present the results of the same questions applied to the vignette database; Table 8.6 presents data that compare "taxes" with "corporate contributions" and "employee contributions."

Table 8.4

Percentages of Respondents Who Support Use of Taxes, User Fees, Lotteries, and Charity as Funding Methods for 6 Social Programs*
(N = 124)

Social Program	Method of Funding			
	Taxes	User Fees	Lotteries	Charity
Alcohol & Drug Rehabilitation Services	72	36	31	31
Job Retraining: Injured Workers	70	9	16	13
Services to Help Immigrants	85	42	20	26
Income Assistance (Welfare)	85	5	29	18
Home Nursing Services	85	31	27	20
Family Allowances	88	7	20	7

* Respondents could choose more than one method of funding a social program.

From these tables we see that in all cases the public shows a preference for public sector funding, as indexed by the votes for "taxes" compared to other sources of funding. In most cases, "taxes" has a large lead over the other options. At the same time, a strong streak of pragmatism is evident in these data. In cases in which user fees, for example, appear to be a practical option, such as in counselling services and services to immigrants, these are frequently checked, but not in cases such as welfare, where user fees are hardly practical. The data on corporate contributions show quite a bit of discrimination among programs, and, again, a healthy respect for the practical, as well as an indication that the respondents expect corporations to be making substantial contributions to funding Canada's social programs.

The message of these data appears to be: primary reliance on the public sector, supplemented by any and all available means of maintaining funding. This is much more pragmatic than it is ideological. But again, it looks much like the traditional credo of comprehensive social security.

Targeting. Targeting, in its most inclusive meaning, refers to giving priority to social programs aimed at low-income groups. The message of the foregoing data, however, is that respondents favour a mix of such programs with other programs, such as universal pensions and unemployment insurance, that provide benefits to middle-income groups. Thus the evidence of these data is against a widespread adoption by the public of targeting proposals.

8.3 Against Programs with Redistributive Aims:
The Argument from Precept

We would expect that if the public had turned towards the neoconservative view of social programs, it would be particularly leery of programs with avowedly redistributive aims. We would expect such programs to be opposed, and to rank well below programs to create business opportunities. In our sample of programs I would count the following two as having clearly redistributive aims: tax deduction for low-income families and income assistance.

From Table 8.1 we see that both these programs are favoured by strong majorities. In overall support, as measured by the percentages of respondents who either strongly favour or favour them, they rank fifth and sixth, respectively: closer to the middle of the ranking than to either end.

Table 8.5

Percentages of Vignettes in Which the Use of Taxes, User Fees, Lotteries, and Charity as Funding Was Supported for Social Programs with Varied Objectives*

Social Program	N	Method of Funding			
		Taxes	User Fees	Lotteries	Charity
Counselling for Personal & Behavioural Problems	192	56	51	11	20
ESL Classes	94	67	40	15	31
Family Counselling	49	67	28	14	34
Homemaker: Care of Children	81	56	38	17	23
Litigation Costs: Suit Against Church for Sexual Abuse of Native Children	23	62	5	5	24
Litigation Costs: Suit against Employer re Gender Equality in Wages	46	65	16	11	9
Litigation Costs: Suit against Government re Discrimination against Metis	40	67	31	11	25
Pharmacare	86	78	27	23	16
Scholarship Grants to College Students	98	67	20	30	17
Supplementary Schooling for Native Children: University Preparation	35	74	17	26	20
School Lunch Program	77	63	33	30	26

Welfare with Job Training	53	77	12	39	18
Retirement Pension, Contributory	83	70	13	13	6
Retirement Pension, Universal	75	83	11	11	10
Subsidized Housing	95	65	25	16	16
Unemployment Insurance	103	64	17	19	14
Voice Box to Replace Cancerous Larynx	72	70	13	13	6
Welfare without Job Training	49	66	14	12	14
Workers' Compensation	37				

* Respondents could choose more than one method of funding a social program.

Table 8.6

Percentages of Vignettes in Which the Use of Taxes, Corporate Contributions Was Supported for Social Programs with Varied Objectives*

		Method of Funding		
Social Program	N	Taxes	Corporate Contributions	Employee Contributions
Counselling for Personal & Behavioural Problems	192	56	34	19
ESL Classes	94	67	29	14
Family Counselling	49	67	36	17
Homemaker: Care of Children	81	56	18	18
Litigation Costs: Suit against Church for Sexual Abuse of Native Children	23	62	19	5
Litigation Costs: Suit against Employer re Gender Equality in Wages	46	65	28	2
Litigation Costs: Suit against Government re Discrimination against Metis	40	67	28	2
Pharmacare	86	78	27	12
Scholarship Grants to College Students	98	67	32	7
Supplementary Schooling for Native Children: University Preparation	35	74	37	5

Program			
School Lunch Program	77	63	21	6
Welfare with Job Training	53	77	46	7
Retirement Pension, Contributory	83	70	35	51
Retirement Pension, Universal	75	83	26	40
Subsidized Housing	95	65	24	9
Unemployment Insurance	103	64	49	64
Voice Box to Replace Cancerous Larynx	72	70	30	20
Welfare without Job Training	49	66	12	14
Worker's Compensation	37	68	9	11

* Respondents could choose more than one method of funding a social program.

Thus, on programs with redistributive aims, the results are again quite consistent with proponents' view and inconsistent with a conservative view. In these data there is no evidence that the neoconservative worries about the disastrous economic consequences of redistribution of wealth to low-income groups are shared by the general public.

Tables 8.1 and 8.2 also show no marked disadvantage for redistributive programs, though the case of welfare without job training illustrates the ambivalence of both proponents of social programs and neoconservatives towards this program: we note that support for this program is about 20 points less than support for welfare with job training.

8.4 Demand that Benefits Be Conditioned on the Meritorious Behaviour of Recipients

To explore this issue I made use of the vignette database described in Chapter 1. In accordance with standard procedures of factorial design, the values of the variables making up each vignette were determined randomly, subject to several restrictions, such as that professionals must have university degrees. Under these circumstances the number of observations for analysis becomes the number of vignettes.[5] We are able to use procedures such as ordinary least squares to estimate the effects on the ratings of support or opposition of different values of the variables contained in the vignette.

One such analysis is to examine the relationship between these ratings and the personal "merits" or "demerits" of recipients as reflected in the vignettes. To explore this relationship, I have constructed a "merit" variable representing those factors that neoconservatives maintain should be taken into account in determining either entitlement, terms on which a benefit is granted, or both. These variables include work record, marital status (married versus common-law), educational achievement, drug addiction, and being on probation for driving under the influence of alcohol.

A variable "merit" was created and initially set to zero, then augmented by one for each of the following values: "married," "high school graduate or better," "steadily employed," "no mention of problems of addiction or drunken driving." This was then decreased by one for each of the following: "common-law," "education less than high school," "never held a steady job," combined with "fit," "on probation for driving under the influence," and "problems of drug or alcohol addiction." This variable was further decreased by one if "never held a steady job" was combined with being a member of a profession or having a university education.

Using the entire database of some 1,700 vignettes, the variable "merit" was correlated with the bipolar rating scale of support or opposition. The results are shown in Table 8.7.

Table 8.7

Part I: Relationship of Variables Merit and Support/Opposition

	Merit
N of Cases	1687
Minimum	-1.0
Maximum	1.0
Mean	0.550
Standard Deviation	0.586

Part II: Pearson Correlation Matrix

	Favour	Merit
Favour	1.0	
Merit	-0.025	1.0

8.5 Correlates of Support for Social Programs

8.5.1 Method

8.5.1.1 Variables
The following variables were construed as indices of support:

- average support score for: alcohol and drug rehabilitation services; child tax deductions for low-income families; job retraining for injured workers; services to help immigrants; income assistance (welfare); home nursing services; and family allowances. This measure was obtained simply by summing the ratings on these variables for each respondent, and dividing by 7, the number of variables that were summed.

- average support scores, arrived at in the same way, for tax deductions for investments and for RRSPs.

I then measured, using multiple regression analysis, the extent to which each of these support indices was associated with each of the following variables, and also with a weighted sum of all of these variables.

An advantage of this method is that the analysis is done in such a way as to assess the independent effects of each of the variables, after the effects of the other variables on the list had been taken into account. The list of variables is as follows:

Sample membership: There were five samples, as explained in Chapter 1: the samples drawn respectively from the high-, medium-, and low-income areas of Vancouver; the random sample of households in the Fraser Valley community of Abbotsford; and the sample of members of advocacy and professional organizations.
Gender: Male, female.
Occupation: We employed a classification based on census categories.
Educational achievement: Highest grade or degree level attained.
Household income: Annual household income, before taxes, from all sources.
Respondents' age in years.

8.5.1.2 Summary of Results

1 The overall effect of all of the above variables on support index (1) listed above was a multiple correlation of .41. This explains about 16% of the variance in the support index, an effect generally considered to be small for the number of predictor variables employed.
2 The overall effect of all of the above variables on support index (2) listed above was a multiple correlation of .44. This explains about 19% of the variance in the support index. This, too, is an effect generally considered to be small in view of the number of predictors employed.
3 Support for RRSPs and Investment Tax Credits was associated with income, but the association was weak: the difference between the top quantile (20%) on household income and the remaining quantiles was less than half of a standard deviation. This is a small difference.
4 The organization sample was more in favour of programs that

redistribute income to low-income groups, as well as Family Allowances, than the Abbotsford sample of households. Again the difference was small, of the order of less than a standard deviation.

5 Support index (1) was positively associated with age. This association was again not strong, about the equivalent of a Pearson correlation of .18.
6 No appreciable differences in the above set of comparisons were found for gender or education of the respondents.

8.5.2 Conclusions

1 The above results are to be expected, given the strong majorities in favour of all programs other than investment tax credits.
2 The conclusion to be drawn is that the data reveal no substantial cleavages in the sample on support for the programs surveyed.

It is evident that in these data there is a weak relationship between merit as indexed by employment record, marital status, drug addiction, and being on probation for driving under the influence of alcohol and the scale of support or opposition. A more general analysis of the relationship of recipient and program variables and the ratings, to be reported in another paper, shows substantial effects for programs and some status variables such as age and gender, but the effects of other characteristics of recipients of benefits are weak or zero.

In these data, one can see no evidence that the neoconservative demand that entitlement be tied to meritorious behaviour is widely shared by the general public.

8.6 Concerns about the Social Services

We have followed two complementary strategies of data analysis: top-down and bottom-up. Our top-down strategy is to identify issues that divide proponents and neoconservative critics of the social services, and to put these issues as questions to our data. The bottom-up strategy is to enquire, more open-endedly, into the agendas that our research participants have for the social services, and then to compare these with the views of proponents and neoconservatives.

Here, using primarily our focus group data, I pursue the bottom-up strategy by a process of coding focus group transcripts for agendas and issues. I conclude this with a comparison of the results with the proponents' and neoconservative views.

I adopted "concerns about the social services" as a master theme because this phrase serves as a good heading for most of the discussion in the focus groups. It is clear that "support for broad-scale social programs," reflected in our survey data, in no way implies a state of satisfaction with the present state of these programs.

Several categories of concern emerged from the data: concerns to *strengthen* the social services through more adequate conceptions of the scope of social policy; needs to *shore up* existing social programs; needs for *rationalization, reorganization,* and *greater attention to efficacy;* arguments that social programs should be made *leaner and more stringent* in their entitlements.

The first three of these themes were major motifs in the data. The last one, which was heard from two members of one focus group, was a minor but clearly contrasting theme, representing the views of about the same proportion of participants (6 to 10%) as we found in the survey.

I have organized the following presentation of the data according to these major themes.

8.7 Shore Up the Concept of Social Policy to Take on Board Some More Fundamental Problems

A good deal of the focus group discussion began with the premise that the social services are not as adequate or effective as we would like them to be, and concluded that to increase the efficacy of social programs we must widen the horizons of social policy beyond programs, program policies, and social services management. A major theme here was the need to recognize the fallacies in existing fiscal policies:

Investment Incentives: We are on the wrong track if we assume investment monies will produce jobs – because investment is no longer producing jobs – it's producing profit. The basic part of society that did produce jobs is now side tracked to multinationals. The rules of government are bypassed by these organizations. The multi-nationals are not paying their share of tax. These investment incentives can also be termed corporate charity.[6]

It is the tax side that creates inequalities – not the distribution side. No longer the individual investor who is the driving force for investment.

Is the existing tax system fair? Low income people pay a disproportionate amount of taxes compared to high income people.

Subsidies to Welfare Rights Groups or Organizations: Concern is raised that in a country like ours there is need to provide such subsidies. Perhaps we need to examine our tax structure more fully.

Investment decisions are still being made with minimal regard to their social benefits and costs. They are treated as purely economic. This omission is the source of many of our social problems as well as of inadequacies in the social service system. We must soften if not eliminate the distinction between the social and the economic.

Also we need to look at the world environment and its economy and start talking realistically about sustainability and what do we need, and what becomes kind of a level of conspicuous consumption.

A related theme was the need to provide more resources for prevention, particularly by addressing the income inequalities, the impacts of poverty, and possibilities for day care as education in our society:

Another member raises the issue of income assistance and the rather negative connotations associated with it, however she feels the major issue to be examined in regard to social issues is poverty. If one can do something with poverty, then you will substantially reduce most of the other issues. We need to begin to do something regarding the growing discrepancy between the high ends and the low ends otherwise we perpetuate the problems of too few services for too many clients.

The issue is raised that the forgoing is really advocating something that seems to be opposite to being crises oriented. Can we give something to people, e.g., support, that makes people feel they're capable or deserving of respect? Maybe income assistance doesn't have that.

Day care for Children: Day care programs, if designed properly, could become the process of education outside the family – like learning how to live in a homogenous or heterogenous mass of different races or cultures. It does not have to be government-run provided there are controls and regulations. It could provide a process whereby we begin to instill in our children certain values and attitudes that carry on through later life.

Two issues here – the physical and the psychological. This leads into a discussion around the issue of services. As our knowledge increases, there is a need for more programs and resources – will there ever be enough resources? Do we need to start educating people to do more for themselves? We can't expect Govt to do everything – It's got to become a total community responsibility.

Finally there were calls for more adequate provision for a number of the existing social programs, without necessarily excluding the foregoing broader concerns about social policy:

Immigration Issue: People are being encouraged to come and when they get here, there are not the necessary services to help them – they are literally abandoned. They are housed by Immigration in hotels, have no money for support – referred to Food Bank by Immigration. Also we tend to take the well educated people from other countries – their own country needs these people and their skill and ability.

We have increased awareness of sexual abuse yet no longer have the staff in our school systems to deal with it. There is both a lack of funding and staff to deal with preventive programs that would help prevent health and social problems in later life – e.g., women now in Riverview who were sexually abused as children, the fetal alcohol syndrome. We are not addressing these type of issues.

We are aware of preventative measures available – but no funding to support staff to follow up on these issues, so thousands of children will need life-long medical care of one form or another.

Strong views were expressed regarding the great need for more public housing and the issue that the Federal Govt was turning full jurisdiction for this issue over to the provinces.

8.8 We Need Better Administration of the Social Services, More Evaluation, More Involvement of the Public

A number of proposals were made for improving the organization of the social services in Canada:

1   *We must replace a plethora of income maintenance programs with some form of guaranteed annual income.*

One senior speaks to a program he has been on for 11 or 12 years – the establishment of a National Base Income. All leaders of federal parties from 1983 have been informed of this initiative – so are the labour groups & – but everyone is "dancing around it": What we desire for ourselves we advocate for others: equality, fairness and responsibility. Our government states that the universality of social services is a sacred trust – yet the programs now in place fall short of this goal. We urge the establishment of a National Basic Income (12,000 per year, indexed to the Consumer Price Index. This fund (NBI) would replace all our current financial programs.

2   *We must make services more inclusive and more accessible, as well as increase the time horizon of funding.*

A major concern is how to provide information, education and access to all services re: Immigrants. Issue of sponsorship of having to be 10 years – can mean great hardship on sponsor if their situation changes – or it can mean the immigrant who come have no place to go as children signed a contract to care for them for ten years.

Issue of concern is the administration of some of the way we do things – we set up bureaucracies to screen people out – and so end up stigmatizing certain population groups.

Day Care – everyone should have access to it and full reimbursement for women who need it.

Aid to Developing Countries – Canadians need to be informed as to how these programs are monitored.

Unemployment Insurance – with the recession and lack of available work in Canada today – need to seriously consider extend unemployment payments rather than force individual to go on welfare – as it is demeaning to the individual and the family.

English as a Second Language – as Federal Govt establishes quotas it should be able to suggest the amount of ESL program – money necessary to these quotas to help integrate these people into both the local community and the overall economic life of Canada. Why could we not offer ESL programs to accepted immigrants in their own country of origin? Another issue Immigration is Federal policy – and education of these people is Provincial – so one can have financial conflict.

Subsidies to Welfare Rights Groups – need long-term funding and should be more flexibility of use by those who administer such funds for the group.

Human Rights Programs – taking too long to implement to do any good for those having such difficulties.

3   *Services must provide a hand up, not a handout: Providing the client with a "hand up" situation rather than a "hand out," which can be demeaning.*

Income Assistance – You can't do anything to help yourself such as go to school while on welfare. The only way you can receive assistance from the government is to sit there and accept this charitable mode. You are forced to lie to cover any earnings or it is taken off your grant. We're making thieves out of our people. People are starting to steal as that is the only option they see open to them.

It's the hardest job in the world to be on welfare.

4   *It's not the cost, it's the wastage. We must rationalize policies, train people to help themselves in some areas such as health prevention and also how to make more effective use of services.*

Concern was also expressed that Govt rather than examining the whole system of social services tends to patch up the services in existence rather than examine the system and make needed change. We are constantly involved in crises management and unless we start applying genuine preventative measures we will continue "throwing good money after bad."

Health Care Programs – being abused by elderly in part out of loneliness. Could have a $10.00 fee which would bring in a large amount of revenue.

Aid to Developing Countries – need to have more control over this – in order to assure that the products we sent actually reach the people who need them and don't fall into hands of Black Marketers, etc. There needs to be a set of Preconditions, Follow up and Reporting Back. In short a better monitoring system must be set up.

Not the cost of programs that will cause us financial difficulty – it's the wastage in the systems – need to curb expenses in our programs. Organizations receiving money most tighten up their delivery service system – we have got to be responsible.

ESL – a good program, essential – but we need to control it. Needs to be available to children. Adults coming into our country owe the country (Canada) for the opportunity we provide, so they should learn our language. Also, if Aid is to be given to developing countries, it should be delivered in a less political manner – provide it through third party international agencies like World Health, Red Cross, UNICEF.

5   *The public must assume more direct responsibility for the effective operation of social programs.*

A theme raised in this group was the importance of people speaking up for their rights, of groups organizing to tell Government what we want. They have to know that it's not good enough to just give them our tax money we want to participate in the process.

The population has become less trustful of politicians and bureaucracies, is demanding a more active voice in the administration of services. Programs must become more independent of the political agendas of governments.

Politicians today are surprised at the cynicism they're getting from the public – people are sick of existing political process, the patronage, arrogance and waste at both the provincial and federal levels of Govt.

Importance of community coming together and jointly working out with different levels of Govt how services may be integrated and costs shared.

8.9 We Need to Re-examine Basics: Many of Our Social Programs Are Not Such a Good Idea After All

In these comments from two participants we find echoes of familiar neoconservative worries about the effects of government programs and their climate of "permissiveness" on the moral fabric of society:

Young people today, not all – but many, growing up in families who have been on welfare for long periods, have no inventive to work, and welfare becomes their "comfort zone." They realize they can just sit and draw welfare. There is no time limit on it. Many others are simply dropping out of school, leaving home and then going to welfare office.

Our youth are seeking work but have no real incentive to work. Schools are not preparing them adequately.

Welfare is business – it started out as a social service and now it's a business.

We are responsible to question how our tax money is being used in our community.

We owe it to ourselves and to our kids and their kids to rejuvenate the fabric of our society, and to create proud communities that work together.

These commentators stopped short of Murray's call for abolition of welfare programs, but advanced a number of suggestions for restricting such programs, including the requirement that welfare recipients who fail to become employed "move on" after a designated period:

Income Assistance – persons should only receive it for three months then have it cut off and they are told to find a job or move on.

Income Assistance – it should not be a free ride. If income assistance is given, it should be reflected in community involvement – in work. Agreement with Mr. Vander Zalm, "Give them a shovel." Work would give them dignity – self esteem: (a) It could be baking for a school lunch program – provide them with the ingredients to do the baking. (b) Come with their child to a day care centre and help out with program and other children.

Unemployment Insurance – program is abused by the seasonal workers – they should be required to pay higher premiums – it should be like household insurance – you make a claim your premiums go up. You make another claim and your premiums go up again.

Unemployment Insurance – need to set it so you could only draw it for four to six months.

E.S.L. – concerns expressed re the high cost of running such programs in the school system. When you move to another country you have an obligation to learn their language.

Old Age Security – have a flat rate, indexed but additional money available for certain people needing extra funding for rent, etc. Perhaps we need to put in place a program like this for those who really need it and not have it "across the board" as it is now.

Appendix 8.1: Results of Statistical Significance Tests

Tests

The medians test was employed to determine whether majorities in favour of or opposed to services are statistically significant, by the selected rules of the test. These rules were as follows: Type 1 error was set at .05, and Type 2 error was set at approximately .047 for analyses involving the entire sample of 128. For subsample analyses, Type 2 error probabilities are substantially larger. We are employing .047 Type 2 error only as a lower bound. This policy is intentionally conservative. That is, to avoid a "liberal" bias in the findings, we insist on a small risk of falsely identifying majorities in favour of programs or minorities opposed to them. The medians test is itself a conservative, i.e., low-powered, test.

In this analysis, a majority is classified as statistically significant if, for the given sample size, it is likely to have occurred by chance alone less often than once in 20 times.

Majorities in Favour of Social Programs
Statistically significant majorities were found to be in favour of the following social programs:

- Alcohol and Drug Rehab Services
- Child Tax Deduction: Low-Income Families
- Job Retraining: Injured Workers
- Services to Help Immigrants
- Income Assistance (Welfare)
- Home Nursing Services
- Family Allowances
- Tax Deduction for RRSP
- Workers' Compensation Pension
- Workers' Compensation Physiotherapy
- Counselling for Individuals
- Family Counselling
- Tax Exemptions for RRSP
- Welfare with Job Retraining
- Unemployment Insurance
- Universal Retirement Pensions
- Pharmacare
- Contributory Survivor's Pension
- Group Home for Handicapped Adults
- Voice Box to Replace Cancerous Larynx
- ESL Classes
- Aid for Plaintiff in Sexual Abuse Case versus Church
- Supplementary College Preparation: Native Students
- Aid for Discrimination Suit: Métis versus Government
- Ombudsman's Suit versus Employer re Equal Pay for Females

Majorities Opposed to Social Programs
Statistically significant majorities were found to be opposed to tax shelters for investment.

Majorities in Favour of Increased Taxes to Pay for Social Programs
Majorities were found to be in favour of paying increased taxes, should these prove necessary, to maintain the following social programs, but none of these majorities was statistically significant by the rules employed:

- Family Counselling
- Universal Retirement Pensions
- Contributory Pensions
- Pharmacare
- School Lunch Programs
- Supplementary College Preparation for Native Students
- Financial Assistance for Native's Suit Against the Church for Sexual Abuse
- Ombudsman's Suit versus Employer re Equal Pay for Females

Majorities Opposed to Increased Taxes to Pay for Social Programs
A statistically significant majority was found to be opposed to paying increased taxes for tax shelters for investment.

A majority was found to oppose paying increased taxes to maintain a program of tax writeoffs for small business, but this majority was not statistically significant.

9
Directions for Social Welfare

9.1 Problem

Amid the chorus of calls for attacking government deficits as the panacea for Canada's economic ills, Canada's social programs are in danger of being made scapegoats. They are being blamed for the deficits and labelled as luxuries that Canada can no longer afford, although the period in which the deficit has increased seemingly beyond control has also seen social spending decline as a proportion of Gross Domestic Product.[1] Thus the correlation, if any, between the growth of the deficit and social spending is more likely negative than positive.

Recently, promoters of cuts in the social services have been much encouraged by the hypothesis of widespread public anger at government and the welfare state. This hypothesis been popular for some years in the U.S. and has more recently emerged in Canada as an explanation of the success of the Reform Party. According to this hypothesis, the Reform Party has "plugged into a ground swell of social resentment, that silently regards the underpinnings of the welfare state – big government, big deficits and big bureaucracies – as costly inanities and legislative inequalities."[2]

If this hypothetical groundswell were to develop into a full tide, this would have far-reaching implications for directions for Canadian social welfare. Our system of comprehensive social security would have to be dismantled, with bits and pieces moved to the private sector, as has happened with other privatization projects. But to put the hypothesis of widespread public anger into perspective, data are required on the following questions:

1 How do Canadians see the role of government in the 1990s? To what extent do they continue to hold government responsible for the traditional functions of the welfare state: redistributing wealth; ensuring that everyone who wants to work has a chance to do so; providing social services; providing housing for those who need it?
2 How effective is government, in the eyes of the public, in carrying out the foregoing welfare functions?
3 Does scepticism about the performance of government in carrying out these functions translate into opposition to public sector social programs? (Recall from Chapter 6 that one of the principal neo-conservative arguments against social programs is that the government is bound to fail in carrying them out.)
4 How satisfied are Canadians with the number, kind, and directions of social programs in Canada? To what extent is dissatisfaction associated with support for or opposition to broad-scale social programs?
5 Does dissatisfaction with government and with social welfare provision appear to be part of a general malaise – with life as a whole, with one's standard of living and prospects, with the economy? What implications can be drawn for directions for social welfare in Canada?

9.2 Role of Government

As we have seen, ideas about the role of government are pivotal both to the support of and opposition to broad-scale social programs. In this section, I present data on the public's views of government responsibility for 11 social welfare functions. Seven functions refer to traditional goals of the welfare state. The other four refer to state responsibility for meeting basic administrative standards. These items are included to enable us to see to what extent they correlate with support or opposition to such provision.

Each item asked the respondent to rate the responsibility of government for carrying out the listed function. The ratings ranged from "none," indicating no responsibility, to "essential." Table 9.1 shows a tabulation of responses to the 11 items.

These data show *strong majorities in favour of governments retaining their traditional welfare-state responsibilities,* such as redistributing wealth and seeking to ensure full employment and adequate housing.

Table 9.1

Tabulation of Government Responsibility Ratings (%)

Government Function	N	None	Some	Important	Essential
Be Careful in Using Public Money	126	0.8	1.6	8.7	88.9
Try to Even Out Differences in Wealth	125	12.0	34.4	31.2	22.4
Provide Everyone a Chance to Make a Good Living	126	1.6	31.0	33.3	34.1
See to It that Everyone Who Wants a Job Can Have a Job	125	4.8	27.2	35.2	32.8
Provide Social Services	126	0.8	11.9	23.8	63.5
Ensure No Social Benefits Unless Entitled	124	2.4	11.3	29.0	57.3
Provide Income Assistance Benefits	125	0.8	17.6	46.4	35.2
Grant No Welfare Benefits Unless Income Is Inadequate	126	0.8	12.7	27.0	59.5
Require Welfare Recipients to Look for Employment	118	3.4	19.5	28.0	49.0
Provide Housing for All Citizens	125	6.4	27.2	26.4	40.0
Provide Compensation for Single Parents Who Stay Home to Raise a Family	126	16.7	34.9	27.0	21.4

There is an equally strong emphasis on basic administrative competence, but evidently concerns about this issue do not translate into questioning the role of government in taking on social welfare tasks. From the qualitative data presented below (section 9.5) it is apparent that there is strong support for expanded and new government programs as well as for keeping intact the present programs.

Table 9.2 presents data on public perceptions of the effectiveness of the government in carrying out the same 11 welfare functions listed in Table 9.1.

Majorities of the public apparently see the government as at least moderately effective in carrying out tasks of being careful in using public money, providing compensation for single parents who wish to stay home to raise a family, requiring welfare recipients to look for employment, and trying to even out differences in wealth. In these areas, performance is by and large consistent with expectations. None of this looks like widespread disaffection with the government.

We also see in the data of Tables 9.1 and 9.2 several stunning contrasts between public expectations of the government and public perceptions of the current effectiveness of government in carrying out these tasks. Thus, 98.4% of the respondents (Table 9.1) hold that the government has at least some responsibility for "providing everyone with a chance to make a good living," and nearly two-thirds believe that this task is a very important or essential task of government. Yet fewer than half believe that the government is even moderately effective in carrying out this task (Table 9.2). We see the same kinds of contrast in "providing social services," "providing income assistance benefits," and "seeing to it that everyone who wants a job can have a job." This powerfully restates a theme that has run through nearly all of our chapters on the survey and focus group data, namely *concern about the inadequacy, ineffectiveness, or weak administration of the public sector social services.*

A question that arises here is: are the majorities favouring a large role for government made up of the same people on each item, or do different majorities emerge around different government responsibilities? To explore this, I looked at the correlations of all items in Table 9.1 and in Table 9.2. The results, not reported in detail here, show mainly small correlations,[3] indicating that different majorities coalesce around different items. *People support a role of government in social welfare out of different and sometimes conflicting agendas.*

Similarly, negative views of government performance are from both the political "right" and "left." The latter focus on the inadequacy of

Table 9.2

Tabulation of Ratings of Government Effectiveness
(%)

Government Function	N	Very Effective	Moderately Effective	Not Very Effective	Ineffective
Be Careful in Using Public Money	124	29.0	44.4	25.8	0.8
Try to Even Out Differences in Wealth	116	31.9	50.9	14.7	2.6
Provide Everyone a Chance to Make a Good Living	123	5.7	41.5	52.0	0.8
See to It that Everyone Who Wants a Job Can Have a Job	116	17.2	54.3	26.7	1.7
Provide Social Services	124	1.6	15.3	67.7	15.3
Ensure No Social Benefits Unless Entitled	120	10.0	36.7	45.0	8.3
Provide Income Assistance Benefits	120	1.7	20.0	67.5	10.8
Grant No Welfare Benefits Unless Income Is Inadequate	123	21.1	36.6	36.6	5.7
Require Welfare Recipients to Look for Employment	120	19.2	42.5	32.5	5.8
Provide Housing for All Citizens	123	21.1	47.2	28.5	3.3
Provide Compensation for Single Parents Who Stay Home to Raise a Family	113	18.6	38.9	37.2	5.3

provision, and the former focus on alleged abuses and waste. Both give the government low ratings on effectiveness.

This brings us to another major question: *does scepticism about the performance of government in carrying out its social welfare tasks translate into opposition to public sector social programs?* To test this, I correlated each of the 11 effectiveness ratings listed in Table 9.2 with a variable "average support," the mean of ratings of support or opposition to nine major social programs provided by government. I had no expectations of finding substantial correlations here, since, as I have said, there are as many critics of government performance from the left as there are from the right. Yet the former group of critics support broadscale social programs and the latter group, at least in theory, question or oppose them.

As expected, there is no substantial correlation of any of the government effectiveness ratings with support or opposition to government social programs.[4] Thus the evidence is that the sceptics of the effectiveness of government performance are demanding better performance, but not that government should be relieved of its responsibilities for social programs.

Using qualitative data, I explore these issues in detail below. First, however, I take a more general perspective on public anger versus satisfaction. One of the questions with which I began this chapter is: does dissatisfaction with government and social welfare provision appear to be part of a general malaise – with life as a whole, with one's standard of living and prospects, or with the economy?

9.3 General Life Satisfaction

9.3.1 Data

To look at this topic, three items from the general life satisfaction scales designed by Alex Michalos[5] were used. These have been extensively tested in various countries and shown by Michalos to have satisfactory reliability.[6] The findings on each scale are presented in the following sections.

9.3.2 Satisfaction with Life as a Whole

- 70% of the sample feel that their lives, considered as a whole, measure up to or exceed what they need; about one-third feel that their lives exceed what they need.

- 76% of the sample feel that their lives, considered as a whole, are about what they expected or better; 43% feel that their lives exceed what they expected.

9.3.3 Satisfaction with Standard of Living
- Nearly 77% report that they are mostly satisfied, pleased, or delighted with their standard of living; about 17% feel mixed satisfaction and dissatisfaction with their standard of living, and 2% feel unhappy or terrible about it.
- 26% feel that their standard of living is better than they hoped for three to five years ago, 55% feel that it is about what they hoped for, and 19% feel that it is worse than what they hoped for.
- More than a third report that they are quite sure that in the future they will achieve what they desire; 42% report that they are somewhat optimistic, and 24% report that they are somewhat doubtful or pessimistic.
- 48% expect to be about as well off in five years as they are now, 41% expect to be better off, and 11% expect to be worse off.

9.3.4 Satisfaction with the Economy
About 37% report that they are dissatisfied with the present state of the Canadian economy, 15% that they are extremely dissatisfied, 37% that they have mixed feelings, about 9% that they are satisfied, and about 1% that they are extremely satisfied.

9.3.5 Remarks
Results on satisfaction with one's personal life are similar to the generally high levels of satisfaction that have been found in other studies in varied settings over the last 20 years. These results hardly look like evidence of profound personal malaise or a boiling, frustrated middle class. Though very few people are satisfied with the present state of the Canadian economy, this apparently does not translate into gloom about the future.

The data on feeling about one's life as a whole compared with what one deserves suggest that a strong personal responsibility ethic is alive and well in the Canadian public. Though the economy may be bad, people still tend to blame or credit themselves for what their lives have brought them. From the findings on support for social programs (Chapter 8), this by no means implies that people should be left to struggle with their own problems, but it does mean that social programs should never be set up in a fashion that takes personal responsibility away from people.

9.4 Directions for Social Programs in Canada: Precepts and Guidelines

9.4.1 Data
We obtained two sets of data dealing with the directions for social programs in Canada:

1   Numerical ratings based on three items. The first item read as follows:

How satisfied are you with the number of social programs that are available in Canada?

1	2	3	4	5	6	7
Extremely dissatisfied			Mixed: Satisified and dissatisfied			Extremely satisfied

This was followed by two items of exactly the same form. One of these items asked about satisfaction with the kind of social programs available in Canada and the other about satisfaction with the direction of social programs in Canada.

2   A data set based on an open-ended item asking what, if any, new programs the respondent would introduce, followed by elaboration probes dealing with the respondent's views as to whether we have too few, enough, or too many social services in Canada.

9.4.2 Coding the Open-Ended Responses
To arrive at a scheme for coding the open-ended responses, the same principle was followed as in Chapters 2 and 4, namely, that the coding categories would be induced from the data themselves. This was accomplished by using, again, the open-coding method of Glaser and Strauss.[7] To do the open-coding, the comments, randomly ordered, were reviewed line by line. Precepts or guidelines pertaining to future directions for social programs in Canada were extracted. The resulting precepts or guidelines were then grouped into the scheme shown in Table 9.3, and this scheme was then used to classify all of the

comments in the file. I then sampled the comments in such a way as to bring out the variation in responses. These examples are shown in section 9.5 below.

Table 9.3

Guidelines for Social Programs in Canada Extracted from Open-Ended Comments on Future Directions

Category	Subcategory	Guidelines
Scope	Expand	• Fill gaps in existing programs • Meet new needs with new programs (e.g., daycare, high-tech training for labour force)
	Keep what we have	• Keep or restore the principle of universality • Take account of real costs of cutting federal transfer payments
	Mixed: expand & reduce	• Increase programs for the poor, but reduce universality • Provide more economic security for the retired; reduce welfare • Reduce the number of physicians; reallocate funds to needs of mental patients
	Reduce	• Reduce eligibility for welfare and/or UIC • Scale down program aims (e.g., provide • only short-term help) • Provide no help to the able-bodied unless they are working
Administration	Strengthen	• Upgrade staffing of social programs; allocate more funding to this • Increase competition, consumer choice, and public input into programs
	Streamline	• Limit objectives to what we can afford • Consolidate programs to eliminate duplication
	Tighten controls; monitor abuse	• Do more to ensure funds are properly spent
	Aim for fairer distribution of benefits	• Alter the tax structure so as to narrow gap between haves and have-nots • Review senoirs' benefits in light of overall needs of population

(continued on next page)

Category	Subcategory	Guidelines
Admin-istration	Reorient services towards self-help and prevention	• Have more proactive programming, less crisis intervention • Have more life skills training programs; tax and social service systems should be coordinated to get better use of funds, sharper focus on self-help, and responsibility for one's own life

The foregoing scheme is used to organize the presentation of comments on future directions. Before turning to this, I present statistical data on levels of satisfaction with the number, kinds, and directions of social programs in Canada. This provides a useful lead into comments on future directions.

9.4.3 Statistical Findings on Satisfaction with Number, Kind, and Directions of Social Programs in Canada
These findings are shown in Table 9.4

Table 9.4

Satisfaction with the Number, Kinds, and Direction of Social Programs in Canada

Count	CUM Count	PCT	CUM PCT	Number of Social Programs
7	7	5.6	5.6	1 Extremely dissatisfied
5	12	4.0	9.7	2
14	26	11.3	21.0	3
43	69	34.7	55.6	4 Mixed: satisfied & dissatisfied
29	98	23.4	79.0	5
16	114	12.9	91.9	6
10	124	8.1	100.0	7 Extremely satisfied

Count	CUM Count	PCT	CUM PCT	Kinds of Social Programs
4	4	3.2	3.2	1 Extremely dissatisfied
6	10	4.8	8.1	2
20	30	16.1	24.2	3

(continued on next page)

Table 9.4 (continued)

**Satisfaction with the Number, Kinds, and Direction of
Social Programs in Canada**

Count	CUM Count	PCT	CUM PCT	Kinds of Social Programs
40	70	32.3	56.5	4 Mixed: satisfied & dissatisfied
33	103	26.6	83.1	5
14	117	11.3	94.4	6
7	124	5.6	100.0	7 Extremely satisfied

CUM Count	CUM Count	PCT	PCT	Direction of Social Programs
10	10	8.4	8.4	1 Extremely dissatisfied
22	32	18.5	26.9	2
18	50	15.1	42.0	3
44	94	37.0	79.0	4 Mixed: satisfied & dissatisfied
19	113	16.0	95.0	5
5	118	4.2	99.2	6
1	119	.8	100.0	7 Extremely satisfied

To summarize: 45% of respondents show some degree of satisfaction with the number of social programs, 21% have some degree of dissatisfaction, and over a third have mixed feelings. The percentages are similar for the kinds of social programs: 44% satisfied to some degree, 24% dissatisfied, and 32% with mixed feelings. The direction of social programs is, however, a source of a great deal of dissatisfaction: a stunning 42% express some degree of dissatisfaction, 37% express mixed feelings, and only 21% express some degree of satisfaction.

An obvious limitation of these items is that *they make no attempt to distinguish between different and perhaps conflicting reasons for dissatisfaction.* Both those who feel we need to expand social programs and those who advocate cutbacks can be lumped together as dissatisfied. Therefore these data are useful in showing overall levels of satisfaction and dissatisfaction, but not in clarifying the reasons for them. To explore this issue, I take up the question of directions for social programs in Canada: if they had their way, in what directions would the respondents take these programs?

9.5 Illustrative Comments on Directions for Social Programs in Canada

In this section, I present samples of the data arranged according to the coding scheme displayed in Table 9.3. In the concluding section, I consider trends and the importance of the data presented in this chapter.

By way of introduction to the comments, I present a statistical summary of the comments regarding scope of social programs, under the subheadings "expand," "mixed, expand and reduce," "keep what we have," and "reduce." These statistics were tabulated from the open-ended comments (for the question on which these are based see section 9.4).

Comments were coded "expand" if they contained suggestions for new programs, for filling gaps in existing programs, or for adding to the groups to be served by these programs. They were coded "reduce" if they called for restricting groups to be served or for the elimination of programs. They were coded "mixed" if they contained both types of comments, and "keep what we have" if they mentioned the need to retain specific programs, or the principle of universality, or other policies that would affect the scope of programs, such as federal transfer payments. These tabulations are shown in Table 9.5.

Table 9.5

Recommendations Regarding Scope of Canada's Social Programs

	No. of Comments	Percent of Total
Expand	40	38
Keep What We Have	46	44
Mixed: Expand & Reduce	9	8
Reduce	11	10
Total	106	100

9.5.1 Scope of Social Programs in Canada

I now turn to examples of comments under each of the categories and subcategories of responses, arranged according to the scheme presented in Table 9.5.

9.5.1.1 Expand
1   Fill Gaps in Existing Programs

#11 – Guaranteed Annual Income – for everyone under a level (economists can figure it out). As their prosperity grows, it should be reduced. No more welfare or UIC. No reductions for work on the side. It would stimulate the economy, higher employment rate. Canada is a self-sufficient entity. It has to be universally applied – paid for by taxes. Day care Centres – Need to be increased especially after school. Need safe, qualified. Too expensive in private one. Govt should pay – by taxes. National Study on Single Parents – it is becoming so widespread. Not only money, but counselling, support groups. Paid by taxation.

#12 – Illiteracy – set up a program for them. People that can't afford it on their own. Today those on welfare are considered to be fraudulent if they go to university. Taxes. Grants – for people that want to be self- employed, ie. tools, equipment. Taxes should pay because when they get going they will contribute back. Drug Rehabilitation – should do more than lock-up. I should be more individual (counselling, job seeking, etc.). Taxes.

2   Meet New Needs with New Programs

UIC – They should provide a funding program to enable those on UIC to create their own jobs or organizations. Their job involvement doesn't lead to permanent work. It's short term and doesn't lead to anything.

#83 – Single Mothers: very often they didn't get much training. They got married – had kids and are not married. They need training so they can get off welfare. They should get education and get off welfare to be productive citizens. Paid for by taxes. Before someone gets welfare – really check them out. Some who really need it don't get it and some who do nothing – sit around and collect welfare.

#32 – Housing a big item. – Supervision of handicapped people (financial and otherwise). – Increase security for single parents (so they can stay home). – Provide counselling/allow for recreation.

#39 – Build in a Structure where parents staying home to look after children can be both encouraged/monitored for effective parenting ie. grandparent/monitoring program, but with training. Also, only for a period of time and with an incentive to retrain or be able to take paid employment when needed, and after children beyond a certain age. Co-operation and monetary support of fathers also need to be explored. No more time, lots of ideas.

#69 – Housing is very important to me. Housing subsidies. Everyone should have a home. Paid for corporate contributions and lotteries and people pay what they can. I'd like to see more co-ops. The gov't should buy up land and designate areas for subsidized housing, if they need it. There are many homeless. It's a vicious cycle. It gives people a sense of belonging. It should be earned. If they can't pay – they should help grounds keep, janitor. Gives a sense of pride. Then they can work themselves out. If things are given, people don't appreciate it as much.

9.5.1.2 Keep What We Have
1 We need to retain and in some cases regain the universality principle.

#101 – ESL classes are essential for people coming in to Canada becoming a contributor. Our university system is becoming harder and harder to become accessible especially for those who don't have a parental source of income. Let's get it back.

2 We must begin to take account of the human costs of cutting federal transfer payments.

#103 – The Social Services we're getting are quite adequate. If we carry on their adequate. If the federal gov't cuts transfer payments – services will be reduced and people will be hurt.

9.5.1.3 Mixed: Expand and Reduce
1 Increase programs for the poor, reduce universality.

#20 – Introduce a program to try to make existing programs more needs based; reallocate funds through reduction in universality of programs. Reallocate money to help those who need assistance most.

2   Provide more economic security for the retired; restrict welfare.

#72 – One program: New Canada Savings Bond. For someone 65+ with fixed interest rate so economy will not bother them so much. Bond cannot be transferred to somebody who is not retirement age (e.g., son – inherits bond at 19% when reality of his time is 7%). Beneficiary has to be 65+. All GST to be paid on deficit principal not on deficit interest. Deficit payments need to be skimmed out of taxes collected at present without tax increase. Welfare Canada – badly mismanaged. Only available to those who can prove need it. A lot could and should be working. Don't need to add programs, programs need to be change; times change, people change.

3   Reduce the number of physicians, reallocate funds to needs of mental patients.

#89 – Spend less money on health programs but use money we have better. I hear highest per capita number of doctors in Canada. Gets to be almost a business for them, not straight with patients, hand-out pills, prescribe remedies when should encourage exercise, more balanced lifestyles. Instead of doing what they can in one visit, do two visits so can get return from government. Day programs for mentally ill. Lot more stress in today's society. Some people need to go into the hospital. They are dumped back into society and nothing in-between to help them go back, maybe need help getting into workplace.

9.5.1.4 Reduce
1   Reduce eligibility for welfare and/or UIC.

#22 – Make all people work before they get social services. No help to healthy individuals capable of work. No cost factor in this new program.

#29 – I would reduce social programs and make them more efficient, e.g., UI making sure people didn't take a vacation and receive benefits they should be looking for work. Should limit amount of times person is able to receive benefits – reduce people's incentive to go on UI.

9.5.2 Administration

9.5.2.1 Provide More Resources
1 Provide resources for earlier intervention in problems.

#47 – Prior to apprehension of children, I'd intervene with family counselling and support programming. Given that huge percentage of adolescents that get in trouble with the law, I'd introduce learning disabled testing in the elementary schools and utilize teachers and counsellors to work with learning disabled little kids. I'd have more preventative programs. Taxes.

2 Increase competition, consumer choice, and public input into services.

#38 – Expand on the ones we already have vs. increase and make services even more competitive: – the available monies are still the same; fighting over the money won't help or make more! – Listen to people re what they want (ie. this survey) and how services should be more accountable.

9.5.2.2 Streamline
1 Limit objectives to what we can afford: we can't provide same lifestyle to everyone.

#130 – I wouldn't introduce any new programs or redistribute resources and [would] probably go for guaranteed income plans done through tax system without bureaucrats (drop UIC, welfare, give guaranteed income securities).

Our lifestyle now requires people have education. We can't provide same levels of lifestyles to everyone and should we even try via UIC or welfare. State can provide basic necessities only for basic survival/life needs. Does it have a responsibility to do more than this; can it even afford this? People need to be more responsible for themselves.

2 Consolidate programs to eliminate duplication.

#93 – We do not need new programs, we have an over abundance of programs already with lots of duplication of services/programs, e.g., War Veterans, special allowances/pension. With an adequate old age pension scheme, we would not require additional services, such as Housing Grants etc.

9.5.2.3 Tighten Controls, Monitor Abuses
1   Do more to ensure that funds are properly spent.

#102 – Tightening up Immigration Policy. Should look closer at health and education. The person should be able to support themselves.

#77 – Welfare: More investigation done, used to years ago. Don't mail cheques, make them come into office. Instead of giving too much money have counsellor for people, teach them things. The more you take out of life the more you have to pay back; work ethic, work for it. Me and my family brought up that way. – Definitely cut down on foster kids. Bring mom and dad in, talk to them, counsel them before, often they're at fault, have them work it out. Foster kids got everything: better clothes, more clothes than tobacco money. My other kids didn't get this. Reduce spending on foster kids and reduce foster kids. – Cut gov't spending on own stuff e.g., ministers: Who do they think they are? We're just as important. – "X" 's so is disabled. Feel so sorry for them, need more services for them. Someone to come in and look at them and see what services they need. Not wait for them to come, e.g., Check for instance his sore feet. He won't ask, very proud, embarrassed to ask. Half time has nothing to eat. Would give anything if could work. – MSP abused: But with someone with lifetime thing e.g., diabetic, should get some help with insulin, should be paid for. Where does diabetic association money go? – Welfare: Put a lot of people on welfare. Half use money for drinking, smoke, would do anyway. If didn't have welfare might shape up. Give too much especially if able to work.

9.5.2.4 Aim for Fairer Distribution of Benefits
1   Alter tax structure and programs to achieve more redistribution.

#59 – I'd try to ensure people and organizations which don't require social services don't get them and for those who need it there should be more funding and comprehensive programs. There should be far higher corporate taxation and gov't spending reallocation so that the gap between haves and have nots can be reduced. I think the infrastructure is there, it just needs to be more directed.

2 Review seniors' benefits in light of overall needs of the population.

#5 – Govt should make a list and see what everything costs to see how they can even our services. Seniors get a lot of services, they're better off than some of the middle age people. It's wonderful to have as much in Canada. Increase of benefits every year is a concern because of what it's costing us.

9.5.2.5 Reorient Programs Towards Self-Help, Prevention
1 More proactive programming, less crisis intervention.

#43 – More money in preventative programs. School age level programs for kids from dysfunctional homes, putting more attention in teaching families how to work effectively, providing support for parents who are stressed, more pro-active approach to social programs. Now we do crisis intervention. Educational programs to people before they get married. More emphasis on family planning, birth control.

2 More life skills training programs.

#68 – I would have classes to teach people to shop wisely, cook nutritional foods, budgeting, etc. Many older people could teach the younger people. Hospitals could encourage young families to attend. Paid for out of taxes. What to expect out of children at different ages, what they should eat, inoculations, etc. The less the gov't has to do with people the better off we are. They look after us from our first breath to our last. People need to be independent.

#6 – Set up an incentive program to help maintain our own citizens before going outside of our borders to get others to come in, ie. encourage families with children, assist in raising the young, taxes, lotteries, joining employee/employer package benefit programs (ie. job training, EAP program).

3 Tax and social service systems should be coordinated to achieve better use of funds, sharper focus on self-help and responsibility for one's own life.

#58 – I would not increase the spending. I would consult with the users and the administrators of the system. I'd require in a short time frame a critique of the programs and recommendations to better use the existing monies to those who truly need it. I'd prefer using the tax return to going through a needs test. Social services is a strange word because that's not where the problem is. The problem is with Canadians. I'd request that ministers change the language to impress upon people the need to depend on themselves and that social net is there for those who can't help themselves. UIC should be based on combined family income. Welfare should be turned into retraining and if necessary lower taxes so welfare is not more attractive than low wages. Why work if they can get welfare and it gives you a greater after tax return. In some of the southern states $5-6/hour jobs are attractive 'cause taxes are low and welfare is not encouraged. Our costs of living are too high because our tax structure is needed to support social services and debt. We have to stop the cycle and start thinking for ourselves, of looking after ourselves and not looking to a gov't.

#102 – try and put more emphasis on a way for the gov't to teach people life skills ie – family planning, financing, achieving goals. This could be done at High School level. Have it mandatory for people that don't get to H.S., they should still require it. Paid for by taxes.

9.5.3 Discussion

In the light of Table 9.3 and the open-ended responses in the previous section, I can now return to the question I raised about the meaning of the evidently widespread dissatisfaction with the directions being taken currently by social programs in Canada. I can approach this question by asking: what changes would the public make?

From the foregoing data it seems clear that there are five major sources of dissatisfaction with Canada's social programs:

1 perception of gaps in existing programs;
2 lack of new programs to meet emerging needs, such as the need for better provision for day care;
3 worry that programs are threatened – concern to keep what we've got;
4 worry about slackness in administration that permits abuses of UI, welfare, and, to a lesser extent, immigration programs;
5 concern that existing programs are too narrowly focused on "problems" and need to be oriented towards more effective prevention and training for competence in meeting problems.

If we ask how these concerns are numerically distributed in the population, our best evidence is the statistical data in Table 9.5. From these data, we see that 82% of the respondents want to either expand the scope of social programs or at least keep what we've got. Eleven percent would expand in some area and reduce in others, and 11% would cut social programs, mainly by restricting eligibility for UI, welfare, or immigration. Thus, from a purely numerical point of view, the major sources of dissatisfaction are clearly gaps in existing programs and the need for programs to meet emerging needs.

Cuts are aimed mainly at two programs that some respondents fear may be undermining the ethic of self-responsibility for one's own problems. This ethic, as I have noted, is alive and well, though fewer than 10% of respondents make a point of it in their comments. This ethic has always been an important part of the agenda of the Reform Party. The Reform Party, having lost the constitutional issue in 1992 as a result of the referendum on the Charlottetown Accord declined in the polls from 20–25% in 1992 to 8–10% in 1993. It regained its base of support in the West by capturing the western alienation vote, promising a new and higher political ethics, and billing itself as the real defender of the social services through its commitment to restore the fiscal integrity of government. By these strategies it was able to augment its core support composed of voters opposed to big government, liberal immigration policies, and comprehensive social services. By our data this core support is about 8–10% of the public.

9.6 Conclusions
Returning then to the questions which this chapter began, the answers provided by our data are unequivocal:

1   Judging by our sample, the public continues to hold the government responsible for the traditional functions of the welfare state. If the public acquiesces in a dismantling of these functions, it is not likely because of any change of heart about them, but rather because the public has been persuaded that there is no choice. But as one of our respondents pointed out, the real costs of such dismantling have yet to be acknowledged.

2   The public has serious reservations about the effectiveness of government, currently, in carrying out its welfare functions. It sees the social programs as full of gaps, unresponsive to new needs, poorly staffed, and needing to be reoriented to prevention, to family services that reach families before the crisis, and to better preparation for dealing with life's developmental tasks.

3   There is no evidence in our data to support the notion that the public has adopted the neoconservative doctrines about the inherent inability of governments to perform social welfare tasks. The major changes the public would make, on our data, would be to fill in gaps and endeavour to meet new needs. Privatizing services was rarely mentioned by our respondents, and then mostly as a problem to be avoided.

4   There is a great deal of dissatisfaction with the direction of social programs in Canada, but this is for the most part unhappiness with stalled development of programs, and fear of losing the programs that we do have.

5   There is no evidence of a general malaise, a "boiling middle class," or any other boiling class, in our data. Our findings on general life satisfaction strikingly resemble the positive findings turned up by the typical life satisfaction survey.

10
National and International Comparisons

10.1 Problem

Ideally one would like to place the principal findings and conclusions of Chapters 2 to 4 and 8 to 9, which were based on a household survey and focus groups in the Lower Mainland of British Columbia, in the context of national survey data on social welfare issues collected at about the same time as our own study. While there is a great deal of data based on national polls in Canada, most of it is the private property of firms like Decima Research, Canadian Facts, Angus Reid, and Environics Research. Findings of this research may be purchased only if one is able to put up $250 or more per poll question. In the public domain, data are too sparse to provide useful evidence on most of the issues we have surveyed.[1]

Particularly hard to come by are descriptive data showing the degree to which the Canadian public continues to hold governments responsible for traditional social welfare goals, the core of our own research. Two of the polling firms, Angus Reid and Gallup, have published summaries or press releases of poll data on Canadians' views of social programs. In this chapter I make use of these publications to draw several general comparisons between our conclusions and those reached by the pollsters. Since the questions the pollsters used are not the same as those we have used, only general trends can be compared. Moreover, as I note below, the quantitative poll data can occasionally lump together persons with opposite views, making the findings hard to interpret.

In spite of these problems it has proven to be possible to draw a number of important comparisons that both generalize our data and place it in context. These comparisons are summarized in the concluding section of this chapter.

10.2 Polling Data

10.2.1 1993 Angus Reid Poll on the Future of Social Programs

This poll was conducted by telephone between 28 July and 5 August 1993, of a "representative cross-section" of 1506 Canadian adults.[2] The data were statistically weighted to be representative of the Canadian population on age and gender.

This poll enquired about Canadians' expectations for the future of Canada's universal health program, Old Age Pension (Security), and Canada Pension Plan. The respondents were asked the following questions:

Let's think about Canada's universal health care program – medicare. Looking ahead to when you yourself are elderly, what do you think the medicare program will be like by that time? Do you think that when you are elderly:

- medicare will be essentially the same as it is today and provide you with access to the same quality of medical services as elderly people now receive;
- medicare program will still be in place but will provide much more limited coverage than it does today;
- medicare as we know it will no longer exist by the time you are elderly?

And what about the future of our Canadian Old Age Pension, which provides benefits to all Canadians when they reach 65 years of age. Do you think that when you are 65 or over:

- benefits that senior citizens get today;
- the Old Age Pension will continue to provide the same benefits, but a good deal less than people receive today; or
- Canada's Old Age Pension will no longer exist by the time you are elderly?

Let's think about the Canada Pension Plan, or CPP, which provides benefits to working Canadians who have retired. Do you think that when you are elderly and retired:

- same benefits that CPP recipients get today;

- the Canada Pension Plan will continue to provide benefits, but a good deal less than recipients get today; or
- the Canada Pension Plan will no longer exist by the time you're retired?

After each of the above questions, the Canadians surveyed were asked: "And, as far as you are concerned, would that be a good thing or a bad thing?"

Medicare
- Only 12% of respondents expected medicare to be essentially the same when they are elderly as it is today. About two-thirds of the respondents expected medicare to be still in place but much more limited than it is today. In all regions of Canada, a majority of the respondents were of this opinion.
- The younger the respondents, the greater the percentages who expected medicare to be either reduced or no longer in existence.
- Among those who expected medicare to disappear, 86% rated this as a "bad thing." 56% of those who expected medicare to be a lot more limited (about 37% of the total sample) viewed this as a bad thing, but 40% of this group (26% of total sample) viewed it as a good thing. 12% of those who expected medicare to disappear (2.5% of the total sample) regarded the projected disappearance of medicare as a bad thing, and 4% of those who expected medicare to remain as is (about 0.5% of the total sample) regarded this as a bad thing. About 25% of those who expected medicare to be greatly reduced (14% of the total sample) viewed this as a good thing
- 94% of those who expected medicare to remain the same (about 11% of the total sample) viewed this as a good thing.

Old Age Pension
Future expectations for the Old Age Pension were similar to those for medicare. A majority (55%) expected the Old Age Pension to be available to them when they retire, but with benefits greatly reduced. 17% of the sample expected to get the same benefits that are provided today. 26% of the total sample, and fully 37% of "baby-boomers," in the sample expected the Old Age Pension to disappear before they reached retirement age.

88% of those who expected the Pension to disappear and 71% of those who expected it to be much reduced viewed this as a bad thing, and 94% of those who expected it to survive as is viewed this as "a good thing."

Canada Pension Plan

Expectations for the Canada Pension Plan proved to be even more gloomy than for the Old Age Pension. 31% of the sample and 44% of "baby boomers" in the sample expected that by the time they reached retirement age the Canada Pension Plan would no longer exist. 50% of the sample expected the Plan to remain but with benefits a good deal reduced, and 17% expected the Plan to remain as it is today.

These predicted changes were viewed as a "bad thing" by 90% of those who expected the Plan to disappear, and by 71% of those who expected the Plan to provided much reduced benefits. 93% of those who expected the Plan to remain pretty much as it is viewed this as "a good thing."

Remarks

There is clear evidence in the Angus Reid data of strong support for social programs coupled with apprehension about the erosion and threatened disappearance of these programs. This evidence closely parallels our own findings and provides support for viewing these findings as typical of the views of the Canadian public.

10.2.2 Gallup Polls, 1991-93

In January 1993 the Gallup organization[3] polled a national sample of some 1100 Canadians on the question: Is government spending on welfare "too much," "too little," or "about right"?

The results are as follows: too little, 26%; about right, 28%; too much, 33%; don't know, 13%. For British Columbia, the percentages are: too little, 41%; about right, 20%; too much, 19%; don't know, 21%. The percentage of the B.C. sample (61%) who feel that the government is spending too little or about enough on welfare is similar to the percentage of our own sample (67%) who support welfare programs.[4]

If the Gallup poll data can be taken as evidence of support for welfare programs, then an important message of the Gallup data is that B.C. appears more "liberal" than the rest of the country. This underlines the need for replication of our B.C. study in other parts of Canada.

Still, one must be cautious in reading meanings into the Gallup poll data. Like most poll data, they lack supporting evidence from open-ended probe questions as to the construction placed by the respondent on the question and the frame of reference in which the answer was given. One could agree, for instance, that too much is being spent on welfare if one believes any of the following:

- Welfare perpetuates dependency and should be phased out, *à la* Charles Murray and his Canadian counterparts.[5]
- Welfare programs are essential but currently are being abused by a few recipients who are getting away with fraud. Money could be saved by dealing with this fraud and abuse.
- Current administrative costs are far too high; too much is being spent on means testing; money could be saved by converting welfare and a number of other programs to a guaranteed annual income administered through the tax system.
- Governments are spending too much on residual aid programs such as Welfare and not enough on preventive programs, such as job creation, job restructuring and sharing, supportive family services, and vocational retraining.

People who hold these very different views are lumped together under the Gallup poll question, and the differences among them are masked. Thus in trying to read meanings about support for welfare into these data, we get on very soft ground. The data can tell us whether the respondent believes that "too much" or "too little," is being spent, but not why the respondent holds this view, and not what this view means for welfare policies and programs.

A second question posed in the same survey was: Could people who receive welfare get along without it, or do most of them really need help?

The national poll results were as follows: could get along, 25%; really need help, 43%; need some help, 28%; don't know, 4%. The B.C. results were: could get along, 15%; really need help, 57%; need some help, 22%; don't know, 6%.

Again, one can see indications that B.C. respondents are more "liberal" on the question than the national sample.

Similar difficulties in interpreting the meaning of the Gallup poll data arise as from the previous question. One could agree that people receiving welfare could get along without it if one believed either of two contrary, if not contradictory, propositions:

- Because of slack administration, people get welfare who don't really need it. The program needs better administration.
- Almost no one in our society really needs welfare. One can always find ways to survive because there are opportunities to survive on casual jobs, help from churches and friends and relatives. We could do without welfare programs.

A number of the American states have adopted this latter view and have announced plans to phase out welfare. The former view is probably more common.

Another difficulty is that a person (common in our own sample) who strongly believes that some people who receive welfare could get along without it, but that the large majority of recipients really need it, will have a problem in answering this poll question. This reflects a problem in the wording of the question: the possible responses are neither exhaustive nor mutually exclusive. One can believe that (some) people who receive welfare could get along without it and also that the large majority really need it. Whether the first part of the question refers to all or some recipients is unclear. It appears to refer to all recipients, but the second half of the question refers to most recipients. The two parts of the question do not match, making it hard to know what the question means.

The underlying problem seems to be that the purpose of the question is unclear: is this a question about welfare administration or the need for welfare programs? As it is framed, the question furnishes no clear evidence on support for or opposition to welfare programs among the general public.

In a poll carried out on 5 September 1991,[6] a similar national sample was asked: Do you favour increased funding for grade school, high school, and post-high school education?

The national percentages favouring an increase were: grade school, 68%; high school, 67%; post-high school, 66%. For B.C., the corresponding percentages were: grade school, 79%; high school, 78%; post-high school, 74%.

This question avoids the ambiguities of wording of the previous two. While our own study includes no question on general education funding, these Gallup findings again parallel our finding of a willingness to pay more for social programs that the respondents consider to be worthwhile (see Chapter 8). This is important support for our findings.

10.3 U.S. Studies of Support for Social Programs

10.3.1 The Cook and Barrett Study

A major study of support for the "welfare state" in the United States was conducted by Cook and Barrett in 1986.[7] The term "American Welfare State" may seem to be an oxymoron, and undertaking such a survey amid the backlash of the rock-ribbed conservatism of the Reagan regime may seem to be a daunting project. Obviously this study was carried out in a political environment hostile to any notions of a welfare state, with a "great communicator" president fond of regaling the public with welfare queen stories. This environment serves in the end to make the findings of the study all the more compelling.

The study was a telephone interview, 45 minutes long on average, with a random sample of 1209 residents of the United States. The "last birthday" method was used to obtain a random sample of household members. The sample proved to be representative, using census surveys for comparison on age, income, race, marital status, and education. Females and the college-educated were slightly overrepresented. Fifty-eight members of Congress were also interviewed.

"Welfare" has for decades been the object of extreme attacks in the U.S., but these intensified in the 1980s. Conventional political wisdom had it that these attacks were a reflection of the public's animosity towards welfare, and had proceeded to generalize this supposed dislike of welfare into a crisis of legitimacy of the welfare state as a whole. One of the many important contributions of the Cook and Barrett study was to explode this conventional wisdom. It looks much like the pundit's wisdom discovered in our own project to have little relationship to public opinion.

As in our study, Cook and Barrett measured "support" not for the welfare state in general but for a sample of programs. Whereas we used 23 programs, they used 7. Although the resulting conceptualization of the welfare state seems a bit narrow, they were on the right track in selecting programs with varied aims and methods of financing. For each program they measured support by the sum of responses to questions about willingness to increase or decrease funding, willingness to take action such as writing a letter to a member of Congress, willingness to pay more taxes, or preference for reduced taxes spent on the programs.

Some of their rather unexpected results:[8]

1   Percent in favour of maintaining or increasing benefits for Aid to Families of Dependent Children (AFDC): 84.5
2   Percent in favour of maintaining or increasing benefits for Social Security and Medicaid, respectively: 96.7, 93.4
3   Percent satisfied or dissatisfied to have their taxes spent for AFDC: 64.5 satisfied, 33.6 dissatisfied
4   Same comparison for Medicare and Social Security, respectively: 78.4 satisfied, 21.4 dissatisfied; 81.4 satisfied, 18.6 dissatisfied
5   Percent opposed to spending cuts: AFDC, 50.8; Medicaid, 63.4; Social Security, 73.1
6   Percent willing to pay more taxes to avoid cuts vs. willing to decrease taxes spent on program: AFDC, 36.2 vs. 15.0; Medicaid, 47.5 vs. 9.3; Social Security, 71.2 vs. 26.9

Some of Cook and Barrett's observations on their data:[9]

The picture painted by these data is hardly what one would have expected given the rhetoric of crisis of the 1980s, when opponents of social welfare argued to the federal administration that social welfare programs had lost their legitimacy in the eyes of the public. Our respondents show little desire for cuts. Instead we find small minorities wanting cuts, and in most cases, majorities favouring increases. Indeed ... 75% of the public want benefits for each of the seven programs to be either maintained at current levels or increased. For Social Security, Medicare and Supplemental Security Income, the proportions expressing such support are even higher, at a level between 96 and 97 percent.

Cook and Barrett's general conclusion:[10]

One of the clearest conclusions we can draw from the data presented in this book is that there is no crisis of support. Judging from the beliefs expressed by the respondents in this study, the crisis rhetoric of the 1980s seems to have been based on the eloquent speech of a vocal few, and an overreliance on responses to a single yearly survey questions about support for "welfare." Although citizens do not always unanimously agree about whom they want to help and how best to do so, there is a shared belief that the major programs of the welfare state should be at the minimum maintained.

Perhaps Cook and Barrett's most important contribution is their effort to avoid the mistake of overreliance on single items, and indeed to develop a full-blown explanatory model of support for the welfare state (though this is not wholly successful, as I shall argue). I turn to this and several other examples in the following section.

10.3.2 The Cook-Barrett Model of Support for Social Programs

Cook and Barrett measure one's support for the welfare state by satisfaction or dissatisfaction with having one's tax dollars spent on AFDC, Medicare, and Social Security, respectively, weighted by one's willingness to sign a petition or write a letter in support of one's views, and by one's willingness to pay additional or reduced taxes for each of these programs.

Cook and Barrett set up a model that explains support by four clusters of variables: self-interest; political predisposition; recipient deservingness, and program effectiveness. Self-interest and political predispositions are assumed to be temporally and causally prior to perceptions of recipient deservingness and program effectiveness. One's opinions on the latter two subjects are assumed to be "shaped"[11] by the former two.

Adjusted R-squared values for AFDC, Medicaid, and Social Security were .556, .701, and .417, respectively. These values are impressive.

As an experimental setup, however, this model looks uncomfortably squishy. In a true experiment, the independent variable is experimentally independent of the dependent variable. The philosopher-physicist Bunge formulated this as the principle of externality of causation: "Efficient causes are, by definition extrinsic determinants ... the external cause is an agent acting on things *extrinseco* and one that cannot act on itself ... an essential mark of (efficient) causation is externality."[12]

In this case, in spite of ingenious arguments advanced (pp. 192-93) by Cook and Barrett to support their proposed causal priorities, their grounds seem to be soft. It is easy to think of plausible counter-examples to their causal priorities. For example, the considerable numbers of Canadian voters who in the last election switched from supporting the New Democratic Party (NDP), a progressive, small-*l* liberal party, to supporting Reform, a fundamentalist conservative party, could be accounted for by these voters coming to believe that many social programs are cost-ineffective and that many of the recipients are not

really in need (one of the key variables in Cook and Barrett's definition of "deserving"). Or, one's conservative views could be reinforced
by reading Murray's book[13] and believing his descriptions of social
programs and their clients. In both of these examples, the causal priorities asserted by Cook and Barrett are reversed.

One consequence of this problem with causal priorities is that one
doesn't quite know what to make of the impressive-looking R-squared
values cited earlier. A better formulation of the Cook and Barrett
model might be a part-whole relationship. Each of the five major
components, including the dependent variable of "support," could be
part of a larger set of beliefs that we could label a "social welfare ideology" (see Chapter 12, where I set forth a dramatistic model of these
variables, which might at some points incorporate a variety of causal
relationships). A better statistical model to represent the relationships
among the components of the Cook and Barrett model might be factor analysis, since we seem to be dealing with a problem of the structure of belief systems rather than one of causation.

Although in this respect they may have gotten somewhat off-track,
certainly their effort to create an integrated model is commendable
and introduces some important components that such model building will need to take into account.

10.3.3 Findings of Other U.S. Studies of Support for Social Programs

During the 1980s, U.S. studies of support for social programs were
many and their foci were various. Since most of these studies relied on
a few National Opinion Research Center items without the kind of
careful conceptual structure devised by Cook and Barrett, they will be
treated more briefly here. I have limited the sample of studies to those
dealing with support for social programs or with taxation to fund
these programs. Because of variations in question wording and differences from the wordings employed in our items, I have limited this
summary to major findings and trends.

Support for Social Programs: Major Findings

1   A most important issue in research on public support for social
    programs in the U.S. has been the stability of public opinion.[14]
2   After extensive enquiry into this issue by a number of authors,[15]
    there is a consensus, as summed up by Shapiro and Young:[16]
    "Specifically, the public opinion data show that support for social

welfare policies has generally remained solid and stable, despite some increase in opposition – mainly to income maintenance and related anti-poverty ('welfare') activities – from the 1970s to the early '80s."[17]

3 Studies during the 1970s and 1980s generally found that the American public not only supported government expenditures to maintain social security but generally favoured higher levels of government spending.[18]

4 Support has included continuing strong approval of indexing social security to the cost of living.[19]

5 Presumably because of the consistently bad press of "welfare," the use of this term in surveys dramatically affects the results.[20]

6 It is of interest that in our B.C. study we found no such effects when we compared the use of the term "social benefits" with "income assistance benefits."[21]

7 Over the eight years of the Reagan administration, there occurred a "liberal rebound" in the U.S., in which support for social welfare programs returned to the relatively high level of the early 1970s.[22]

8 This rebound appears to have been stimulated or reinforced by the recession of 1982.[23]

9 More generally, there is evidence that public opinion on social welfare issues is affected by the state of the economy. Worry about loss of social programs becomes more pronounced during recession periods.

10 The clearest trend in the latter 1980s was towards a middle position in which there was majority support for government intervention on behalf of the poor coupled with a strong emphasis on individual and family responsibility for problems.[24]

11 This is in one respect the same finding we arrived at based on a variety of quantitative items and the open-ended comments associated with them. See particularly Chapters 8 and 9.

12 On the other hand, our sample, as shown in Chapter 2, is much more inclined to think of social programs as being for everybody, not just the poor or special groups.

Taxation Policies

1 A major unsettled issue in U.S. research is how to explain an apparent contradiction in the American public's attitudes towards taxation and government services.[25] Whereas the public has generally favoured cuts in taxation, it has also favoured increases in

spending for social, health, and defense programs.[26] This contradiction dates back to the 1930s.[27]

2 Shapiro and Young attempt to resolve this contradiction by suggesting that questions about taxes and services have rarely been asked together, and not often in the same survey. Thus the contexts in which the responses are made vary.[28]

3 Cook and Barret dealt effectively with this seeming contradiction by bringing taxes and spending together in the same questions, such as "would you be prepared to pay more taxes to permit AFDC benefits to be maintained?"[29] Their findings strongly suggest that when this is done service increase takes precedence over tax cuts.[30] While excellent evidence, this of course needs to be replicated.

4 Again, the findings of the Cook and Barrett study raise questions about much conventional wisdom concerning the public's attitudes towards taxes and services.

5 Other U.S. studies have shown that personal income taxes are less popular than more regressive forms of taxation, such as sales and property taxes.[31]

6 This seeming contradiction may be explained as follows. A number of authors have presented evidence that there is substantial public confusion in the U.S. about taxes, in part because of the ways in which information before the public is manipulated.[32] In our project, we found little evidence of this confusion, although a number of our respondents had difficulty seeing that a tax shelter or other tax deduction has a cost in lost revenue that has to be made up. The more important contrast between our data and the U.S. data is the salience of the tax issue: it was rarely brought up by our respondents, but seems to have been a more serious concern of the American respondents.

U.S., U.K., and Canadian Studies of Correlates of Support
In their massive time-series reanalysis of 28 years of research in the U.S. on demographic correlates of public opinions on social programs and issues, Luttberg and Martinez found that only the effects of black-white racial differences were substantial.[33] On other variables they report:

> ... we are struck by the fact that gender, although increasing [in its correlations with opinions] still fails to provide much information about the opinions of a person. Other demographic distinctions are mildly useful in attributing opinions, but hardly justify the broadcast

and print media's overanxiousness to paint groups such as baby-boomers or women as sharing a single and distinct set of opinions as a result of shared experiences. The same point can be made relative to those living in our largest cities, Midwesterners, Protestant Fundamentalists, and the poor.

On a similar though less statistically elaborate analysis of studies in Britain, Taylor-Gooby reached a similar conclusion:

Opinions follow a complex pattern which is clearly influenced by personal circumstances [age, social class, occupation, gender]. The pattern, however, is a subtheme: the dominant theme is the consistency of ordering between the various subgroups. Opinions about state welfare display the strong homogeneous public support that Klein and Whiteley identify in this country and Cooke and Fifield in the United States of America, especially the high-spending services for deserving needs ... opposition to the state is taken to imply support for the market and vice-versa. But the pattern of data indicates that attitudes are more complex.[34]

No comparable body of research exists in Canada. One useful study is the work of Kopinak on gender and support for social welfare interventions by government.[35] Using a database compiled at York University on Canadian attitudes on a wide variety of social and political issues, Kopinak analyzed the effects of gender on views of government responsibility to improve social welfare. She found that when a range of variables (especially variables of class, ethnicity, and region) are controlled, gender has no independent effect on political ideology. Women's attitudes towards efforts to give women greater power in the workplace interacted with income: women of higher income were more inclined to support such efforts. The reverse was true of men. Her conclusion is that no simple grouping of opinions by gender can be made. This is similar to the conclusions reached by the American and English researchers on gender and other demographic variables.

10.4 Concluding Observations

1 An important problem both for policy and research methodology is the stability of the public's views of social programs. The implication for policy is that a stable public opinion is a much more consistent source of policy guidance than a fluctuating public opinion.

2   The problem of research methodology is that of reliability of measurement. Recall my "research hired gun" critic whose view is that "John Q Public" is influenced most by what he happened to see on TV the previous evening (see Preface). If he happened to see a touching case of physical disability, he is all for assisting the disabled, but his interest could just as well have been seized by some different touching case.

3   While this can be dismissed as a professional's stereotype of the public, the problem of reliability of public opinion on social welfare matters is highly important. In a survey such as the present one, with samples taken at only two points in time, we must rely on evidence from other sources concerning the stability of social welfare opinions.

4   Fortunately, as I have shown in this chapter, there is substantial evidence available on the stability of these opinions. Relatively high levels of support for social welfare commitments by government are, in the words of Cook and Barrett, "firmly rooted and consistent."[36] Our own data on the meanings of the social programs to Canadians and their views on future directions for social programs strongly support the conclusion that opinions are deeply held.

5   The other main issue on which our national and international comparisons are able to throw some light is the problem of how our data compare with Canada-wide and B.C.-wide data. Here we found close similarities between out data on support and directions for social programs and the trends we were able to infer from the Angus Reid and Gallup polling data for B.C. Thus the evidence is that our data are representative of British Columbia.

6   There is also, however, clear evidence in the polling data comparing the Canadian provinces of a greater "liberalism" towards social programs in B.C.

7   Because the polling data on which this observation is based are sketchy, not much can be inferred in the way of explanations for these differences. This problem can be tackled adequately only by further regional studies carried out in depth, studies that replicate, at least in part, the present study.

8   Cook and Barrett are right, I believe, in pointing out the inadequacies of polling-type studies that rely on a few items. What is required is further efforts at building conceptual structures to serve as models of social welfare ideologies to guide further enquiry. I make proposals for further work on this problem in the final chapter.

Part V:
Conclusions

11
Social Policy Implications

11.1 Seven Myths about Canada's Social Programs

Will Rogers once said: "It's not the things we don't know that hurt us but the things we know that aren't so."

Findings from several previous chapters cast doubt on much of the conventional wisdom on social programs with which we are barraged by various media. In this section, I call into question seven examples of this wisdom.

The following appear, in light of the data, to be examples of things we know that aren't so:

1 *There are large savings to be had by "targeting" social programs to the poor, for whom the programs were intended.*

   DATA: 98% of the sample, presented with a standard list of social programs, reported using at least one of them during the previous 12 months. Half the sample reported using between two and six of the programs. 77% of the sample rated the impact on their lives of one or more of these encounters as major. It is clear that the social programs play a major role in the lives of the whole population, not just the "needy." For further details, see Chapters 3 and 4.

2 *Canadians are angry at the government* and, to quote a recent paper on Preston Manning and the Reform Party, there is "a groundswell of social resentment, that silently regards the underpinnings of the welfare state – big government, big deficits and big bureaucracies – as costly inanities and legislative inequalities."[1] Therefore Canadians want government to cut back on its social policy commitments.

   DATA: Strong majorities favour the government's continuing its commitment to such goals as redistributing wealth, ensuring that the population is housed, and providing social services. For further details, see Chapter 8 and the data on responsibility for funding social programs in Chapters 8 and 9.

3   *There is a widespread anti-welfare backlash in the population.*

DATA: 6% of respondents say they are opposed to welfare programs. There *is* evidence of serious concerns about weak administration, both from friends and opponents of welfare. For further details, see Chapters 8 and 9.

4   *The baby boomer generation had better provide for its own retirement, as Canada Pension Plan will have gone broke before this generation reaches retirement age.*

DATA: A small minority of baby boomers have ample retirement portfolios. The large majority have slim retirement packages. The median gross household income of the latter group is well below the median for the boomer population. The advice to these people to provide for own retirements is a counsel of let-'em-eat-cake. For further details, see Chapter 3 and section 11.2.1.

5   *Public support for the comprehensive social programs put into place in the post-World War II period has seriously declined.*

DATA: Strong majorities favour a list of 29 major social programs. Only tax breaks for business investments were opposed. For further details, see Chapters 8 and 9.

6   *The public is unwilling to pay more taxes to support social programs.*

DATA: Majorities were willing to pay more taxes to enable a number of major programs to continue. (It has often been found that the public favours tax cuts in general, but is willing to pay more taxes for specific purposes that they see as worthwhile.) For further details, see Chapter 8.

7   *On welfare issues people vote with their pocketbooks, supporting mainly those social programs from which they themselves directly benefit. Thus social programs are examples of the vulnerability of governments to special interest groups.*

DATA: In the present study, as in other studies that have looked at self-interest and social welfare preferences, there is very little correlation between income, age, gender, and other demographic variables and support for social programs. Support cuts across all such categories. The comments of most of the respondents implicitly defined "self-interest" in very broad terms: for example, they justify universal health care as an essential part of being Canadian. For further details, see Chapters 8 and 9.

The implication for policy makers is the need to have a much more sceptical attitude towards conventional wisdom about social programs and to find ways to stimulate and publicize research that will explode popular mythologies. A good starting point would be to replicate the present study, first in several regions and then nationwide, as originally planned.

11.2 Public Opinion and Fiscal Realities

As we have seen, our respondents expressed remarkably little concern about Canada's famous deficit and seldom echoed the chorus of pundit voices calling for cutbacks in Canada's social programs. Indeed, our respondents are calling for expansion of social programs to meet an overwhelming advance of social needs to which the policymakers seem to be giving scant attention.

This raises again the problem of the public's tendency to ignore the issues that have preoccupied professionals and interest groups. We saw this tendency in the lack of reflection in the public's thinking of the neoconservative tenets concerning social programs, and also the rarity with which we heard in our interviews and focus groups echoes of social welfare issues currently debated in the press, and issues promoted by campaigns like the Social Charter movement.

This takes us back to the two experts who challenged me on whether it is worthwhile to research the public's views.[2] These experts argued, in effect, that the public doesn't really know what's going on, and therefore can hardly be expected to give intelligent direction to public policy. To these experts, public opinion is a set of variables to be taken into account in the same way that an agricultural researcher in planning an experiment on crop growth would take into account fluctuations in local climates. The major concern of the researcher, argued my friends, has to be with the reliability and validity of the opinion data. They, the experts, could not be comfortable with the idea the public should be consulted for policy guidance. For them, the wisdom required for policy direction resides only with the experts: public opinion studies produce data; experts, people like themselves, produce wise policy advice.

From this perspective, the explanations of our respondents' apparent lack of concern with the deficit are first that few respondents have a full grasp of the workings of compound interest and the possibility that debt payments will take over the lion's share of government budgets. Therefore the public doesn't yet realize the full significance of the deficit. Second, the public is living a happy dream: it expects, re-

gardless of deficits, to go on receiving the benefits to which it has become accustomed.

I shall argue here for an alternative thesis, which can be formulated
in the following way. The public mind has the advantages of its limitations. This mind is less likely, for example, to run down the grooves
of currently fashionable economic models. As a result it ignores some
of the variables captured in these models, but is also aware of other
variables that the models leave out: especially the real costs of the
proposed cuts to social services, costs that are not being adequately
accounted for by the advocates of cuts.

From its closer-to-the-ground, less specialized, more "holistic" perspective, the public sees the future more clearly than the experts do. It
has a sense of the disastrous consequences of tearing the social safety
net. This too, it recognizes, will bring frightening economic costs.
Moreover, the public, as we know from much recent research,[3] is less
trustful of experts than it used to be. It knows that the government
policies that brought us to the deficits were also under the guidance of
policy experts. It knows that we have had cheery economic indicators
for three years now, but not much of the predicted cheery economic
news.

The claim that the public doesn't clearly see what is coming, does-
n't yet realize the consequences of budget shortfalls, and expects to go
on receiving the same services as in the past is easily dismissed. A major theme in our own data is public concern about erosion of programs and a fear that these are gradually disappearing.[4] More recently,
the Angus Reid polls cited in Chapter 10[5] make it abundantly clear
that the public is pessimistic about the future course of the social services and is well aware of what is happening to them.

In our study the public has expressed some loud and clear concerns
about the erosion of Canada's social services. The task for the remainder this chapter is to explore some of the policy implications of these
concerns. For this purpose I select two themes from our data that
show public worries about the problems, both economic and social,
that will be the legacy of an exclusive preoccupation with expenditure
cuts. I explore this legacy in enough detail to demonstrate the validity
of the public's concerns, and to suggest that there are other approaches, besides cutting programs, that need a better hearing.

The first theme is the increasing difficulty of retirement planning,
and the second is taxes.

11.2.1 Retirement Planning

We saw in Chapter 3 that of a sample of 125 respondents, 89 had few significant sources of retirement income other than government pensions. This is apparently typical of the Canadian workforce. According to Heather Compton, an investment advisor with Levesque Securities, fewer than 40% of Canadian workers have company insurance plans, but *fewer than 10% of these ever collect full benefits from such plans.*[6] As we have seen in our data and in the Angus Reid polls, few Canadians expect that adequate government pensions will be available when the middle-aged and younger members of our sample reach retirement age. This issue obviously demands priority enquiry, policy development, and program planning in the public sector.

A recent study by Statistics Canada shows that *even today the percentage of retirees who have the resources to finance their own retirements is minuscule.* The data are as follows:

Table 11.1

Financial Capacity of Canadian Retirees, 1900
(%)

Men		Women
1	Wealthy	1
8	Financially secure	2
14	Financially insecure, must work past age 65	11
24	No longer alive	4
53	Require government assistance	82

As these data show, for every 100 men and every 100 women·born 65 years ago, 76 men and 96 women reach the age of 65 years. If we limit this sample to those who survive to age 65, we find that of the 76 male survivors, 53, or a stunning 70%, require government assistance. Of the 96 female survivors, 82, or an even more stunning 85%, require government assistance. Of the 172 survivors, both men and women, 135, or 78%, require government assistance. This again raises serious doubts about the prospects for large gains from "targeting" pension plans.[7]

Are there prospects for improvement in the years to come? As we saw in the Angus Reid poll data,[8] a substantial majority of Canadians expect government pension and Old Age Security prospects to get worse.

Not only the general public sees problems ahead. A recent study by the Canadian Pension and Benefits Conference points to a coming crunch in the Canada Pension Plan.[9] The problem arises from the increase in the number of retirees projected for the first decade of the 21st century. To maintain present levels of benefits, steep increase in pension contributions will be required. Younger contributors will have little hope of recovering even the amount they contribute, and will therefore likely resist these increased contributions. It will become necessary to cap contributions to avoid a revolt by those who will lose out. Consequently, benefits will have to be lowered. Recall that in any case, 20% of our subsample with limited pension resources (89 of 125 respondents on whom we had data) had no access even to Canada Pension Plan.[10]

The solution being urged on the public is to take more responsibility for its own retirement planning, through the private sector. Many investment firms are strongly promoting RRSPs on the basis that public sector pension plans cannot be relied on. The following illustration is taken from a newsletter put out by one of these firms.[11]

The newsletter points out that investing $10,000 per year for 20 years in an RRSP that pays 10% will build a retirement fund of $630,025. Assuming that inflation averages 3% over the 20-year period, I discount this amount to approximately 55% of $630,025, or $346,513.[12] If this were invested at 6%, it would yield some $20,790 per year in today's dollars, a barely adequate pension. The assumptions built into this calculation are, however, very optimistic, especially the requirement that $10,000 per year be saved for retirement.

In evaluating the realism of this assumption, we need to consider income and employment security, since each of these variables has a major effect on one's ability to save money consistently. A useful statistic on income is that the 52% of tax filers in 1986 earned between $18,000 and $30,000 per year in 1992 dollars.[13] If we use just the top figure here of $30,000 and assume an income tax rate of 29%, we find that the after-tax income is $21,300. Assume substantial tax exemptions and set the tax rate at just 20%, and the after-tax income is $24,000.

If $10,000 of this income is being set aside for retirement, the remaining net after-tax income is about $10,000 to $14,000, depending on the tax deductions one allows for the RRSPs. The recommended $10,000 saving amounts to 40 to 50% of a net income that at least in most areas of Canada is barely enough for a family to survive on. To achieve this level of saving consistently over a 20-year period would require, for most Canadian families, a heroic feat of household economics. 10% of one's gross income is generally considered to be a reasonable rate of savings.[14]

The ability of the Canadian workforce over the coming years to finance its own retirement will obviously depend a great deal on the quality of jobs available. Here again the signs look ominous. A useful summary of the evidence has been compiled by Geoffrey York in a series of *Globe and Mail* articles on social policies.[15] The following is adapted in part from York's article.

There is increasing downward mobility in the Canadian workforce. This is illustrated by York's example of Derrick and Ivana Balan. Derrick Balan's income has shrunk from a high of $120,000 per year in the 1980s to a present level of $9 per hour, or some $17,100 per year. This resulted from the loss of his business income, due to declining prospects, as a construction subcontractor in Ontario. His wife, Ivana, presently earns $6.50 an hour as a part-time clerk in a supermarket. To survive on this income, the Balans have had to obtain an income supplement from the welfare department.

Their jobs have "no benefits, no paid vacations, no pension plans and no assurance for the future." In York's words:

Like twigs in a hurricane, the Balans have been swept up in the massive economic restructuring of the 1990s. They have been forced to enter the twilight world of the "non-standard work force." It is an uncertain life of part-time jobs, short-term contracts, low-paying temporary work and tiny kitchen-table businesses.

Growing legions of workers are tumbling into this murky world. In the 1980s, half of all new jobs were of this irregular type. Almost a third of the Canadian workforce is now locked into this life.

Other facts of life for workers in the non-standard work force are:

In the early 1990s the number of part-time jobs grew by 266,000. Yet at the same time almost 500,000 full-time jobs were lost. Nearly 70% of the new jobs have been part-time ... A job-killing wave of technology is beginning to hit the service sector, which has accounted for 90% of net employment growth in the past two decades ...

When the country's network of social programs was rounded out in the 1960s and 1970s there was an assumption that private and public employers would provide a growing share of pension and insurance needs. But policy analysts never anticipated the rise of the "contingent" labour force.

Some economists are recommending "a more targeted system of retirement income":

> When these people reach retirement, we'll have an older generation that is very polarized. A big chunk of the population will be dependent on CPP and the Old Age Security programs. Another group of rather wealthy people will have private pensions and everything else. We'll need a much more targeted system of retirement income.[16]

Clearly, from our data, there are questions to be raised about what "targeting" the retirement system means. We have noted that even today 78% of retirees need government assistance. Our grouping analysis of pension plans in our sample of respondents already mirrors closely the kind of bimodal distribution between the affluent and the impoverished that Maxwell is talking about.[17] But we must add to Maxwell's comments that since Canada Pension Plan (CPP) is built into the occupational structure, the changes projected by York and others in the job market *will also erode CPP. Again: 20% of our respondents with limited retirement resources had no access even to CPP.*

A large gap in York's otherwise excellent analysis is his treatment of the "contingent work force" as something new. For generations there has been a large marginal workworld in the Canadian Maritime provinces, where Unemployment Insurance has served the tacit purpose of providing this work world with a supply of workers by enabling them to exist year-round on seasonal work. Attempts to rationalize Unemployment Insurance in accordance with its official objectives will destabilize this workforce and add enormously to the population of "contingent workers blown in the hurricane" that York is describing.

Unless ways are found to meet the income and retirement needs of this contingent labour force, we can expect that in Canada there will develop an underclass, not likely in the style of the American black ghetto, but more like the underclass of Victorian England, described by Henry James in *The Princess Cassamassima* (Harper Perennial Classics Edition, 1968, p. 242):

> ... for the season was terribly hard; and as in the lower world where one walked with one's ear near the ground the deep perpetual groan of London misery seemed to swell and swell and form the whole undertone of life. The filthy air came into the place in the damp coats of silent men, and hung there until it brewed to a nauseous warmth, and ugly, serious faces squared themselves through it, and strong-smelling pipes contributed their element in a fierce dogged manner which appeared to say that it now had to stand for everything – for bread and meat and beer, for shoes and blankets and the poor things at the pawnbrokers's and the smokeless chimney at home ...
>
> People go and come, and buy and sell, and drink and dance, and make money and make love, and seem to know nothing and suspect nothing and think of nothing ... and the misery of half the world is prated about as a "necessary evil" ...

Though the public may not perceive all of the details, its intuitions about the disastrous costs of a loss of the social services are valid. *In the clamour for cuts, and in the stampede of governments to off-load responsibilities onto the private sector, these insights of the public are being lost.*

11.2.2 Taxes

Three strong and consistent messages of our data are: the public's willingness to consider paying more taxes for programs that it deems to be worthwhile; the need for a more cost-effective administration of the social services; and the need for a shift in emphasis in social programs from provision to prevention over the life cycle, particularly in the form of more family supports.

Here I consider some of the policy possibilities in the public's willingness to look at the revenue side of current fiscal problems. As we saw in Chapter 8, majorities of our respondents are prepared to pay increased taxes to maintain the following programs:

- Family Counselling
- Universal Retirement Pensions
- Contributory Pensions

- Pharmacare
- School Lunch Programs
- Supplementary College Preparation for Native Students
- Financial Assistance for Native's Suit Against the Church for Sexual Abuse
- Ombudsman's Suit versus Employer Re Equal Pay for Females

Majorities were opposed, on the other hand, to tax shelters for investment.

By "increased taxes" most respondents were probably thinking of income or sales taxes. But their support for increased taxes coupled with their perceptions of the disastrous consequences of loss of the social programs implies the need for a comprehensive look at the revenue base of government. We are constantly told that "taxes" is a scare word and that increased taxes will produce a tax revolt. Yet we should keep in mind that tax revolts are carefully nurtured and stage-managed, not unlike the popular American images of the Boston Tea Party. Though the stage managers of tax revolts rush to define the issue as one of overtaxation, our data strongly suggest that the public is greatly concerned about the fairness of the taxation system.[18]

The policy implication of the public's views concerning taxes is the need for voices to be heard that are recommending that attention be given to a more effective and more equitable tax system. An example is the tax reform proposal of the International Institute for Sustainable Development, based in Winnipeg.[19]

This proposal points out, though not in these words, that "welfare" permeates the entire tax system in the form of subsidies to selected population subgroups. There is, for example a host of subsidies to the resource and energy industries. Commonly these subsidies take the form of cleaning up, at public expense, the environmental damage caused by these industries. To offset these expenditures, as well as create incentives to reduce damage to the environment, "green" taxes would be imposed on water and air pollution, on noise and waste, on environmentally destructive products such as batteries, and on household garbage, for which higher fees would be charged to households that generate larger quantities of garbage.

The proposal of the International Institute for Sustainable Development also points out that the Canadian energy sector is subsidized to the tune of $4 billion per year, and that Canada has the second lowest energy taxes in the world.[20] It claims that savings of $10 billion annually are possible in subsidies that artificially underprice natural resources.

A set of proposals similar in some respects to those of the International Institute for Sustainable Development have been made by the Auditor General of Canada and academics such as Neil Brooks, professor of tax law and policy at Osgood Hall Law School.[21] These are proposals for recovering revenue lost to corporations who find ways to avoid taxes in Canada by operating subsidiaries abroad. Brooks claims that by a more aggressive tax policy towards corporations, $8 billion in revenue could be obtained without discouraging corporations from operating in Canada. He points out that for every dollar of tax revenue given up to corporations, only 20 cents worth of investment is created, and that tax considerations play at most a secondary role in corporate decisions about where to locate.

Such claims need independent evaluation, but the points to be made here are that they are consistent with the direction in which the public evidently wishes to take tax and welfare policy, and deserve attention on the same footing as the louder voices arguing for sole reliance on cuts in the social services.

11.3 Challenges to the Social Welfare Policy Community

1 It is clear that there is a very large challenge to the social welfare community to respond effectively to the myths that we pointed out earlier. That is probably the most important implication of the present study.

2 There is a clear challenge to policymakers for a more aggressive articulation of unmet needs.

   Comments of respondents on directions for social programs clearly show that a major source of public concern is unmet needs about which nothing is being done by government. A wealth of examples are provided in Chapters 8 and 9. There is a challenge here to policymakers not just to accept passively the necessity of cutbacks but to point out the real costs of ignoring unmet needs in areas such as dental care, mental health, family services, and day care. The public appears to be acutely aware of these gaps.

3 There is a large challenge to administrators to reorient social services towards secondary prevention, by better equipping the population to deal with developmental problems over the life span.

This emerged as a major public concern in the comments of respondents on future directions. For further details, see Chapter 9 and also Chapter 4.

4 Finally we hear from our respondents major notes of warning about the certain aftermaths, economic and otherwise, of governments' apparent scramble to unload their responsibilities for the social services.

12
Research Implications: Towards a Model of Social Welfare Ideologies

12.1 Aims

I begin this chapter by reiterating what was said in Chapter 1 about the objectives of this Report.

A first stage in analyzing the data of our study is to explore, describe, and classify our respondents' judgments concerning programs and policies, and to compare these with the trends noted in our documentary materials. The present Report is primarily concerned with this first stage. Beyond this, however, there is a need to explore the ideological structures that underlie these judgments. The present Report makes a beginning on this task by working out a conceptual model and offering a proposal for further research.

Given this general objective, the present chapter has two major aims. The first and primary one is to propose a theoretical elaboration of the concept "social welfare ideology."

This theoretical elaboration is designed to supply a number of critical dimensions of the "construct social welfare ideologies" around which the comparisons can be made. The immediate practical value of this is to facilitate comparisons among different theoretical approaches, and, of more immediate importance to our current research, to permit popular views of welfare to be compared systematically with writings of theorists and policy researchers dealing with the welfare state and related topics. In the light of our theoretical construct, one can, for example, lay out the essentials of the neoconservative, liberal, and communitarian perspectives and see along what dimensions these compare and contrast with one another and with popular views. The series of comparisons one can make along these lines also facilitates critical appraisal of the different views by permitting us to compare the aspects that are dealt with effectively in some perspectives and perhaps overlooked or misunderstood in others. Each position, one can assume, is a mixture of well-articulated positions, gaps, and ambiguities that can be seen more clearly in the light of what other systems have accomplished.

The second major aim of the chapter is to propose an approach to the widely recognized problem of effectively integrating quantitative and qualitative methodologies within a single study. Over the last two decades, qualitative methods have established themselves as equal partners of quantitative methods, but in practice the two methods have remained largely separate.

The present chapter offers an approach to this problem through a parallel and complementary use of two models that seldom, if ever, appear together in research reports: a causal model relying primarily on quantitative data and controlled experimental design, and a dramatistic model that uses an exploratory design, draws heavily on grounded theory methodology, and uses mainly, though not exclusively, text data.

In pursuit of these objectives, this chapter is primarily concerned with research design, in the broad sense of the "logical strategy of a study."[1] Work in progress is concerned with the further testing of techniques of comparative analysis within and across the two models.

12.2 Theoretical Construct

The term "ideology" is employed herein in Diesing's sense,[2] as a standpoint and perspective deriving from membership in a given social location or world. This is contrary to a number of commonly held definitions of this term, from which it is useful to distinguish it. Thus Shils saw as essential features of ideology a high degree of explicitness of formulation and a demand of complete subservience to the ideology on the part of adherents.[3] Harry M. Johnson saw ideology as "distorted or selective ideas about a social system or class of social systems when these ideas purport to be factual."[4]

Diesing's definition belongs rather in the tradition of social studies of science, in which scientific activity is no longer treated as a thing apart from other kinds of human problem-solving behaviour. Scientific logic is thought to be continuous with the practical reasoning of everyday life, not a precious preserve of scientists. Claims to a unique scientific method are disputed, in agreement with Bridgman, who said that a scientist's only method is doing his damnedest. Like collective problem solving in any human realm, science has ideological components, especially science in the public realm.

Diesing, in his comparative study of nine major policy science perspectives,[5] set himself the task of identifying the main ideologies to be found, and showing how these ideologies affect the several theoretical systems that have developed in the policy sciences. An important accomplishment of this work is to recognize the significance of Subject, Object, Perspective, and Standpoint in the policy sciences, and to apply this discovery creatively in comparing the different theoretical systems. Diesing explains the terms Subject, Object, Perspective, and Standpoint in the following way:

> We conceive the scientist or school of scientists as identifying with or relating to a certain location in society and viewing society spread around that location. This location I call the standpoint. The location is where "We," people like ourselves, are. Like ourselves, the people there are active; they plan, make decisions and act; they are selves or subjects. The surrounding world is the object to be acted upon, the other, the system. The object takes on certain characteristics from the fact that it is Object, the to-be-acted-on; it takes on other characteristics from the fact that it is studied from a certain standpoint; and takes on yet other characteristics from its degree of sameness or difference with the Subject.[6]

> The Perspective is the angle of vision from the standpoint: it is the way the world looks from that standpoint. Perspectives are always embodied in a set of categories that distinguish the main features of Society. One feature that is almost always prominent is the Subject, the part of the world that is where we are. Another feature is the Object or System. The System in turn is usually divided into several interacting parts. The Subject, the part that is here, may be a prominent interacting part of the system or may be more sharply distinguished from the System as its opposite. Finally, there must be a category that locates the scientist and relates him or her to both Subject and Object.

>   An important feature of the different perspectives is the assumed freedom of different parts of the social system to act on, deal with, respond to problems as opposed to being influenced or even determined by them. In some systems, for example, government is treated

as Subject – free to act on problems and thus to be major consumer of research, but in other systems, such as Galbraith's, government is to a large extent inhibited or controlled by problems and circumstances, and becomes an Object rather than a Subject.[7]

Diesing's achievement is thus to break out of psychological and methodological criteria of comparison of works of different scientists, such as the work of Mitroff and Kilman,[8] into a social systems or social worlds perspective on policy researchers. This enables him to see more clearly the parts of a problem area to which the different research perspectives are sensitive, and those aspects of a problem that persons identified with particular perspectives find hard to see or invisible.

These ideas are briefly summarized in Table 12.1.

Table12.1

Subject	Object
• Self	• Other
• We	• They
• My social worlds	• Social world(s) of my research
• The domain of free will, decision making, planning, acting	• The world to be acted upon, controlled; a world governed by laws explainable by my theories

12.2.1 The Perspective

In Diesing's formulation the Perspective is how the world looks from a particular standpoint. A Perspective has cognitive, moral, and cathectic elements. Since a Perspective provides categories for filling in the properties of the Object to be studied, and since this is also the job of theory, I find it hard to distinguish, in Diesing's formulations, Perspective from theory. That is, in its empirical aspect, theory would also be defined as an approach to filling in the properties of the Object.

Diesing is anxious not only to preserve this distinction but also to somehow isolate the effects of ideology on theory, as if the former were a set of independent variables that could be isolated and experimentally studied. He feels that otherwise the term "ideology" becomes synonymous with system of beliefs, which he considers to be too broad. His concern here seems to be to keep the boundaries of his subject within practical limits.

I prefer to tackle this problem by more clearly limiting the Object to be studied. Whereas Diesing sets no particular limits on this, in my study I have attempted to limit the Object to Social Welfare Provision, or the Social Services.[9]

The upshot is to leave Ideology as a part of any theoretical system. Unlike Diesing, I am not especially troubled by this, nor do I particularly worry about the negative connotations that the term "ideology" holds in the minds of many people. On page 10 of his book, Diesing drops the term "ideology" because it might induce negative responses to his work, asking, "Who needs enemies?" Yet he continues to use "Ideology" in his title. Though there may be some risk in doing so, I prefer to try to make the case that Ideology is an aspect of all theory building, and that it is not particularly profitable to try to erect a wall between Ideology and Theory. I am encouraged in this by McCloskey's lovely demolition job on a similar wall in economics.[10]

Another major change I have made in Diesing's system is to elaborate his broad and somewhat vague categories into a much more detailed scheme. This is summarized in Table 12.3.

12.3 Design Overview

Table 12.2, reproduced in part from Chapter 1, displays the elements of a research design for the comparative use of two models of social welfare ideologies. In the remainder of this chapter, I elaborate this design by taking up first the concept of "social welfare ideologies," then the properties of each of the two models, and finally some of the ways in which the two models can be employed in a complementary fashion.

It should be noted that the particular samples used could be different from the ones described, as long as they are capable of being analyzed by the methods of the respective models. It is assumed that both models are applied to at least a subset of the samples used, in order to facilitate comparisons. Note that in Table 12.2 the household and organization samples appear under both models.

12.4 The Causal Model

12.4.1 Ideology as a Preferred Social Welfare Function

In the causal model, ideology is represented as a preference for a

Table 12.2

A Comparative Design for Study of Social Welfare Ideologies

Theory	Models	Sampling Units	Patterning of Observations	Analysis
Construct of Ideology[1]	Causal[2]	• Households • Organization members	• Factorial experiment • Descriptive survey	• Ordinary least-squares • Hierarchical grouping
	Dramatistic[3]	• Organization members • First Nations • Policy science • Writings • Newspaper file • Households	• Exploratory • Formulative	• Grounded theory coding

Exchanges between Models:

a Use of theoretical scope sampling in dramatistic model to generate comparison groups for ordinary least-squares (OLS) analysis.

b Use of grounded theory coding within dramatistic model to generate additional variables for OLS analysis.

c Use of narrative analysis within dramatistic model to clarify nature of linkages between independent and dependent variables in OLS analysis.

d Use of OLS analysis to estimate strength of relationships identified in the grounded theory coding (constant comparative method of Glaser and Strauss).

Notes:

1 P. Diesing, *Science and Ideology in the Policy Sciences* (New York: Aldine, 1982); J. Schumpeter, "Science and Ideology," *American Economic Review* (1949) 39(2):345-59; K. Mannheim, *Ideology and Utopia*, tr. L.Wirth and E. Shils (New York: Harcourt, Brace and World, 1936).

2 P.H. Rossi and S.L. Nock (eds.), *Measuring Social Judgments: The Factoral Survey Approach* (Beverly Hills, CA: Sage, 1982).

3 K. Burke, *A Grammar of Motives* (New York: Prentice Hall, 1945); J. Gusfield, "The Literary Rhetoric of Science," *American Sociological Review* (1976) 41(1):16-33; Northop Frye, *Anatomy of Criticism* (Princeton, NJ: Princeton University Press, 1957); B. Glaser and A. Strauss, *The Discovery of Grounded Theory* (Chicago: Aldine, 1968).

specified "social welfare function," an expression employed by econo-mists to refer to social welfare as a function of a set of variables (utili-ties). A preferred social welfare function for a particular person is one in which the values of the variables are "optimum" in the view of that person. One can then compare different persons or groups as to their optimum social welfare functions. The causal model contains no method of creating the groups to be compared, but, as noted, this can be achieved through the use of the dramatistic model. This is taken up below.

In this section, I outline a method of creating the required social welfare function. I represent this welfare function by a set of three re-gression equations, in which support for an instance or example of so-cial welfare provision and allocations of responsibility for this provi-sion are regressed on variables representing properties of persons served, program aims, and attributes of the person expressing the preference. These equations are as follows:

$$S = aX1 + bX2 + cX3 + e \tag{1}$$
$$I = aX1 + bX2 + cX3 + e \tag{2}$$
$$C = aX1 + bX2 + cX3 + e \tag{3}$$

in which, for a sample of N observations:

- $X1$ is a $k \breve{} N$ matrix of values of variables referring to persons served by social welfare programs
- $X2$ is an $l \breve{} N$ matrix of values of variables referring to attributes of programs
- $X3$ is an $m \breve{} N$ matrix of values of variables referring to persons making the judgments
- a, b, and c are $1 \breve{} N$ vectors of weights applied respectively to the $X1$, $X2$, and $X3$ matrices
- S is a $1 \breve{} N$ vector of scores representing support for an instance of social welfare provision
- I is a $1 \breve{} N$ vector of scores representing support for individual and family responsibility for social welfare provision
- C is a $1 \breve{} N$ vector of scores representing support for local commu-nity and voluntary association responsibility for social welfare pro-visions
- e is a $1 \breve{} N$ vector of random errors (e.g., idiosyncratic personal preferences) added to the S, I, and C vectors.

One can postulate that underlying the social welfare preferences is a set of more general value commitments, such as a commitment to individual responsibility for consequences of one's actions, and also to community and to mutual caring and dependence. I use the term "values" in its ordinary meaning as a social good that a person will prize to some degree. I am referring throughout our discussion to social rather than personal values or preferences, though the value profile of any one person will reflect not only social values but, to some extent, personal and idiosyncratic preferences.

A social welfare function can also be thought of as a valuation schedule. By a valuation schedule I mean a rank ordering or set of tradeoffs that a person will make in situations that call forth several competing values. Following the cognitive psychologists, I think of a valuation schedule as a more or less stable hierarchy of desiderata that underlie a person's social judgments. I suspect that valuation schedules are stable for individual persons over samples of judgment tasks and over populations and subpopulation of persons. It is a reasonable working assumption, as well, that most social judgments involve not only stable values but stable ways of combining different and sometimes conflicting values. I believe that underlying the judgments there exist identifiable structures, in the form of profiles of weights attached to different values. The aim of the causal model of ideology is to map these structures when they are expressed as valuations of alternative patterns of social welfare provision.

To make use of the causal model, we devise an experiment in social judgments by which the independent variables are rendered orthogonal, as explained further below. This permits us to make estimates of the independent contributions of each independent variable when the others are fixed at their means. The experiment thus provides us with not only the relative weights attached to each independent variable but also the patterns of interactions among the variables, free of multicollinearity.

In this experiment in social judgments, the stimuli presented to the respondents take the form of "vignettes," each one embodying a particular mix of the variable values that are hypothesized to influence the judgment. Each judgment is considered to be a weighted combination of an individual's social welfare valuation schedule. As noted, these weighted combinations may be linear or nonlinear, as in polynomials and multiplicative relationships.

The judgment, usually in the form of a rating, is regressed on the variables of which the vignette or other stimulus package is composed. Because the variables on which the judgments are made are presented in random patterns, the independent variables are experimentally independent, and simple or OLS regression may be employed to estimate the weights to be assigned to each value, represented by one or more measured variables. For an individual or group, the corresponding profile of regression coefficients may be interpreted as an individual or collective social welfare value schedule. An economist might refer to this as a social welfare function. Our primary interest at this stage is to compare social welfare functions across a number of sample subgroupings.

Thus, by experimentally separating the effects of the various values by presenting them in the form of vignettes in which they appear as randomly combined independent variables (subject to some restrictions, such as "no professors of English in ESL classes"), the model aims to provide stable estimates of the independent weights assigned to each independent variable in the judgment process. As noted above, interactive or multiplicative effects may be studied, but not relationships among the independent variables, since these have been made orthogonal by the experimental procedure. The major gain from this procedure is the ability to study the effects of the independent variables free of multicollinearity, and thus to estimate with some confidence the effects of each value after the effects of the others have been allowed for. Repeated judgments over many combinations permit reliable estimates to be made.

The regression coefficients attached to each independent variable may be considered to be measures of the social consensus on these variables, since these coefficients will be larger the greater the similarity of weightings made by different persons. The error terms, on the other hand, reflect both individual differences in valuation schedules and inconsistencies in the application of these by individuals. A number of other sources of error, such as measurement error and the influence of variables omitted from the equations, are also reflected in the error terms.

12.4.2 Variables

Given the objective of mapping social welfare ideologies, not values systems in general, we must obviously be able to choose as independent variables those variables that are important in social welfare ideological systems. While there is no well-established body of research that identifies such variables, the work of Alves and Rossi[11] is especially useful.

Alves and Rossi studied public ratings of fairness of earnings and showed that these judgments varied according to the needs, merits, and social statuses of the earners. Judgments of fairness of earnings are a class of variables likely to be part of social welfare ideologies. One would expect, for example, the statistical distribution of such ratings to be wider for neoconservatives than for liberals or social democrats, and perhaps less uniform in shape.

Since fairness of earnings, which in the Alves and Rossi study included welfare as income, seems to be an example of the kinds of social welfare judgments in which we are interested, I opted to employ independent variables similar to those of Rossi and Alves, with some additions to both the variables and indicators employed. I also added an array of variables representing the values that I judged to be sought by 24 social programs selected to cover financial benefits, benefits in kind, compensatory benefits, rectification of injustices, and counselling for a variety of personal and family problems. The social welfare values embodied in these programs include security in old age, floor income protection, health protection, rewards for economic enterprise, support in dealing with personal problems, compensation for injury, and rectification of injustices.

Computer software to perform this operation, randomly combining variables to create the vignettes, was prepared in Fortran and is available for subsequent uses. The random combinations were subject to several restrictions. For example, if the variable "occupation" given in the vignette were engineer, the variable "education" must show a University degree.

Response Variables

Respondents were asked for the following responses to each vignette:

- general reactions to the vignette (open-ended)
- a seven-point bipolar rating of their support or opposition to the benefit or service described in the vignette
- preference as to how the service should be paid for, if in favour of it (checklist included taxes, user fees, lotteries, and several kinds of voluntary contributions)

- preferences as to entitlement (checklist ranged from universal to specifically targeted)
- even-point rating of willingness to pay more taxes to support the service
- likelihood of a range of actions they might take (e.g., writing to their MPs) in support of the service.

Each respondent received a unique package of 15 vignettes. The responses to the vignettes were obtained as part of the household survey.[12]

12.5 The Dramatistic Model

12.5.1 Grounded Theory Coding Paradigm

Perhaps the best known qualitative coding paradigm is the one generally employed in grounded theory studies:

causal conditions → phenomenon to be studied → contexts
intervening conditions → action/interaction strategies →
consequences

Since this paradigm reflects the emphasis on human action around problems arising in experience, and the processes and outcomes of the actions that are an important part of the philosophical background of grounded theory,[13] it is a valuable source paradigm for the study of social welfare ideologies.

"Human action, its process and outcomes" well describes the focus of a comparative study of ideologies. Such a study might seem to be concerned only with the static structure, organization, and content of the belief systems. There is good reason to believe, as I elaborate below, that popular ideologies of social welfare take the form of stories, incidents, and character analyses. We require, therefore, a paradigm that is well adapted to the analysis of materials of these kinds, and that at the same time will be sufficiently structured as to permit different belief systems to be readily compared.

We recall that ideologies are a blend of cognitive, moral, and cathectic statements. A dramatistic paradigm readily accommodates all three of these kinds of statements and brings out their interrelationships, whereas a causal model has difficulty in including moral and cathectic statements and also references to the social locations from which ideologies develop, except as explanatory variables or phenomena to be causally explained. It is awkward to include these within the basically causal framework of "causal conditions," "consequences," and so on of the grounded theory paradigm. The resulting analysis leaves out too much. I now turn to an alternative, a dramatistic paradigm.

12.5.2 Dramatistic Paradigm: A Larger Framework

In view of both these advantages and limitations of the grounded theory paradigm, in what follows it is incorporated into a larger framework that casts ideologies of social welfare into a narrative form, which may then be analyzed using dramatistic tools that have been developed for this project as an extension of some of the ideas of Kenneth Burke, Joseph Gusfield, Northrop Frye, and others.

The beginning of a dramatistic analysis of a batch of data is to identify the story line of social welfare provision that is contained in the data. Having laid out in summary form the story line, one proceeds to analyze the story as a piece of drama, concluding with a brief schematic representation and an examination of strengths and limitations of the example, compared to other examples.

The complete analytic scheme is outlined in Table 12.3. Since space limitations of this chapter preclude a detailed presentation, I make use of an example, a dramatistic analysis of Murray's exposition of the neoconservative ideology of social welfare. I begin by summarizing the story line of Murray's case study, and then show how the dramatistic analytic categories may usefully be applied to bring out essential features of the neoconservative ideology in a way that facilitates comparison with other viewpoints.

The main advantages I claim for this dramatistic paradigm are as follows:

- *Fit*: As the neoconservative example illustrates,[14] the ideologies of welfare found in academia as well as those that are found in everyday life can very clearly be expressed in dramatistic form. In the case of popular ideologies, a case in point is the wide circulation in the American public of stories of welfare clients, some favourable but most of them critical, such as the "welfare queen" myth that President Reagan was reportedly fond of repeating (a story of welfare clients arriving in luxury automobiles to collect their welfare cheques).

- *Communicability*: Because they are close to the original data in which popular ideologies are expressed, dramatistic accounts are comprehensible and make sense to the persons who hold them.
- *Inclusiveness*: An ideology as an account of social welfare and its workings embodies a variety of different kinds of causal systems and explanations, not just one. A dramatistic paradigm does justice to this complexity.
- *Generality*: We are seeking a paradigm that may be used with equal accuracy to depict academic and popular frameworks, to make comparisons of these different sorts of ideologies that make sense to their proponents.

On all of these requirements a dramatistic model ranks highly.

12.5.3 A Neoconservative Ideology of Social Welfare

The neoconservative ideology of social welfare is well represented in the work of Charles Murray and several other authors who have carried out case studies of the American social welfare system.[15] The following account is mainly from the work of Murray.

The story line of Murray's work is built around the theme of the alleged failure of the Great Society programs of the 1960s, introduced by the Johnson administration to achieve the objective of relieving poverty. These programs, according to Murray, were introduced on the advice of a "new class" of intellectuals from Harvard and other Ivy League institutions who had arrived in Washington in the years following the Second World War, become an entrenched part of the Washington power elite, and achieved an extraordinary and undue influence over Washington politicians.[16]

These academics were pursuing an agenda derived from social science theories that are, in Murray's view, at odds with the common-sense credo of the vast majority of American citizens, are of doubtful validity and practical value, and, worse, by encouraging government to undertake projects beyond its means to achieve, posed an indirect threat to the continued effectiveness of the American system of government. Moreover, the theories of the "new class" of politically active academics were, in the eyes of neoconservatives, a threat to the governability of America, inasmuch as they were broadly supportive of the "counterculture," a movement to undermine many of the basic precepts of the "American way of life."[17]

By Murray's account, the Great Society programs not only failed to alleviate poverty but made it worse and, as well, worsened the problems of educational failure, adult and child delinquency, and family breakdown. In addition to all of these negative effects, these programs tended, according to Murray, as a result of their obvious failure, to lessen respect for government and, by rewarding irresponsible behaviour, to reduce the status rewards to the "responsible poor" for their hard work and faithfulness to ordinary norms of responsible behaviour.

The means by which all of these disastrous outcomes were brought about was the series of changes in law and regulation that constituted the Great Society program. A few items in Murray's bill of particulars against these enactments are as follows: the liberalization of benefits, the elimination of the "no man in the house" rule for AFDC recipients, and the relaxation of work requirements.[18] A similar bill of particulars is given by Marsla and Segalman, who discuss the following consequences of a welfare state set up along Great Society lines:[19]

- high unemployability
- high unemployment
- high government deficits
- a huge body of centralized bureaucracy resistant to cutting
- an extensive pathology in the form of low educational achievement, increased illegitimacy, criminality, addiction, alienation, intermittent riotous behaviour, emigration of skilled employees.[20]

12.5.4 Dramatistic Analysis
To illustrate dramatistic analysis, in the following paragraphs I have listed major categories, such as Prologue, and subcategories of the dramatistic coding paradigm.

PROLOGUE
Murray's credentials and claim to authority are implied in his role (social researcher with a background in social program evaluation) and the sponsorship of his work by the Manhattan Institute. The latter body is presented as entirely disinterested, with no stake in the results except the general social good (the business connections of the Manhattan Institute are unmentioned).

The theme of the work, as we have seen, is the failure of the Great Society programs with an implied tone of distress at the unfortunate outcomes of these programs. The knowledge claims of the study derive entirely from its research data interpreted according to economic principles, those of neoclassical economics, that are taken as established beyond argument (as we show in the final section of this analysis, the data can readily be interpreted otherwise, but not by Murray). There is no appeal to firsthand experience of the author, who is distant from the action, a distressed spectator. The game theory analysis on which the data rests makes no direct connection to the data of the study but rests entirely on a metaphor of "economic man." The tone varies between windowpane (the author as transparent, invisible, merely a medium through which the research findings transmit themselves) and that of distressed viewer of bad government and social policy making.

The backdrop of the story is federal social policy making and liberal politics, especially the emergence of a more assertive federal role in social policy in the latter 1950s, the increasing influence of social science and social scientists in government and the judiciary, and the movements for social and civil rights that developed around the same time. As we have seen, there is special concern in Murray's work with the completely unrealistic and even dangerous (as seen by the neoconservatives) applications of liberal social science to policy making.

SCENARIO

The action of the story is largely centred in the dealings of welfare agencies, schools, and the courts with their clientele. The principal actors are social scientists (referred to as the establishment), who are background architects of the action; politicians, who enact the agenda of the social scientists; and clients of agencies, who respond to the resulting policies. While the agendas of the liberal establishment and politicians are to remake society in a more just form and to remedy social problems, the agendas of the clients, the intended beneficiaries of the reforms, are to survive as comfortably as possible in a rather hard environment with limited prospects, to make critical choices in such a way as to maximize short-term gains and gratifications while minimizing effort. These are universal human tendencies and people will respond in predictable ways, holds Murray, to the options that are made available to them by social policy makers.

The key to the neoconservative story line, as illustrated in Murray's work, is thus the neoconservative concept of agency. This concept of agency is a very simple games theory model of human behaviour, presumably derived from neoclassical economics.[21] The game itself is a set of rules governing payouts and penalties to welfare clients. Though the game is operated by welfare staff, to the client it is much like playing against a machine, the welfare bureaucracy being faceless. The players are assumed to be rational, governed by the simple rule of maximizing short-term financial gain. Playing the game is simply a matter of learning how to manipulate the eligibility rules to one's financial advantage.

Being devoted to this goal and valuing short-term gains over long-term ones, clients will choose to go on AFDC if it is financially attractive compared with working, even if the long-term consequence is to reduce their employability and hence long-term income. Similarly, they will choose to live together rather than get married, regardless of other considerations, if this will entitle them to AFDC or mean fewer deductions from their benefits.

Propositions derived from this system are illustrated by Murray's contentions about the effects of the Great Society programs of the Johnson administration:

- Increasing AFDC rates made welfare an attractive alternative to working.
- This effect was magnified by the extension of benefits to unemployed husbands.
- Allowing increased non-deductible earnings by recipients increased the work incentive for welfare families, but this was more than offset by the increased enrolments on welfare to which it led.
- This was further magnified by the relative relaxation of eligibility checks, the liberalization of residence requirements, and a Supreme Court decision striking down the practice of midnight raids in search of live-in men.

Schematically, this theory of welfare can be represented as in Figure 12.1.

EPILOGUE

Appraisal of the Neoconservative System

To establish a convincing connection between the claimed universals of behaviour on which the action rests and the data of his study, Murray relies on a quasi-experimental argument. He treats the Great

Figure 12.1

A Schematic Representation of the Theory of Welfare, in Which the Arrows Represent Causal Relationships

Variables, Causes, and Consequences

Welfare Eligibility Rules:

↓

Family Decisions:
- short-term advantages
- destruction of status rewards

↓

Specific Decisions Concerning:

↓

- work
- marriage
- children   →   reduced earnings

↓

increased poverty

Society reforms as a social experiment and purports to show from an array of statistical data the net effects of the reforms. However, this line of argument is dependent on assumptions that are not given by the data and need not even be consistent with it. They are assumptions of the neoconservative ideological system itself, as the following example shows. Here I make use of Giere's formulation of the logic of hypothesis testing.[22]

Murray's Test of the Neoconservative Theory
Applying the neoconservative theory to a part of the Johnson War on Poverty of the 1960s, Murray endeavours to show that its result was to increase poverty. Using Giere's framework, his logic is as follows:

INITIAL CONDITIONS (IC)
Official poverty rate at the point of initiation of the War on Poverty Programs of the Johnson administration in the U.S. (1965): about 13%.

HYPOTHESIS (H)
The War on Poverty Programs of the Johnson Administration of

the 1960s constituted a neoconservative welfare system.

PREDICTION (P)
In spite of the massive intervention entailed in the War on Poverty, the poverty rate in the period 1965-80 will fail to decline or will increase.

AUXILIARY ASSUMPTIONS (AAs)
Contexts: liberal political climate; emergence of the powerful "new class" – the liberal policy elite.
Conditions: prosperity; rising GNP; increasing population of elderly. *Contingent events*: the 1970s oil crisis; dislocations of the Vietnam War; inflation.

Murray provides extensive data purporting to rule out each of these contingent events as plausible explanations of his claimed increase in the poverty rate. This evidence and argument have been challenged by a number of authors,[23] but my focus here is not in the IC or in the specific prediction and its outcome but in some implicit AAs, or auxiliary assumptions, to which I turn after a brief look at the outcomes of the test.

Reflections on Murray's Analysis:
The Neoconservative Credo in Murray's Research

Outcomes of the Test
By Murray's account, the liberalization of welfare benefits became a reality in the late 1960s, but poverty failed to decline: in 1980, it was about what it had been in the early 1960s. This he describes as the "spending-poverty paradox," the failure of large increases in spending to appreciably reduce poverty. There is much room for doubt as to whether Murray's account of the outcome of the test, let alone his explanations of it, are accurate. This has been shown in detail by critics such as Jencks.[24] For this chapter, this debate is beside the point, since our interest centres on showing that the auxiliary assumptions Murray is forced to make place him exactly in the position of the alleged new class: forcing data to conform to theories. Thus to use this research to guide policy on any significant scale requires the establishment of a neoconservative "new class." As noted, the problem arising from this is not that it shows a kind of hypocrisy on the part of the

neoconservatives but what it presages for the profession of social research.

Additional Auxiliary Assumptions

In this section I show that a commitment to parts of the neoconservative credo is required in order to accept Murray's findings. This is reflected in the additional auxiliary assumptions that are required if the confirmation of the prediction is to be a valid test of Murray's hypothesis. Murray mentions none of these:

1   To be faithful to the neoconservative credo, Murray must maintain that the principal, if not the sole, important determinant of increased rates of applications for welfare is the enhanced benefits of welfare stemming from the war on poverty. Thus one of his key assumptions is that the reforms of the 1960s greatly increased the economic attractiveness of going on welfare and that this condition held true until 1980, the end of the period over which Murray tested his prediction. If welfare benefits actually declined in real value, for instance, over this period, the failure of the poverty rate to decline could clearly not be taken as confirmation of the hypothesis: a first condition for a good test would have disappeared. In fact, this is what happened.[25] Therefore, the increase in enrolments is in conflict with Murray's hypothesis, not in support of it.

2   By Giere's logic, the predicted outcome must be most unlikely should the hypothesis be false, but, as subsequent points show, this assumption is untenable.

3   The most obvious of these points, which was understandably leaped upon by critics of Murray's work, is that "changes occurred in factors in the economy that affected" the number of new welfare cases and the duration and prevalence of welfare assistance. Murray did endeavour to rule out this possibility with data showing an increase in gross GNP for the 1970s. He contended that since the real dollar increase in GNP in the 1970s was half again as large as it was in the 1950s, changes in the economy, far from helping to explain why poverty failed to decline, actually added to the poverty paradox.[26] However, in relying on this evidence Murray ignored factors in the economy that are well known to be more strongly and consistently correlated with the poverty rate than GNP, especially the median wage rate. This, as Jencks and others showed, correlates about .99 with the poverty rate over the 30-year

period from 1950 to 1980.[27]

4 To make use of this, Murray would have had to admit into his analysis a problem in the distribution of the benefits of the gains in GNP to which he points. This would have been to admit that at least in part "the system is to blame," an unacceptable violation of one of the principles of the neoconservative credo, namely that the socioeconomic structures of the capitalist system cannot in any significant degree be held accountable for problems such as poverty. Poverty is to be regarded instead as evidence of a cultural and moral crisis, a decline of traditional values. That Murray subscribes to this principle is repeatedly made clear in the book.

12.5.5 Summary of Dramatistic Model
The major elements of a dramatistic analysis are as follows:

- *Main Categories*: Prologue, Scenario, Epilogue. These categories provide the basic organizing scheme for the materials to be analyzed. This is a way of showing the interrelationships of the various elements of the ideology by means of a story line.
- *Subcategories*: For example, Credentials, Action, Agency: an elaboration of the elements of each main category.
- *Codes*: Applications of the categories and subcategories to a particular substantive area, such as the neoconservative ideology (e.g., the "new class" as a code for one of the major sets of actors in social welfare as seen by the neoconservatives).

In Table 12.3 these elements of the scheme are summarized with illustrative codes drawn from the neoconservative ideology of social welfare.

Table 12.3

Dramatistic Coding Matrix with Illustrative Codes from the Neoconservative Ideology

Category	Subcategory	Codes (Illustrative)
A: Prologue		
Form, Format	Conversation	Interview
		Focus Group
	Paper	Articles, Academic Journal
		Op-ed Article
	Book	Social Research

Category	Subcategory	Codes (Illustrative)
Prefaces	Author's Identity	Researcher, Manhattan Institute, Members of Native Education Centre
	Author's Authority Credentials	
	Themes, Theses	Failure of the Great Society Decline of Government
B: Senario		
Backdrop	International National Provincial	New Global Economic Order Welfare State Declining Provincial Economy Bureaucratic Encounters
Scene (Vision)	Images	Federal Social Policy Making Academic Liberal Establishment Alliance of Liberal Academics & Politicians Welfare Bureaucracy
Point of View	Close-up Distant	Outsider's View Distressed Spectator
	Personal Knowledge Reflected Knowledge	Social Statistics
Style	Windowpane	Reporter Social Scientist
	Personal	
	Argument	From Economic Laws From Laws of Behaviour
Agency	Personal	Personal Moral Decisions Government Rulemaking The New Class The Adversary Culture Homogenization of the Poor Incentives to Fail Incentives to Succeed
	Impersonal	Change in GNP Oil Supply Crisis of 1970s
Actors	We all	Canadians, Americans
	We	Silent Majority The Responsible Poor

(continued on next page)

Table 12.3 (continued)

Category	Subcategory	Codes (Illustrative)
	They	Friends of the Adversary Culture The Irresponsible Poor
Agendas	Universal Ours	Benefits/Costs Effectiveness Maintain Status Rewards Control Socialization Remediation
	Theirs	Remake Society Maximize Short-Term Goals Minimize Effort
Problems	Universal	Making a Living Family Decisions Career Decisions Obeying Norms, the Law
	Ours	Growing Poverty Failure in Educational, Judicial, Welfare Systems Growing Social Problems
	Theirs	Limited Choices Limited Prospects Hard Living Conditions Short-Term Gains vs. Long-Term Losses
Story Lines	Contexts	Climate of Great Expectations of Government Climate of Permissiveness
	Conditions	Increasing (Decreasing) GNP
	Strategies: Universal	Play the Rules to One's Advantage
	Ours	Toughen the Rules
	Theirs	Soften the Rules Liberalize Benefits Maximize Short-Term Gains
	Actions	Strike Down of "Man in the House" Rule
	Events	OPEC Meetings

Category	Subcategory	Codes (Illustrative)
Outcomes	For All	Loss of Respect for Government Ungovernability Increased Personal Danger
	For Us	Destruction of Status Rewards Increasing Costs of Government Unsafe Public Places
	For Them	Trapped in Poverty Long-Term Losses, Hardship
C: Epilogue		
Moral	Ideals Principles Precepts	 Billions for Opportunity, Nothing for Outcomes
	Imperatives Valuations Lessons	 The Law of Unintended Rewards
	Problematics	The Law of Imperfect Selection
	Goals	Restore Public Expectations of Personal Responsibility
	Priorities	

Cathectic	Positive Feeling
	  Expressions
	  Towards Actors,
	  Actions, Policies	

	Negative Feeling	Dismay at Policy Failures

Story: Reconstruction and Commentary
1 Story
2 Commentary: tightness of structure; uniformity; themes and variations; consensus; disagreement; problem areas; ambiguities; gaps; acuities, insensitivities; unique strong and weak points
3 Comparisons with other systems, descriptive and evaluative

12.6 Between-Model Comparisons

12.6.1 Linking Functions of Qualitative Data
We are accustomed to thinking of the comparative use of multiple research approaches as primarily a means of using one approach to

check on another, in order to reveal gaps, ambiguities, and errors. In the present case this is only a lesser part of our purpose. Our two models have different but complementary purposes: one, the causal model, is primarily a device for specifying clearly and estimating hypothesized relations among concepts; this is accomplished by turning concepts into variables and using the least-squares algorithm to develop the estimate.

The dramatistic model, on the other hand, is primarily a device for concept and theory generation. Beginning, as we have, with a partially specified causal model and the broadly defined construct "ideology," we can develop at least three sorts of complementary exchanges between our two models. I briefly illustrate these exchanges; many more examples could be given:

- *Use of the dramatistic model as a device for theoretical scope sampling, as in grounded theory development, by which subgroups can be created whose profiles of regression coefficients can be compared.* Suppose, for example, that we have an open-ended survey question such as, "What does the term 'social services' mean to you? The replies can be coded to reveal the inclusiveness of the definition: does the respondent see the social services as intended to serve the entire population, or only subgroups with special problems? Does the respondent include self as one of the beneficiaries, as an outsider to social services, or even, in a sense, a victim, stuck with paying the bills? A related line of coding deals with the evaluative tone of the remarks concerning intended beneficiaries: e.g., favourable, neutral, disapproving. The former coding can provide a typology of respondents who related themselves in different ways to the social services: beneficiaries, non-users, victims. This can be extended to include three major subgroups (favourable, neutral, pejorative) based on evaluative tones. The typologies created in this manner can be employed to construct sample subgroups whose profiles of regression coefficients may be compared.

   Similar examples can readily be constructed using data on the respondents' patterns of utilization and evaluation of different branches of the social services.
- *Use of the dramatistic model to identify variables to be added to the regression equations of the causal model.* As is well known, the results of regression and related forms of causal analysis may be greatly affected by a change in one or two of the variables that are entered

into the regression equations. Nothing in regression methodology provides any rigorous method of identifying such variables. Therefore, as is often pointed out, they must come from theory or practical experience.[28] Grounded theory coding provides a far superior alternative.

- *The interpretation of variable relationships.* A problem in regression clearly related to the foregoing one is that a regression analysis, while it measures variable relationships, usually indicates little of the mechanism by which the variables are related. Yet it is precisely this mechanism on which the interpretation of the relationship hinges. The regression model by itself provides only an estimate of the fit of the model to the data.

For two reasons this estimate seems insufficient: first, in the event of an unsatisfactory fit, we are left with nothing to fall back upon; second, in the case of a good fit, simply knowing that the data are consistent with the model is hardly enough in itself to affirm the model. A sound strategy is to distrust all models and methods until they have earned our confidence by performing better than alternative models and methods. Ever since the classic paper by Campbell and Fiske on the multitrait-multimethod matrix, it has been well known that, in ANOVA terms, method as a source of variance often outweighs substantive variables. Therefore, to permit us to take the effects of method into account, the dramatistic model provides a companion procedure that enables us to explore in a more open-ended fashion the variables to which respondents are giving primary weight when they make judgments on social welfare issues.

From this exploration, in which we compare, for instance, actors, agency, and plot line as revealed in the dramatistic analysis with regression coefficients attached to the independent variables, we can determine whether the variables that have agency in the dramatistic analysis are the same ones that have explanatory power, as estimated by the regression weights, in the causal model. If not, our interpretations of the variable relationships probably do not correspond closely with the interpretations our respondents are making.

These comparisons have several values that go beyond the exploration of method effects. First, respondents' spontaneous reactions to the vignettes on which their judgments are based give us good evidence of the variables that they are taking into account. With this evidence in hand, we can compare the findings from the two methods, using each to challenge and modify the other. Each identifies variables that the other omits.

To add new variables we can transform text data into categories or numbers and move them across to the quantitative data file to provide additional variables that have already been shown to be relevant and important.

Conversely, as in the preceding example, we can move quantitative values into the text file to group respondents, in order to apply the constant comparative method of Glaser and Strauss, with confidence that the grouping variables have explanatory power. Thus the way is opened to a more systematic version of the theoretical scope sampling methodology that has long been a part of grounded theory methodology. We can progressively identify portions of the database on which further qualitative coding can be performed in such a way as to map variations in the public's views of social welfare provision.

12.6.2 Social Standpoints and Preferred Welfare Functions
The "output" of these analyses will be a series of matrices showing sample subgroupings in the columns and regression coefficients in the rows. Thus we will be able to compare the social welfare value profiles, or, in economic terms, utilities and welfare functions of our subgroups. We will use gender and other demographic variables to create the subgroups, but our claim to originality in this aspect of the analysis is in using theoretical scope sampling of the database to create the subgroups.

12.7 Work in Progress
The work presented in this chapter is still in its early stages. The model presented here is ready, in the next stage, for application to a variety of research productions. Work in progress is along two lines: applying the model to qualitative and quantitative items in the vignettes database and applying the model to additional examples of neoconservative writings, with a view to comparing them with liberal and conservative approaches. Once the model has been further tested through these efforts, it will be a guide to further combined analysis of quantitative and qualitative data.

Notes

Preface and Acknowledgments

1 See John A. Crane and Chris McNiven, "A Review of Survey Research on Support for the Welfare State" (unpublished paper, School of Social Work, University of British Columbia, September 1989).

2 Rachel Marks, "Research Reporting," in *Social Work Research*, edited by Norman Polansky (Chicago: University of Chicago Press, 1975), pp. 284-301.

3 B. Scott, "The Social Charter Movement in Canada" (unpublished paper, School of Social Work, University of British Columbia, 1992).

Chapter 1: Directions for Social Welfare Project

1 See Table 1.1. For further details see: John Crane, "Public Support for the Welfare State: A Research Proposal. Appendix 2: Models of the Judgment Process" (September 1989; submitted to Welfare Research Grants, Health and Welfare Canada, Ottawa); John Crane, "Modelling Social Welfare Ideologies: A Comparative Approach" (draft, School of Social Work, University of British Columbia, June 1992).

2 See Chapter 8, and section 1.3.2, below.

3 Glenn Drover and Pat Kerans, "The Social Construction of Welfare: Progress Report" (School of Social Work, University of British Columbia, December 1991).

4 A detailed conceptual frame for comparing ideologies is developed in Chapter 12.

5 The social welfare values that we judged to be embodied in these programs include security in old age, floor income protection, health protection, rewards for economic enterprise, support in dealing with personal problems, compensation for injury, and rectification of injustices.

6 Details of methodology are described in several papers: "Working Paper II: Models of Social Judgment" and "Working Paper V: Design of a Factorial Experiment to Estimate Effects on Support for the Welfare State of Program and Client Variables and Characteristics of the Rater."

7 John Crane, "Technical Note on Sampling for the Directions for Social Welfare Project" (School of Social Work, University of British Columbia,

1991); City of Vancouver Planning Department, *Vancouver Local Areas, 1986* (Vancouver, 1989).
8 Jacob Cohen, *Statistical Power Analysis for the Behavioural Sciences* (New York: Academic Press, 1976); B.J. Winer, *Statistical Principles in Experimental Design* (New York: McGraw-Hill, 1962).
9 Peter S. Rossi and Stephen L. Nock (eds.), *Measuring Social Judgments* (Beverley Hills: Sage Publications, 1982).
10 The complete set of vignette variables is listed in Chapter 8.
11 Peter S. Rossi and Stephen L. Nock, *Measuring Social Judgments.* See n. 11.
12 Methodology is described in the papers on "Modelling Social Welfare Ideologies ..." and "Design of a Factorial Experiment ..." See n. 2.
13 A note on reliability:

Our major interest in reliability is in these ratings of the public's support for social programs. Reliability was estimated by the statistic theta, a multivariate generalization of Cronbach's alpha. See: E.g., Carmines and A. Zeller, *Measurement in the Social Sciences: The Link Between Theory and Data* (Cambridge: Cambridge University Press, 1980).

This was applied to the nine items measuring support for social programs presented in Chapter 8 (see section 8.1). Further details of the reliability analysis are available in the unpublished paper: John Crane, "A Technical Note on Reliability of Support Ratings" (October 1992), available from the author.

Principal components factor analysis of the nine items revealed a substantial general support factor accounting for some 40% of the total variance. Theta for this factor was .88. Since theta provides a lower-bound estimate of reliability, .88 is highly satisfactory.

A second factor, accounting for 12% of variance, loaded on two items referring respectively to tax deductions for RRSPs and to investments, and to a third item referring to child tax deductions. This was clearly a "fiscal welfare" factor, but its theta value was only .38. Thus it is not particularly reliable, probably because of the small number of items referring to fiscal welfare.

Our ratings of support for social programs, however, do appear to be highly reliable.
14 The method is described in a draft paper by H. Goodwin and C. McNiven, "Report on Focus Groups" (School of Social Work, University of British Columbia, August 1992).
15 M. Patricia Marchak, *Ideological Perspectives on Canada,* 3rd ed. (Toronto: McGraw-Hill Ryerson, 1988).
16 Ramesh Mishra, *The Welfare State in Crisis* (Brighton: Wheatsheaf Books, 1985); Ramesh Mishra, *The Welfare State in Capitalist Society* (Toronto: University of Toronto Press, 1990).
17 P. Diesing, *Ideology and Science in the Policy Sciences* (New York: Aldine, 1982).

Chapter 2: Meanings of Term "Social Services"
1 C.E. Osgood, C.J. Suci, and P.A. Tannenbaum, *The Measurement of Meaning* (Urbana: University of Illinois Press, 1957).

2 Linda McQuaig, *The Wealthy Banker's Wife* (Toronto: Penguin Books, 1993).
3 J. Citrin, and D.P. Green, "The Self-Interest Motive in American Public Opinion," in *Research in MicroPolitics 3,* edited by S. Long (London: Jai Press, 1990); see also P. Gooby-Taylor, *Public Opinion, Ideology and Social Welfare* (London: Routledge and Kegan Paul, 1985).

Chapter 3: Encounters with the Social Services
1 I have omitted here an item dealing with student fees, as these do not present an option of "use" of "nonuse."

Chapter 6: Neoconservative versus Proponents' Views of Social Programs
1 G. Radwanski and J. Luttrell, *The Will of a Nation* (Toronto: Stoddart, 1992), pp. 4-5.
2 Ramesh Mishra, *The Welfare State in Crisis* (Wheatsheaf Books, 1985); Ramesh Mishra, *The Welfare State in Capitalist Society* (Toronto: University of Toronto Press, 1990); Robert Reich, *The Resurgent Liberal* (Vintage Press, 1991); Brendan Martin, "Privatization and the Developing World" (paper presented at the Public Services International Privatization Conference, Geneva, Ontario, 26 March 1991); Ministry of Intergovernmental Affairs, Ontario, *A Canadian Social Charter: Making Our Shared Values Stronger* (September 1991).
3 Peter Steinfels, *The Neoconservatives* (New York: Simon and Schuster, 1979).
4 Adapted from Charles Murray, *Losing Ground* (New York: Basic Books, 1984), p. 146.
5 Steinfels, *The Neoconservatives,* p. 66 (see n. 3).
6 Quoted in Steinfels, *The Neoconservatives,* p. 124.
7 E.C. Banfield, "Policy Science as Metaphysical Madness," in R.A. Goldwin, *Bureaucrats, Policy Analysts, Statesmen: Who Leads?* (Washington D.C.: American Enterprise Institute, 1980); Banfield's views are echoed in current productions of the Fraser Institute of Vancouver, Canada. See Chapter 7.
8 Frank Fischer, "Policy Expertise and the 'New Class': A Critique of the Neoconservative Thesis," in F. Fisher and J. Forester (eds.), *Confronting Values in Policy Analysis: The Politics of Criteria* (Newbury Park, CA: Sage Publications, 1987).
9 William Simon, *A Time For Truth.* (New York: Reader's Digest Books, 1979).
10 Ibid.
11 Ibid.
12 Irving Kristol, *Two Cheers for Capitalism* (New York: Basic Books, 1987), pp. 141-45.
13 Murray, *Losing Ground,* p. 212.
14 Radwanski and Luttrell, *The Will of a Nation.*
15 Tom Kent, *Social Policy for Canada* (Ottawa: Policy Press, 1962), p. 17.
16 Radwanski and Luttrell, *The Will of a Nation,* p. 18.
17 Ibid.
18 Kent, *Social Policy.*
19 Radwanski and Luttrell, *The Will of a Nation,* p. 19.
20 Similar lists are provided by Ralph Segalman, *Cradle to Grave,* Chapter 2 (University of Oregon, 1989).

21 Radwanski and Luttrell, *The Will of a Nation* (see n. 1); Robert Reich, *The Work of the Nations* (Cambridge, MA: Harvard University Press, 1989); Robert Reich, *The Resurgent Liberal;* and Andrew Schotter, *Free Market Economics, a Critical Appraisal* (New York: New York University, 1991).
22 Mel Hurtig, *The Betrayal of Canada* (Edmonton: Stoddart, 1991).
23 Economic Council of Canada, *The New Face of Poverty: Income Security Needs of Canadian Families* (Ottawa: Economic Council of Canada, 1992).
24 See the neoconservative summary of "popular wisdom," above.
25 Summarized in Michael Walzer, "Life with Father," *New York Review of Books* (2 April 1981), pp. 3-4.
26 George Gilder, *Wealth and Poverty* (New York: Basic Books, 1980).
27 Discussed in John Crane, *Policy Science Perspectives on Support for the Welfare State.* Working Paper I (1989). Drawing on a variety of writings in the policy sciences, this paper develops concepts concerning the societal processes that influence support; Appendix 1 of *Public Support for the Welfare State: A Design Proposal,* p. 46, submitted to Health and Welfare Canada, September 1989.
28 Murray, *Losing Ground.*
29 Ibid., p. 156.
30 Ibid., p. 160.
31 See for example, Michael Walker, "The Reasons for Poverty," *The Chronical Journal* (Thunder Bay, ON, 13 February 1987).
32 M. Patricia Marchak, *Ideological Perspectives on Canada,* 3rd ed. (Toronto: McGraw-Hill Ryerson, 1988), p. 195.
33 E.g., Clinton Proposes Welfare Overhaul Emphasizing Work. Headline in the *New York Times,* 10 September 1992.
34 See the account of this episode in Mishra, *The Welfare State in Capitalist Society.*
35 Similar examples are given in Hurtig, *The Betrayal of Canada,* pp. 16-118 (see n. 22).
36 The view of Canadian Manufacturers Association president Lawrence Thibault. Quoted in Hurtig, *The Betrayal of Canada,* p. 118 (see n. 22).
37 Hurtig, *The Betrayal of Canada,* p. 118 (see n. 22).
38 Lawrence Mead, *Beyond Entitlement: The Social Obligation of Citizenship.* (New York: Free Press, 1986).
39 J. Crane, *Models of Social Judgment,* Working Paper II (1993). This paper identifies quantitative and qualitative models of the social judgment process that may be applied to judgments of welfare programs and policies; *Design of a Factorial Experiment to Estimate Effects on Support for the Welfare State of Program and Client Variables and Characteristics of the Rater,* Working Paper V. Lays out a model of a factorial survey-experiment. See also J. Crane, *Public Support for the Welfare State: A Research Proposal, Appendix 2: Models of the Judgment Process,* and *Modelling Social Welfare Ideologies: A Comparative Approach* (Vancouver: School of Social Work, University of British Columbia, 1989).

Chapter 7: Against Social Programs
1 Tim Gallagher, "Leading Edge on the Right: The Fraser Institute Helps to Shape the New Economic Conservatism," *Western Report* (1987) 2(29):19.
2 Each issue: *Fraser Forum.* Vancouver: Fraser Institute.

3 Walter Block and Michael Walker, *Lexicon of Economic Thought* (Vancouver: Fraser Institute, 1989), p. 159.
4 Gallagher, "Leading Edge," p. 16. See n. 1.
5 *Brief Summary of Fraser Institute Operations* (Vancouver: Fraser Institute, 1992), p. 5.
6 *Fraser Institute Endowment Fund* (Vancouver: Fraser Institute, 1983), p. 5.
7 Cliff Stainsby and John Malcolmson, *The Fraser Institute, the Government and a Corporate Free Lunch* (Vancouver: Solidarity Coalition, 1983), p. 3.
8 Ben Swanky, *The Fraser Institute: A socialist analysis of the corporate drive to the right* (preface, unpaged) (Vancouver: Centre for Socialist Education, 1983).
9 "Capitalism," *International Encyclopedia of the Social Sciences 2* (New York: Macmillan Company, 1968), p. 298.
10 Debate: Glenn Drover and Walter Block, "What, if any, social services should the public sector provide and/or deliver?" Videorecording. (Vancouver: University of British Columbia, 1988).
11 Block and Walker, *Lexicon,* pp. 78-79. See n. 3.
12 *Fraser Forum,* October 1991, pp. 6-7.
13 *Fraser Institute Endowment Fund,* p. 6.
14 *Fraser Forum,* July 1989, p. 20.
15 *Fraser Forum,* January 1992, p. 8.
16 *Fraser Forum,* February 1988, p. 19.
17 As quoted in *Fraser Forum,* August 1992, p. 10.
18 Ibid., p. 9.
19 Radio commentary for CHQM, taped 17 September 1987.
20 Conversation with Dr. Walker, February 1993.
21 *Fraser Forum,* July 1991, p. 26.
22 Chronicle journal, 13 February 1987.
23 Block and Walker, *Lexicon,* pp. 290-91. See n. 3.
24 Walker, CHQM commentary, 30 September and 1 October 1985.
25 *Fraser Forum,* January 1990, p. 33.
26 *Fraser Institute Endowment Fund,* p. 11.
27 *Brief Summary,* pp. 1-2. See n. 5.
28 *Fraser Forum,* January 1990, unnumbered insert.
29 *Fraser Forum,* September 1991, pp. 5, 7-8, 10.
30 *On Balance: Media Treatment of Public Policy Issues* (Vancouver: Fraser Institute, February 1992), p. 8.
31 Ibid., p. 4.
32 Robert A. Hackett, William O. Gilsdorf, and Philip Savage, "News Balance Rhetoric: The Fraser Institute's Political Appropriation of Content Analysis," *Canadian Journal of Communication* (1992) 17:31-32.
33 *Fraser Forum,* February 1993, pp. 27-29.
34 Stainsby and Malcomson, *The Fraser Institute; Canadian Dimension* 18:24; MLA, p. A15.
35 *Fraser Forum,* March 1992, p. 21.
36 *Vancouver Sun,* 13 September 1992, p. D10.
37 Fraser Institute, *Annual Report, 1991* (1992), p. 15.
38 Debate, concluding remarks. See n. 10.

Chapter 8: Public Support for Comprehensive Social Programs

1 The vignettes are displayed in Chapter 1.
2 See section 8.5 for treatment of the regression analysis.
3 T.W. Kent, *Social Policy for Canada* (Ottawa: Policy Press, 1962), p. 17.
4 Ibid.
5 Peter S. Rossi and Stephen L. Nock (eds.), *Measuring Social Judgments* (Beverly Hills, CA: Sage Publications, 1982), Chapter 1.
6 This quotation and the following quotations in this section are from Harold Goodwin's summaries of Focus Group transcripts.

Chapter 9: Directions for Social Welfare

1 Don Mazankowski, Minister of Finance. 1992, February 25. *Budget Papers Tabled in the House of Commons* (25 February 1992) , pp. 11, 15.
2 Andrew Nikiforuk, "The Manning Reformation" *Globe and Mail Report on Business Magazine* (May 1992), pp. 46-60.
3 Of the 231 correlations involved, only 5 had Bonferonni-adjusted probabilities of less than .05, and these were expected.
4 I produced a matrix of 66 correlations, involving all possible pairs of the variables. Only one of the Bonferroni probabilities for these correlations was less than .05.
5 A.C. Michalos, "Multiple discrepancies theory (MDT)," *Social Indicators Research* (1985) 16:347-413.
6 Ibid.
7 A. Strauss and J. Corbin, *Basics of Qualitative Research* (Newbury Park, CA: Sage Publications, 1980).

Chapter 10: National and International Comparisons

1 This is evidence of the commodification of policy research in Canada today, and an illustration of Galbraith's *public squalor and private affluence.* For a recent treatment of this topic by Galbraith see his *The Culture of Contentment* (Boston: Houghton Mifflin, 1992) pp 44-46.
2 The National Angus Reid Poll, *The Future of Canada's Social Programs,* press release, 13 August 1993.
3 Gallup Canada, *The Gallup Report,* January 1993.
4 See Chapter 8, Table 8.1.
5 Charles Murray, *Losing Ground* (New York: Basic Books, 1984). For Canadian echoes of Murray's views, see Chapters 6 and 7.
6 Gallup Canada, *The Gallup Report,* September 1991.
7 Fay Lomax Cook and Edith J. Barrett, *Support for the American Welfare State: The Views of Congress and the Public* (New York: Columbia University Press, 1992).
8 Ibid., p. 65.
9 Ibid., p. 63.
10 Ibid., p. 218.
11 Ibid., p. 193.
12 Mario Bunge, *Causality and Modern Science,* 3rd rev ed. (New York: Dover Publications, 1979), pp. 173-74.
13 Murray, *Losing Ground.*

14 B.I. Page and R.Y. Shapiro, "Changes in Americans' Policy Preferences, 1953-1979," *Public Opinion Quarterly* (1982) 46:24-42; E.C. Ladd Jr. and S.M. Lipset, "Public Opinion and Public Policy," in *The United States in the 1980s*, edited by Peter Duignan and Alvin Rabushka (Stanford, CA: The Hoover Institution, 1980); R.M. Coughlin, *Ideology, Public Opinion and Welfare Policy* (Berkeley, CA: Institute of International Studies, 1980).

15 Coughlin, *Ideology, Public Opinion and Welfare Policy.*

16 R.Y. Shapiro and J.T. Young, "Public Opinion and Welfare Policies," in *Research in Micropolitics. Volume 3: Public Opinion,* edited by S. Long (Greenwich, CT: Jai Press, 1990), pp. 143-86.

17 Shapiro and Young, "Public Opinion," p. 148; E.C. Ladd, "Public Attitudes Towards Policy and Governance: Searching for Sources and Meaning of the 'Reagan Revolution,' ' in *The Reagan Presidency and Governing America,* edited by L. Salamon and M. Lund (Washington D.C.: Urban Institute Press, 1984); J.R. Kluegel, "Macroeconomic Problems, Beliefs About the Poor and Attitudes Towards Welfare Spending," *Social Problems* (1987) 34:82-99.

18 R.Y. Shapiro and T.W. Smith, "The Polls: Social Security," *Public Opinion Quarterly* (1985) 49:561-72.

19 Ibid.

20 It is of interest that the term "welfare" compared with "assistance for the poor" produced a 44% swing in percentages of respondents in favour of the program. Data are from a National Opinion Research Center survey cited in Cook and Barrett, *Support,* p. 27.

21 See Chapter 9, Table 9.2.

22 Shapiro and Young, "Public Opinion," p. 160.

23 Shapiro and Young, "Public Opinion," p. 148.

24 R.Y. Shapiro, K.D. Patterson, and J.T. Young, "The Polls: Public Assistance," *Public Opinion Quarterly* (1987) 51:120-30.

25 Hansen, S.B. 1983. *The Politics of Taxation: Revenue Without Representation* (New York: Praeger, 1983).

26 Ibid.

27 Ibid.

28 Shapiro and Young, "Public Opinion," p. 160.

29 Cook and Barrett, *Support,* p. 65.

30 Ibid.

31 *Volumes for 1975-1986. Changing Public Attitudes on Government and Taxes* (Washington D.C.: Advisory Commission on Intergovernmental Relations).

32 Hansen, *Politics of Taxation;* D. Stockman, *The Triumph of Politics* (New York: Harper and Row, 1986).

33 N.R. Luttberg and M.D. Martinez, 1990. "Demographic Differences in Opinion, 1956-1984," *Research in Micropolitics: A Research Annual* 3:83-118 (Greenwich, CT: Jai Press).

34 P. Taylor-Gooby, 1985. *Public Opinion, Ideology and State Welfare* (London: Routledge and Kegan Paul, 1985), pp. 21-52.

35 K. Kopinak, 1987. "Gender Differences in Political Ideology in Canada," *Canadian Review of Sociology and Anthropology* (1987) 21(1):23-35.

36 Cook and Barrett, *Support,* p. 215.

Chapter 11: Social Policy Implications

1 See Andrew Nikiforuk, "The Manning Reformation," *Globe and Mail Report on Business Magazine,* May 1992, pp. 46-60.
2 For an account of this, see the Preface.
3 Allan Gregg and Michael Posner, *The Big Picture* (Toronto: McFarlane Walter and Ross, 1990), p. 59.
4 See the concluding sections to Chapters 3, 4, 9, and 10.
5 See Chapter 10, section 10.1.
6 Quoted in Melanie Collison, "Self-Employed Need Special Pension Plans," *Vancouver Sun,* 14 February 1994, p. D10.
7 See also section 11.1, "Seven Myths About Canada's Social Programs."
8 See Chapter 10.
9 News release by Canadian Pension and Benefits Conference, dated 10 February 1994.
10 See section 3.4.3.
11 This example, one of many, is from the *Mackenzie RRSP Reporter* (1994) 3:1.
12 D. Hart, *College Algebra* (Boston: Heath, 1953) p. 445 (table on present value of an annuity).
13 Gregg and Posner, *The Big Picture,* p. 121.
14 *Mackenzie RRSP Reporter,* p. 1.
15 Geoffrey York, "A Family Still Needs Welfare When 2 Jobs Give No Security," *Globe and Mail,* 22 January 1994, p. A1.
16 Quoted in York, "A Family Still Needs Welfare," p. A6.
17 See section 3.4.3.
18 This is evident in the opposition to tax shelters and in the many suggestions in our qualitative data of the need for greater tax equity.
19 See Nelle Oosterom, "Green Tax Will Slice Deficit," *Vancouver Sun,* 6 February 1994, p. D12, release by Canadian Press.
20 Ibid.
21 Cited in Valerie Casselton, "Mechanical Pigs Should Remind Us There Is No Free Lunch," *Vancouver Sun,* 1 February 1994, p. D2.

Chapter 12: Research Implications

1 A. Kahn, "The Design of Social Research," in *Social Work Research,* edited by N. Polansky (Chicago: University of Chicago Press, 1975), Chapter 3.
2 See P. Diesing, *Ideology and Science in the Policy Sciences* (New York: Aldine, 1982), pp. 1-20.
3 Edward Shils, "Ideology and Civility: On the Politics of the Intellectual," *Sewanee Review* (1958) 66:450-80.
4 Harry M. Johnson, "Ideology and the Social System," *International Encyclopedia of the Social Sciences* (1968) 7:76-85.
5 Diesing, *Ideology and Science,* pp. 1-20.
6 Ibid., p. 10.
7 Ibid., p. 11.
8 J. Mitroff and J. Kilman, *Methodological Approaches in the Social Sciences* (San Francisco: Jossey-Bass, 1979).
9 See J. Crane, 1992. *Memo #3: How Science and Ideology Woke Up In Bed: Remarks*

on *"Science and Ideology" by Paul Diesing* (working paper on data analysis, School of Social Work, University of British Columbia).

10 Donald N. McCloskey, *The Rhetoric of Economics* (Madison: University of Wisconsin, 1983).

11 P.H. Rossi and S.L. Nock, *Measuring Social Judgments* (Beverly Hills, CA: Sage, 1982).

12 Directions for Social Welfare Project, *Project Report* (Vancouver: School of Social Work, University of British Columbia, 1991).

13 A.L. Strauss, *Qualitative Analysis for Social Scientists* (Cambridge: Cambridge University Press, 1987), p. 99.

14 J.A. Crane, *Public Support for Broad-Scale Social Programs: Some Preliminary Evidence.* Report No. 1: Directions for Social Welfare in Canada Project (Vancouver: School of Social Work, University of British Columbia, 1992).

15 C. Murray, *Losing Ground* (New York: Basic Books, 1984).

16 Peter Steinfels, *The Neoconservatives* (New York: Simon and Schuster, 1979).

17 Murray, *Losing Ground*, Chapter 14.

18 Ibid.

19 R. Segalman and D. Marsla, *Comparative Perspectives on the State of Welfare* (Whitehall, London: The Social Affairs Unit, 1989).

20 A striking feature of the list of "pathologies" is what it implies about the neo-conservative expectations of a "welfare state." Most of the items on the list refer not to hazards of industrial society, such as poverty, illness, loss of bread-winner, injury at work, working conditions hazardous to health, and child labour, against which the bulk of the welfare state legislation was designed to protect, but to personal problems, especially those that can be attributed to individual character deficiencies.

21 Here the complementary use within a single project of both grounded theory and regression analysis can be of enormous help, since the former procedure identifies variables with a clear connection to data, providing solid grounds for their selection for the regression analysis.

22 R. Giere, *Understanding Scientific Reasoning* (New York: Holt, 1979).

23 Especially Christopher Jencks, "How Poor Are the Poor," *New York Review of Books*, 9 May 1985, pp. 41-48.

24 Ibid., p. 43.

25 R. Aponte and K. Neckerman, "Joblessness Versus Welfare Effects," in *The Truly Disadvantaged*, edited by W. Wilson (Chicago: University of Chicago Press, 1987), pp. 92-106.

26 Murray, *Losing Ground*, p. 58.

27 Jencks, "How Poor Are the Poor," p. 43.

28 W.S. Brown, *Introducing Econometrics* (St. Paul, MN: West Publishing, 1991).